Female Fetishism

D0809524

Female Fetishism

Lorraine Gamman
&
Merja Makinen

New York University Press
WASHINGTON SQUARE, NEW YORK

NEW YORK UNIVERSITY PRESS
New York and London

First published 1994 in the U.K. by Lawrence & Wishart, London

Library of Congress Cataloging-in-Publication Data
Gamman, Lorraine.
Female fetishism / Lorraine Gamman and Merja Makinen.
p.   cm.
"First published 1994 in the U.K. by Lawrence & Wishart, London."
Includes bibliographical references and index.
ISBN 0-8147-3071-X (cloth : alk. paper) —
ISBN 0-8147-3072-8 (pbk. : alk. paper)
1. Sexual deviation.   2. Feminist theory.   3. Bulimia.
I. Makinen, Merja.   II. Title.
HQ79.G25 1995
306.77—dc20   92-28488
                              CIP

New York University Press books are printed on acid-free paper,
and their binding materials are chosen for strength and durability.

Manufactured in the United States of America.

10   9   8   7   6   5   4   3   2   1

Sex is the thing that bugs English people more than anything else, so that's where I attack ...

Vivienne Westwood

Contents

Acknowledgements

Special thanks are due to Lon Fleming, Head of Gender Studies at Middlesex University, who persuaded us to write up an 'article' on fetishism we had been discussing with her; and also to Suzanne Moore who read and commented on drafts and passed on contacts, after it dawned on us all that it was a *book* on fetishism we were writing; and to Caroline Evans who patiently ploughed through many manuscript drafts without complaint and at all times made us think about what we were trying to say. These three women in particular gave us encouragement, friendship, and intellectual guidance when we asked for it. More importantly, through the general decency of their own behaviour, they reminded us at all times why we got into feminism (if not fetishism) in the first place.

Acknowledgement is also due to other friends, colleagues and loved ones who read and commented on early drafts of this book and/or who were generous to us with their help and time. Thanks to Helen Birch, Ian Birchill, Peter Booth, Paul Burston, Barry Curtis, Lynne Gamman, Jane Graves, Stella Kane, Martin King, Janet Lee, Mandy Merck, Francis Mulhern, Gilda O'Neill, Claire Pagaczkowska, Yasaraf Pilang, Matt Seaton, Sophia Chauchard-Stuart, Andrea Stuart, Judith Williamson, and not least Sid Wragg.

We should also like to thank Parveen Adams and Bernard Burgoyne for suggesting relevant texts; Jane Collins for translating some of them from French to English; the generous and helpful editors behind *Skin Two* magazine, who gave us their time, ideas and copies of the magazine for free, with no regard to profit logic. In particular, Tim Woodward (publisher), Michelle Olley (main feature writer) and Grace Lau (until recently official photographer), were most helpful. They have all creatively documented and inspired the activity of many British women involved in some of the sexual subcultures we have looked at in this book.

We would also like to acknowledge the support of Central St. Martin's students who attended seminars about social and sexual subcultures with Lorraine Gamman. There are too many to name but in particular thanks to Sean O'Mara, Amanda Ross, Karen Sainsbury and Joe Vell, who gave us obscure references and images on fetishism, and helped us photocopy research material (as did Natalie Gamman). We also very much appreciated the help of Martin Tothill, formerly from MA Industrial Design at Central St. Martin's School of Art and Design, who assisted us with picture research and copyright clearance.

We should also thank the students who participated in the Female Fetish Competition which ran at Central St. Martin's School of Art and Design in 1992, particularly Dean Hollowood and Kelly Harrison who allowed us to use images of their work in this book. Thanks also to the sponsors of this competition; *Skin Two* magazine, Lawrence & Wishart Ltd. and the Institute of Contemporary Arts, who donated the prizes, and sent representatives to judge the winners; and to Caroline Dakers of Central St. Martin's who helped us organise the whole thing.

Helena Reckitt of the ICA allowed some of the students mentioned above to exhibit their art work at the conference, *Preaching to the Perverted: Are Fetishistic Practices Politically Radical?* which ran at the ICA in July 1992. We would like to thank her not only for inviting us to contribute papers to the conference, but for giving us encouragement and support during the writing of the book.

This book wouldn't have been finished without the testimony of the women who completed our survey on food fetishism. Many thanks to all those anonymous women for agreeing by proxy to let us use their material in our book, and for entertaining us. Thanks are also due to staff at the *North Circular Magazine* at Middlesex University who circulated publicity for us about the survey. We would also like to acknowledge the help of the staff at the British Library, for their patience and ability to remain straight-faced when we asked them to chase up some of our more obscure references on erotica.

Not least on our long list, thanks are due to Sally Davison our editor at Lawrence and Wishart, for her guidance, intellectual integrity and particularly for her love of heretical argument. We of course bear responsibility for any mistakes that may inadvertently appear herein, but many of the good bits owe a lot to Sally's patient editing.

Introduction

Compare the stories told by women and those by men. The differences have many ramifications. *Deborah Tannen*

a fetish is a story masquerading as an object *Robert Stoller*

When we started to write this book about female fetishism we were surprised that the idea that women do *not* fetishise was still taken for granted. It wasn't just the images of Madonna and other female celebrities wearing fetish fashions and enjoying what is often called 'kinky sex' (on their own terms) that made us want to question this. We wanted to make the case for 'woman as fetishist' because we found so much empirical evidence that shows her existence.

What women are doing inside sexual subcultures; the often bizarre behaviour of some female 'fans'; as well as women's obsessive relationship to food; all these phenomena persuaded us that orthodox thinking on the subject of female fetishism was grossly inadequate. It certainly couldn't explain what many young women were up to: neither could it conceptualise the female activities going down on what *Skin Two* magazine describes as 'the international fetish scene'.

But what do we mean by fetishism? Do we really think the stereotypes of 'kinky' sex that film stars like Kim Basinger, Sharon Stone, Michelle Pfeiffer – to name but a few – have been associated with in the last five years, illustrate all female experiences of fetishism? The straight answer to that question is 'No,' though most people, when they think about fetishism, think of sex with whips and being tied up with bondage gear. So we recognised that any discussion on the subject of fetishism needed to clarify from the outset the differences between the different types of fetishism and various sexual subcultures. To separate fetishism from bondage, sado-masochism, exhibitionism, voyeurism, transvestism, and cross-dressing seemed absolutely vital.

It also improved our incentive to go to the British Library, at the British Museum in London. There is nothing like reading about sex to keep the research stimulating.

When starting to identify the different types of erotic magazines available on the UK market, and then meeting women involved in sexual subcultures on the London night club scene, we heard many fascinating stories about fetishism. But overall there seemed to be a lack of consensus, among the people we talked to, about what actually constitutes *sexual* fetishism. So to find a theoretical framework to account for the whole range of female behaviour being described seemed vital. We found so many confused definitions of fetishism that we felt it was inappropriate to employ a single academic model or to rely on any one group of women fetishists to simply tell the 'truth' about their experiences. Our emphasis in this book therefore, on the idea that women can and do fetishise in the sexual sense, employs a model of 'stages' of sexual fetishism. We felt we needed to be able to conceptualise different stages (and intensities) of sexual fetishism because not all the female sexual fetishists we found got all of their sexual stimulation from objects. This model helps refine some of Freud's observations and, of course, is substantiated with reference to many clinical case studies and academic observations about fetishism.

In the chapters that follow details are given about the different types of female fetishism we found. This, includes the discussion of women who do experience sexual fetishism in its most extreme intensity, that is women who orgasm over objects such as silk, mackintoshes, cars, string, books, plaster casts and white socks... So what? you may well ask. Even if we have found some women who are clearly sexual 'orthodox' fetishists, how is this useful to feminism? Legitimating the idea of women as perverts, by making the case for them as sexual fetishists, may not seem like a grand step forward towards a brave new feminist world. In a context where the tabloid press in Britain frequently has 'moral panics' and portrays feminists as being 'perverted' *per se* (usually for demanding equal civil rights or sexual equality) perhaps caution is needed when claiming that fetishism is something that women might do.

Our argument is that activities like fetishism that are labelled 'perverse' have the capacity to subvert dominant discourses about sexuality, and the social order. Culture, as anthropologist Mary Douglas has argued, has always had to maintain the purity of its ideas about the sacred and the profane and the purity of its categories that define sexuality; the female fetishist breaches many of those boundaries and 'binary oppositions' about sexual difference. These levels of 'subversion' often align sexual fetishism with what is being called 'Queer' politics. An insistence on fetishism as a different but common sexual practice, as gay writer Michael Warner suggests, disturbs ideas about sexual normality. Clearly it is not true that only heterosexual men are fetishists, and by showing fetishism as a more common sexual practice than may have been previously imagined we hope to disrupt preconceptions of 'deviant' sexual behaviour being associated with any one group. These stereotypes are seen by some as so oppressive that they 'do violence' on individuals informed by them.[1]

So we feel that arguing for sexual diversity is politically important. To make the case for sexual fetishism as a common practice demands a deeper understanding, and a broader model altogether, of female sexuality. And looking at female sexual fetishism as part of today's sexual practice puts on the political agenda the question of problematic – and often outdated – medical and legal definitions in regulating ideas about 'normal' sexual practices.

Despite these significant political objectives, some feminists have questioned whether it is sensible to suggest that individual sexual activities, like those of the female fetishist, can in themselves be 'transgressive' or 'progressive'[2]. Clearly, since Conservatives of all shades of blue have so wholeheartedly participated in diverse sexual practices, fetishism in itself is obviously not 'radical'. But admitting to being a fetishist, in certain contexts, can be subversive... And we think that for women to engage in fetishism is often both pleasurable and radical.

To be able to consider the politics of fetishism or other sexual variations, it is necessary to understand why these practices have been designated 'perverse' in the first place. We discuss this in chapter one, when looking, for example, at women's involvement in sado-masochism, genital piercing, scarification, and many other activities, and considering whether or not they constitute sexual fetishism. To assess this material it has been necessary to read beyond the prejudices of the past and present in order to understand both male and female behaviour under scrutiny. Recent legal precedents, particularly those focusing on the implications of the Operation Spanner case, have got in the way of our ability to do this, and have worrying political consequences for fetishists and any other people who enjoy sexual variations that involve consensual, diverse sexual practices. The British legal judgments on Operation Spanner, and on the under-age anorexic's right to starve, demand urgent political evaluation of the issue of consent as a civil right. New legislation is needed so that our right to give our consent cannot be overturned by the courts if the individuals involved can prove they were of sound mind and that their actions did not endanger life. From the anorexic to the sado-masochist, this political issue of consent cuts right across 'cultural politics' and ultimately affects the sexual practice of every individual in society.[3] This is why we think understanding sexual fetishism is relevant to radical sexual politics and why we object to labels like 'pervert' being used not in a playful way but to pathologise and criminalise consensual sexual practices (like S&M or fetishism). To make this political point it was good to join gay, lesbian, heterosexual and other activists, as well as the editors and contributors to *Skin Two* magazine, at the 1992 ICA Conference *Preaching to the Perverted*. If the British establishment intends to continue to criminalise or pathologise sexual behaviour, it would be far more appropriate for them to focus on nonconsensual sexual practice. Rape, paedophilia and bestiality, for example, seem perverted to us because by their very nature they cannot involve consent.

Despite the way terms like 'perve' are being reappropriated by some subcultural groups, as a positive statement about diverse sexualities, nevertheless the origins of legal and medical definition and regulation of perversity is problematically connected with the beginnings of psychoanalysis in the nineteenth century. Consequently, any focus on definitions of perverse behaviour reveals a cultural history associated with the earliest writings on sexuality, and our focus reviews that history. We found that even before Freud, nonconformity to dominant sexual norms has been categorised as unhealthy or as an abnormality. Sexual diversity and sexual variation have not been popularly recognised as part of normal sexual practice at any time in Western culture, but rather connected to ideas about degeneracy. We think it is about time this changed.

We inevitably found ourselves, as a consequence of our political perspective, aligning ourselves with radical historians of sexuality such as Jeffrey Weeks and Jonathan Dollimore, in challenging nineteenth century definitions of perversity and gender. In order to understand even the meaning of contemporary dress codes (leather and rubber gear, drag and vogueing outfits for instance), as well as the role of some women in London clubs, we found it necessary to challenge many definitions, including those which define what constitutes 'feminine' behaviour. As Caroline Evans, writer on fashion, has pointed out, 'ideologies about femininity, that are taken for granted in our society, are often more perverse than sexual variations, like transvestism'.[4] We pursue this line of argument in chapter two to introduce the familiar figure of the so-called 'feminine' woman and name her as a possible 'female homeovestite' – a woman who 'dresses up' as a caricature of a woman, for example Barbara Cartland or Barbara Windsor.[5]

This type of categorisation would make such women 'perverts', if we accept dominant psychoanalytic definitions of perversity and Joan Riviere's idea that the so-called normal femininity that appears all around us unchallenged is often nothing more than a sham, a masquerade. The drag queen Rupert Charles has summarised this point more simply – 'Honey, if you're in clothes, you're in drag...' We try in this book to explain the implications of this statement by considering how masculinity and femininity are culturally constructed.

'Natural' femininity is not all we found ourselves questioning when looking at ideas about female fetishism and female perversity. In the literature that defines fetishism there is a lot of confusion and terms have been muddled. Indeed, it became clear that the study of fetishism raises theoretical problems associated with ideas about 'conflation'. How did erotic excitement associated with leather or rubber relate to religious rituals, or consumer publicity for washing powders, or identifying ourselves with 'pepsi people'?[6] We found the term 'fetishism' was being used to describe everything from totem poles to advertising, as well as the visually erotic. So we began to look at the history of the word itself and found three types of fetishism: anthropological fetishism and commodity fetishism as well as sexual fetishism. These terms are analysed and defined in detail in chapter one.

Writers on anthropological and commodity fetishism have always acknowledged women as practitioners, but women disappear from debates about sexual fetishism . We couldn't understand this because the case studies we came across contradict the view that female sexual fetishism is 'rare' and, in fact, show many women doing it. Indeed, our examples destabilise the certainty of conceptual thinking which underlies the Freudian model of sexual fetishism. Moreover they demand a new look at the issue of gender within the theoretical analysis of sexual fetishism.

In the course of arguing that women's sexual desire is as 'active' as men's, we couldn't help but fall over some of the 'axioms' about female sexuality laid down by Freud. Traditional theories of *sexual* fetishism have usually discussed women as passive objects of fetishism, not its subjects. In the nineteenth century, Freud suggested that the 'fetish' develops out of an unconscious urge to protect the penis (castration anxiety) due to the young boy's first realisation that his mother does not have one too. Since a woman does not have a penis to protect, why would she need to fetishise?

Not surprisingly with this sort of logic informing debates, we came up against what has been called the 'phallocentrism' of psychoanalysis: it didn't just 'pop' up now and again but permeated the whole canon from beginning to end. Something else began to strike us too about the clinical data on fetishism: women made up a significant number of the case studies cited and yet the clinicians each claimed their own female patient was a 'rarity'. Why didn't they notice that female sexual fetishism, when conceptualised and analysed in the active sense, recurred again and again? Why wasn't it a 'troubling' problem to those trying to analyse it?

It wasn't just the Freudians that seemed to us to be blind to this particular female desire. Other psychoanalytic schools, Kleinian for example, also concurred with the idea that women do not fetishise sexually, despite the evidence of their own case studies. This surprised us, because the Kleinian privileging of the breast, and the infant's anxiety about being separated from the mother, could have provided a further way of explaining sexual fetishism. Yet none of these subsequent analysts thought to challenge 'penis envy' (the idea that female sexuality is determined by lack). They simply accommodated ideas about female sexual passivity into their own findings. Neither the British nor the American followers of Klein make very much of the shift of emphasis we find in their case studies of women fetishists. So it became necessary to provide a re-reading of theories of fetishism by reconsidering the female behaviour examined.

From the 1960s onwards, the enormous influence of Lacanian psychoanalysis compounded the theoretical impasse. In the last twenty years Lacanian formulations have entered the consulting rooms and the academic institutions across the world. Even feminist film critics have used his ideas to explain erotic representations of women in film. In the Lacanian model, once again, fetishism is linked to castration anxiety and it is argued women do not fetishise. We argue against this way of thinking. We feel important ideas about 'castration anxiety' and 'penis envy' have been overemphasised, and this overdetermination has contributed to a blindspot about women. The female gaze at women's sexuality, which demands recognition of female desire and female libido as active is often simply not noticed or seen.

The reader may well ask why, when feminism has now permeated the academy, psychoanalysis continues to deny agency to women? Using the insights of writers such as Jacqueline Rose, Parveen Adams and the French Feminists, Luce Irigaray, Hélène Cixous and Julia Kristeva, we concluded that in describing women as sexual fetishists, we found ourselves disagreeing and undermining dominant explanations of female sexual desire. In chapter three we examine psychoanalytic writing on fetishism and prepare the ground for our challenge to phallocentric theories which take exclusive male agency for granted. We argue that acknowledging female fetishism leads to a need for a new psychoanalytic representation of the female erotic. To some extent these demands for a new model of the female erotic, in different subject areas, have been made before.

Some critics might argue that female fetishism has also been 'done' before and that, previous to our discussion, this topic has been subjected to rigorous analysis, by notable and insightful critics such as Mary Kelly, Naomi Schor, Emily Apter and Marjorie Garber. In chapter six we discuss all the feminist writing on female fetishism that we could find. Every text we looked at, despite the best intentions, stumbled with Freud and Lacan in the same places, no doubt as a consequence of underlying theoretical formulations about female passivity. So we had to start from scratch and reconsider other case studies which appear to show women as active agents of fetishism, without too much prejudice.

Our re-examination of the theory of sexual fetishism made us look at important psychoanalytic writing about sexual fetishists that appeared to us to have been either overlooked or ignored by the feminist writers mentioned above. This material made us re-think our own ideas about sexual fetishism as being solely a post-Oedipal response. Our re-reading of the case studies stresses pre-Oedipal elements which allow the entry of women as sexual fetishists into the theory. This new reading of fetishism involves recognition of:

1. underlying anxiety about separation from the mother;
2. an oral component;
3. the need for a new theoretical representation of female desire.

This approach also enables us to stay within the psychoanalytic paradigm when considering food as a possible object of fetishism.

Many cultural arguments have been made about food 'fixations' or 'obsessions'. Feminist critics such as Ros Coward have discussed food recipes and representations aimed at women, which eroticise chocolate cake or other dishes, as a form of 'pornography' for women.[7]

But previous feminist arguments about food and sex are not very precise and in our opinion do not go far enough. Discussion of bulimia, for example, is full of statements that require further consideration. In psychoanalytic terms, we suggest that many of the clinical findings on bulimia usefully compare with both the symptoms and the cultural manifestation of sexual fetishism. But popular figures from Princess Di to Jane Fonda are said to be bulimic. Does this mean that these icons are doing something similar to sexual fetishists?

We believe food can be the object of fetishism by women. As we know, a very diverse range of 'discourses',[8] from Freudian theory down to current adverts which virtually show women doing fellatio on Cadbury's chocolate flake, acknowledge the closeness of the oral and sexual drives. Food, we argue, can become a fetish object: in some, though not all, cases of female bulimia, it can be the object of something similar to sexual fetishism.

Our connection of bulimia with sexual fetishism has shocked some people.[9] Some women ask how their feelings of being out of control, when they binge on food, and their sense of 'worthlessness' when they do this, can equate with men's sexual pleasure in fetishism? One woman we interviewed summed up this position;'I do not believe that bulimia can be regarded as the ultimate female fetish, as something so linked to self-destruction cannot be regarded as OK.'[10] This was also certainly the view of many of the women who attended the talk we gave at the *Preaching to the Perverted* conference. In response to questions put to us about bulimia being linked to feeling out of control we argued that many sexual fetishists feel equally out of control when compulsively procuring, or masturbating over, knickers or shoes. They too may measure themselves against society's model of the normal, and find themselves wanting. We argue that food fetishism for some women is a disavowal of dangerous anxieties, involving a pleasurable release via the oral impulse, and that it therefore constitutes a fourth type of fetishism, a *food* fetishism. Bulimics clearly play out the fetishistic doing-and-undoing strategy via their bingeing-and-purging syndrome. We believe it should be placed alongside the other three categories of anthropological, commodity and sexual fetishism, although it clearly has the closest links with sexual fetishism, as we explain in chapter four.

Much of the material which refers to women's food obsessions has never been conceived as fetishism before. While Meret Oppenheim's shoe sculpture, featuring high heels adorned with noisettes exhibited on a silver platter (see Illustration 1) – links traditional fetishism with

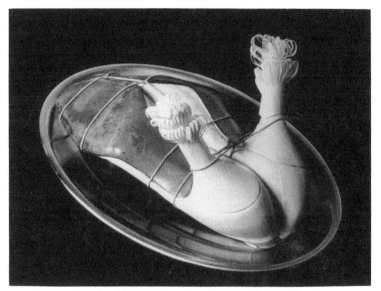

Food fetishism? Shoe Sculpture on a Silver Platter,
by Meret Oppenheim, copyright DACS 1994

food, no one has suggested that women could actually be food fetishists.[11] Nor have they suggested that women are as 'pathological'
in relation to food as men are seen to be with objects appertaining
to the female anatomy.

Such limited arguments about women and food seem quite astonishing to us. The diet industry is estimated to be worth at least
£850 million a year in Britain alone and growing, despite the current
economic recession.[12] Though not all women in Britain suffer from
eating disorder, or obsessions with chocolate, it has been argued by
many therapists, particularly those from the Women's Therapy Centre,
that women are more preoccupied than men with calories, eating,
recipes and food preparation.[13] Some women may genuinely be
addicted to food. But we rule out addiction, as an alternative to
fetishism, or as an explanation of bulimia, because addiction uses a
specifically chemical 'high' to fix onto. Food fetishists do not. Imagine
an alcoholic drinking a bottle of whisky and then vomiting it up before
she feels drunk – and you'll see why a bulimic needs a psychoanalytic
rather than a chemical explanation.[14]

Most of our arguments about the fetishism of food by women are
cultural as well as psychoanalytic, since psychoanalysis recognises that
culture mediates and regulates our relationship to the self. But when
we started to question the *epidemic* proportions of women suffering
from eating disorder, we felt the cultural factors needed to be given
more thought. Psychoanalytic discourse rarely discusses the implications of cultural shifts upon female identity and avoids cross-cultural
comparisons or analysis of cultural images and values, but we feel a
material analysis of the female unconscious is important, and raises
questions beyond individual case histories (the usual style of psychoanalytic writing), questions that impact across the terrain of race, class,
gender and generation. Such an analysis would engage with many
important theoretical concerns voiced by other critics, about the way
the unconscious is structured.

We must register our surprise that in the context of so much activity
by the medical and psychiatric profession about 'eating disorder', the
idea of food as the object of fetishism by women has not entered the
discussion. When contemporary epidemics of eating disorders like
anorexia, bulimia and compulsive eating (90 per cent female) are being
written about by journalists and medical writers as symptoms of a
'perverse' culture, it is astonishing perhaps that the idea of food
fetishism hasn't been discussed before now.

Women are being urged to consume more and more, as specific

targets of capitalist consumerism; consumer fetishism has invested food with messages of desirability, pleasure, wealth and harmony. Yet as objects of consumer fetishism in their own right, bodies of women are expected to be impossibly thin. Could it be that women unconsciously play out these impossible social contradictions upon a body that allows the *pleasure* of satiation, while simultaneously escaping some of the dangers by vomiting food?

In a world where 800 million people are threatened every day with starvation, in focusing on the Western female beauty aesthetic as either oppressive or dangerous, we lay ourselves open to charges of cultural relativism or even Eurocentrism. We would not deny the restricted nature of our investigation, but we would still argue that within our culture of 'plenty', where traditional moral ideologies have been replaced by the ethics of obsessionality, problems of self-regulation bear historical and political scrutiny. We feel in particular the need to examine the thinking behind the Western idea that 'you can never be too rich or too thin'. For as Heather said to her mate after consuming too much then deliberately making herself vomit, in the film *Heathers*: 'for Christ's sake ... bulimia is such an eighties fetish ...'.

In a culture which over-promotes the female slender ideal, food is often presented as being, and is indeed found to be, more erotic and dangerous for women than sex. But even when faced with this sort of behaviour we don't think that images of skinny women are at the bottom of it all and have *caused* eating disorder or food fetishism. We would argue, however, that thin female representations, particularly in the West, have informed ideologies about femininity and the language that structures desire. Food has become associated with pleasure, danger and the erotic by women who oscillate between engagement with and resistance to the thin ideal. We feel the fetishism of food may well become more common if the tyranny of slenderness continues to frame women's comprehension of their bodies and their ph/fantasies.

Is it a wonder that Western women form fetishistic relationships with baby food or chocolate, as was revealed by the survey we undertook for this book, discussed in chapter four. In a culture that constructs female fat as 'sin', but equates orgasm with eating great quantities of Belgian chocolate or Häagen Dazs ice cream, it is perhaps inevitable that food fetishism should occur in women. It is as if the perverted logic of advertising has actually mapped onto the unconscious of the female population, and eating, metonymically, appears as a way of achieving orgasm. Food, the chosen object of fetishism, for some women, provides a more satisfying, a more 'naughty but nice' relationship than the rest. This book explains that women do fetishise in the sexual sense, with a number of inanimate objects, and that they also fetishise food, using the oral pleasure principle.

Madonna's music, photos, performances and bondage outfits and her book *Sex* have drawn attention to changing sexual practices of some of today's young women. Madonna has her feminist critics as well as champions, but none of them seem to disagree that her attitudes towards sexuality have literally put female desire on the international stage. We hope in our own small way we can also contribute to international debates about female sexuality. By discussing the active dynamic of female desire that is central to female fetishism, we hope to align ourselves with women who wish to challenge sexual stereotypes in cultural representations, as well as within psychoanalysis. Both arenas still seem to be unable to understand the broad extent of female *agency* as well as female desire.

We anticipate that some readers may glimpse in the wild mental copulations of the female fetishists we describe, some of their own thoughts, desires and behaviour. Today's female comics, from Victoria Wood to Roseanne Barr, with their jokes about food, sex and desire, draw attention through humour to 'perverse' female activities that most women know about but which are rarely addressed (or completely understood) by the media or the clinicians. We wait for those who regulate ideas about fetishism to catch up with today's female performers as well as the sexual imaginations and secret food fetishes of the rest of us women. Meanwhile, *bon appetit?*

Notes

1 Michael Warner in 'Fear of Queer Planet', quoted in Cherry Smyth, *Lesbians Talk: Queer Notions*, Scarlet Press, London 1992, p11.

2 Questions raised at the *Preaching to the Perverted* Conference, ICA, 12 July 1992.

3 'Cultural politics' is defined by Michèle Barrett as being about 'the struggle over meaning', in Ros Brunt and Caroline Rowan (eds), *Feminism, Politics and Culture*, Lawrence & Wishart, London 1982.

4 Caroline Evans, 'Femininity as Perversion', paper at ICA, July 1992.

5 Louise Kaplan, *Female Perversion*, Pandora, London 1991 provides definition of the concept of 'homeovestism' on page 250. It should be noted that it was George Zavitzianos ('Homeovestism: Perverse Forms of Behaviour Including the Wearing of Clothes of the Same Sex, *International Journal of Psychoanalysis*, 53: p471–7, 1972) who introduced the term to psychoanalytic debate in 1969 after reading Joan Riviere's arguments ('Womanliness as a Masquerade', *International Journal of*

Psychoanalysis, 10:303–13) published some 40 years earlier. We discuss this fully in chapter two.

6   See discussion of 'pepsi people' by Judith Williamson, *Decoding Advertisements: Ideology and Meaning in Advertising*, Marion Boyars, London 1978.

7   Ros Coward, *Female Desire*, Paladin, London 1984.

8   Catherine Belsey in *Critical Practice*, Methuen New Accents, London 1980, p5, defines the concept 'discourse', use of which is usually associated with Michel Foucault's writing, as follows: '*A discourse* is a domain of language-use, a particular way of talking (and writing and thinking). A discourse involves certain shared assumptions which appear in the formulations that characterize it. The discourse of common sense is quite distinct, for instance, from the discourse of modern physics, and some of the formulations of the one may be expected to conflict with the formulations of the other. Ideology is *inscribed in* discourse in the sense that it is literally written or spoken *in it*; it is not a separate element which exists independently in some free-floating realm of 'ideas' and is subsequently embodied in words, but a way of thinking, speaking, experiencing'. Throughout this book we hope this usage will become clear and familiar.

9   Response to paper delivered at *Preaching to the Perverted*, ICA, July 1992.

10   Interview with Sophia Chauchard-Stuart by Lorraine Gamman, August 1992.

11   This sculpture is featured on the front cover of Ros Coward's book (1984, *op cit*). This image and discussion, in our opinion, clearly hints at the idea of food fetishism in connection with shoe fetishism by men, but Coward doesn't use the word or a conceptual framework to discuss fetishism.

12   Figures quoted by Penny Chorlton in 'Where Do the Pounds Go' *Observer*, 20 January 1991, pp24–36.

13   E. Gleick, 'Food on the Brain', *New York Woman*, 1990.

14   We would not necessarily agree with the view that men who ritually binge on beer and vindaloo, and then vomit the whole lot up, should be compared to bulimics. This male braggadocio perhaps does warrant closer scrutiny, but in relation to notions of the masquerade – a masculine masquerade, in this case (living up to machismo images of the 'hard drinking man') – and to the anthropological badge of belonging ('being one of the lads').

1

Three Types of Fetishism: a Question of Definition

The word 'fetish' derives from the Portuguese 'feitico', a name given to popular talismans in the middle ages – often illegal and/or heretical. The word subsequently developed in popular usage to mean fated, charmed, bewitched. Originally, the word 'feitico' came from the Latin ('facticium'), which meant 'artificial', before it came to mean 'witchcraft'. As William Pietz has identified, the Portuguese words most often used to designate witchcraft were 'feitico', 'feiticeiro' and 'feiticaria' and were part of the vocabulary of the fifteenth-century Portuguese who sailed to West Africa'.[1] Earlier accounts of daily life in Portugal in the Middle Ages, where Catholic religious ideas determined Christian witchcraft law, indicate a prior connection between witchcraft and fetishism.[2] This can be seen in the extract from the anti-witchcraft edict issued by King John I of Portugal in 1385:

> No person may use or effect fetishes [obre de feticos], nor bonds [ligamento], nor summoning up of devils [chamar os diabos], nor incantations [descantacoes], nor casting spells [obre de veadeira], nor making cabalist figures [obre de carantulas], nor evil spells [geitos], nor interpreting dreams [sonhos], nor working enchantments [encantamentos], nor may he cast lots [lance roda], nor read fortunes [lance sortes], nor practice divinations [obre d'advinha-mentos] in whatever guise that may be forbidden.[3]

Historically, it appears that the origins of the word 'fetishism' had always addressed the behaviour of women. William Pietz reminds us that in the *Forum Turolij* of 1176 the use of amulets [ligatures] by women 'upon men or animals or other things' is referred to as part of the law dealing with crimes of women, which also included punishment for other acts such as the practice of abortion.[4]

The word 'fetish' did not enter the English language until the seventeenth century (the OED gives 1613 for its first known usage) when it appears to have been used by writers to describe any object used by 'The Negroes of the Guinea coast and neighbourhood as an amulet or means of enchantment.'[5]

Discussion about fetishism as the province of non-European 'savages' is found in some of the earliest popular voyage 'travelogues' such as: Ramusio's *Viaggio e Navigazion* (1550), de Bry's *India Orientalis* (1597), Purchas's *Hakluytus Posthumus* (1625), Churchill's *Collection of Voyages and Travels* (1732), Astley's *A New General Collection of Voyages and Travels* (1746) and Prevost's *Histoire generale des voyages* (1748).[6] These discussions of fetishism rarely focussed upon the analysis of European 'good luck' amulets or activities of medieval non-Christian Europeans. More usually they posited fetishism as part of heathen rituals found in 'black' Africa. Anthropologists such as Nicholas Villaut writing in the seventeenth century,[7] and philosophers such as Charles de Brosses writing in the eighteenth century,[8] went on to define many rituals by diverse cultures involving inanimate 'magical' objects as 'fetishism'.

By the nineteenth century the term 'fetishism' had entered popular language and was being used more generally by writers to refer to anything reverenced without due reason; 'Public opinion, the fetish even of the nineteenth century' (Lowell, 1837).[9] Marx, in an early article 'Theft of Wood' (1842), went on to make the analogy between the tribal fetish made of wood, and the peasant's right to the forest. He developed this idea further in 1859 when he described commodity fetishism in 'A Contribution to the Critique of the Political Economy', and then more substantially in *Capital* Volume One, first published in 1867. Krafft Ebing first used the term fetishism in 1886 in a criminal/sexual sense of obsession:[10] it was then used by Alfred Binet in 1888 with the sexual connotation we now associate with Freud's writing.[11]

Historically, and in our present culture, then, 'fetishism' is used in three distinct and, we would argue, separate ways: 'commodity fetishism'; 'anthropological fetishism'; and 'psychiatric' or 'pathological' fetishism. (We will refer to the latter as 'sexual' fetishism throughout since we find the term 'pathology' in this context problematic.) Confusion often arises when discussions of fetishism do not clarify exactly which kind of fetishism is being considered, and a conflation of the types often leads to muddled analysis. In what follows, while it is not our purpose to offer a complete history of the idea of fetishism, we do begin to try to define three distinct types of fetishism. (For more historically detailed discussion see articles by William Pietz[12] and Alisdair Pettinger).[13] These definitions aim to prepare the reader for our additional analysis of *contemporary* behaviour by women that we believe best illustrates the different types of fetishism under scrutiny.

Anthropological Fetishism

Anthropological fetishism, originating from the Portuguese 'feitico', is the first concept of fetishism to enter Western thought. As we have already indicated the concept has an ethnocentric history of usage, associated with imperialist ethnography. Indeed, much early usage of the concept of fetishism can be said to represent a misunderstanding, undervaluing or denigration by one culture of the rituals and practices of another.

Even though the word 'fetishism' originated in connection with Christian ideas about 'pagan' practices in Europe (ie, idolatry and witchcraft), as already mentioned, it was more commonly applied to describe 'heathen' religious forms and practices of non-European cultures. This is because the Portuguese traders who travelled to the West Coast of Africa in the sixteenth century, and subsequently the Dutch traders who arrived in the seventeenth century and ejected them, were disturbed and fearful of the religious practices of the new cultures they encountered, and sought a 'rational' explanation for them. According to Willem Bosman, a Dutch merchant writing in 1703, this situation was complicated by the fact that the Dutch Calvinists found the Portuguese Catholics nearly as barbaric as the Africans. They were as much disgusted by the Catholic idolatry as they were by African attribution of talismanic powers to inanimate objects.

William Pietz's fascinating articles published in the anthropological journal *Res* introduced the analysis of these voyage accounts to us; he suggests that it was the writings of Willem Bosman about New Guinea that led the philosopher Charles de Brosses towards his general conceptualisation of 'fetishism' published in the eighteenth century.[14] By the late nineteenth century anthropologist E. B. Tylor was using the word 'fetishism', in his influential book *Primitive Culture* (first written in 1871) in order to distinguish the practice of 'fetishism' from 'idolatry', and to explain and define the worship of inanimate objects:

> To class an object as a fetish demands explicit statement that a spirit is considered as embodied in it or acting through it or communicating by it, or at least that the people it belongs to do habitually think this of such objects; or it must be shown that the object is treated as having personal consciousness and power, is talked with, worshipped, prayed to, sacrificed

to, petted or ill-treated with reference to its past or future behaviour to its votaries.[15]

Tylor observes the use of fetish objects in many cultures – African and Indian among others – which are believed to hold a peculiar or special power because of their links to a deity. Slightly later anthropological writings make a distinction between 'totemism' and 'fetishism' which is also worth identifying here. In the twentieth century the word 'fetishism' was used by J.G. Frazer, the author of the twelve volume *Golden Bough* (written between 1890–1915) but it was his earlier book *Totemism and Exogamy*, in which he first specifically uses the word 'fetish' to 'distinguish it from a totem'.[16]

Frazer argued that the 'fetish' is often 'an isolated individual object', whereas the totem is 'always a class of objects generally a species of animal'.[17] His book explains in great detail how totemism is both 'a religious and social system'. Clansmen and women find themselves (as a consequence of inheritance through the male or female line) in a sacred relationship to a totem object. The object (animal, plant or whatever) has a special relationship to the whole clan. The clan find themselves under a holy bond not to eat, destroy, or disrespect their totem. The totem forms the basis of all the clan's obligations and religious understandings. It also determines tribal membership: men and women from different clans are not allowed to have sex with, or 'marry', each other. This taboo, known as 'exogamy', is found alongside totemism.

This analysis of exogamy constructs a major difference between anthropological fetishism and the totemism of clans, a distinction blurred in previous discussion. Both totemism and fetishism have different functions but a common social purpose, and are believed 'to allay anxieties of the individual and group, and to promote social cohesion through joint rituals and common belief'.[18] Only totemism contained sexual taboos against mating with members of alternative clans. By the twentieth century there were many theories, some of them conflicting, but they started to consolidate the separation of the concepts of 'fetishism' and of 'totemism' in anthropological literature.[19]

The French philosopher Alfred Binet, writing in his 1888 treatise, 'Le Fetichisme dans l'amour', had also started to make distinctions within fetishism that directly addressed the issue of sexuality. He was the first to divide fetishism into 'religious' and 'sexual' categories. But his main interest lay in the use of the term to describe cultural practices of nineteenth century France.

Binet's definition of 'religious' fetishism displays similar characteristics to 'anthropological' fetishism: the idea that a fetish object may derive power from a deity. He applied it to explain rituals within the Catholic church, especially in connection with relics or with the worship of statues of saints. Binet went on to argue that, in his experience, women practised 'religious' fetishism even more than men.[20]

This idea of religious or 'anthropological' fetishism, as we have explained, had more usually been applied to discussion of so-called pagan or 'primitive' amulets or voodoo dolls, but Binet now included the Catholic sacraments in the definition.

But the concept of anthropological fetishism, the idea that the fetish object may derive power from a deity, is also appropriate for understanding other behaviour in the contemporary West. It could be applied to explain many European forms and practices. As one example we concentrate on the behaviour of female fans. We believe the concept of anthropological fetishism can usefully be employed to discuss the way some young women fans are said to 'fetishise' pop or film idols.

Fetishism (Anthropological) and Female Fans

We are all 'fans' of someone or something, although we may not choose to describe ourselves in this way, and we derive a multiplicity of pleasures from looking at or enjoying our chosen objects of worship or desire. Neverthless, popular representations of fans in films like *Play Misty For Me* (1971), *King of Comedy* (1983) and *Misery* (1991), as Lisa A. Lewis has pointed out, tend to associate fans, particularly female fans, not with 'us', but with 'danger, abnormality and silliness' as well as 'pathological deviance'.[21] We feel that these meanings associated with female fans are largely inappropriate, and sexist, in the way they represent women, as we go on to explain.

Fan worship often mimics religious behaviour (though not always). The concept of 'anthropological' fetishism enables critics to consider the behaviour of fans separately from psychological or consumer explanations about such behaviour.

So what is a fan? How is the definition of fan to be distinguished from spectators, aficionados, consumers and/or general audience members? In the collection, *The Adoring Audiences: Fan Culture and Popular Media*, edited by Lisa A. Lewis, there are many essays which attempt to define fans, none conclusive. John Fiske's article is among the best of these and in this and other writing he uses the phrase 'fandom',[22] and defines it 'as part of … proletarian cultural practice in contrast to the bourgeois, distant, appreciative, critical stance to texts',[23] and as something positioned in between 'High' and 'Popular Culture'.[24] Fiske goes on to argue that fandom is characterised by 'discrimination', and since it involves choice, 'productivity', since fans produce their own 'texts', for example their bedrooms or hairstyles.

Discrimination and productivity may be components of fan behaviour exhibited when fans engage with various practices which help them summon up the star's presence, such as constructing their own 'temples' in honour of the star. These temples often consist of rooms in their own homes and sometimes even their own bodies (in the case of lookalike 'wannabees'), behaviour which has parallels with some other forms of worship.

Male and female 'Elvis lookalike' fans en route to Gracelands are one of the most haunting spectacles of the age, since love for a pop star is perhaps harder to understand than love for a spiritual figure. Such worship, articulated through reproduction of the star's image or hyperconformity to the star's image, on such a massive scale, may simply show that acute 'similarity' is as threatening (if not more so) than 'otherness' and difference. But these human 'Elvis' texts, as well as offering visual evidence of anthropological fetishism in homage to the deity (Elvis himself),work almost as tribal signs of 'allegiance' that are communicated to onlookers. This point about mediated collectivity through shared understandings of the Sacred (in this case Elvis) should not be overlooked. Fandom involves 'recognition' by other fans in the community. This recognition is often as important to fans as enjoyment of the music or other products associated with the star in question. The fan's room, objects, and personal appearance, which often have a relation to the identity of the star, may help to cement a shared obsession, a sense of belonging, or in some cases even, communicate to onlookers through the use of specific signs and symbols certain knowledge that Elvis isn't really dead ... .

Fred and Judy Vermorel summarise many case histories of different female (and male) fans who have exhibited such 'tribal' behaviour. Such fans have become preoccupied, and/or fallen in love with pop stars, and subsequently engaged in unusual behaviour to accommodate that love interest.[25] As can be observed from the following quotation this behaviour often involves experiencing their idols as gods or beings on a higher plane:

[Female Fan of Barry Manilow]: 'As he walked into the hotel all the guests stood up and applauded.I was holding onto the back of his Fox Fur jacket and he turned and saw me and said "Hi". I was so stunned I opened my mouth to speak but couldn't say anything. I couldn't move. My legs just wouldn't take me any further. When he spoke I was in a daze and I remember hearing his voice in slow motion.'

[Julie (14) won a competition]. 'The night we met Kajagoogoo I could hardly sleep. I sort of hurt inside. I felt sick every time I thought about them. I felt like crying because I knew it wouldn't last. I'd see them and I would be there for what would seem like a second and then we would be leaving London. We went backstage. I walked in. They were strangers we had never met before but they treated us really nice. I was in a daze. It was absolute paradise. We had made it. I just felt stunned and couldn't believe it. It just wouldn't sink in.'[26]

While some fans live from one concert to the next, with years in between, what sustains them through these 'empty' periods, as Suzanne Moore has pointed out, 'are in fact fetish objects – a poster, a ticket stub, a video, a doll, an exact replica of the jacket HE wore'.[27] As one Buck's Fizz fan, who checked each night the order of his memorabilia, explained 'I really enjoy my collection because it feels like I have a piece of them in my possession.'[28]

We would argue that this metonymic substitution of the *part*, (a lock of hair or other objects more distantly removed but nevertheless associated with the star) standing in for the *whole* (the idol), constitutes anthropological (religious) rather than sexual fetishism. The fan's primary desire is to be in the star's presence and to pay homage to the star. Fetish objects such as ticket stubs, like the anthropological fetish doll or totem, are utilised to bring the deity closer. Some fans even search for more of these 'trinkets' or treasures by going through the rubbish bins of stars as part of the phenomenon known in the USA as 'trashcanning'.

It is surprising given the sexual charge that often seems to accompany the behaviour of some adolescent female fans, that after going to such effort to collect their mementos and 'memorabilia', that all the fan can often do, once they get near their idol, is scream, sit stunned, or cry. One Bay City Roller fan, who had a collection of their dog ends, spare plugs, and an identity bracelet, turned down the opportunity to have sex with one of her idols because 'it would be like a groupie and I wouldn't want to be one of those'.[29] This fan's refusal of the opportunity of sex with the object of desire should not surprise the reader. Cheryl Cline, in her insightful writings about female rock music fans, makes the point that the sexual fantasies of fans, when stated, should not always be read as literal desire for sex with the idol, but may accommodate other desires and fantasies.[30]

This point is corroborated by research undertaken by the Vermorals. Many fans they interviewed indicate that the objects they collect associated with the idol provide a way of coping with dissatisfaction generally. If the fan's idol is male, perhaps the fandom may also provide a way of coping with the disappointment a real heterosexual relationship might offer. This speculative point is supported by Barbara Ehrenreich, Elizabeth Hess and Gloria Jacobs, who in their analysis of Beatlemania have suggested that female pop fans often choose the male stars that represent more 'subversive' versions of heterosexuality,[31] because the men they have access to do not fulfil their 'needs' or 'dreams'.

Many fans, whether of the Beatles, Barry Manilow or heavy rock musicians, join some form of unofficial or official fan club, and are found to congregate in groups to talk about their idols with other fans. Or, if that proves geographically impossible, fans often resort to writing to a series of fan pen pals. In many of the discussions presented by the Vermorels it is clear that stars cannot become tarnished through such interaction (criticism is taboo). The most common phrase used by fans to describe concerts and meetings – the times when the fans are in their idol's presence – is 'it was just like living in a dream'. And the most common dream is of being proposed to, of being the 'chosen one' of the idol:

'I never actually imagined marrying him. I only imagine him asking me to marry him and that's as far as I go. Cos when you are married, there's nothing much more to think about. You've got there.'[32]

Some fans of male pop stars do imagine an afterlife. This involves having a baby – usually a boy (!) – which makes their idol very happy. How they get the baby is left extremely hazy when the fantasies are recounted. Conversely, the fantasies of female fans of female pop stars are imagined to be rather different. Indeed, we were troubled that Ehrenreich, Hess and Jacobs could simply accommodate dominant gender stereotypes in their analysis. For instance, they argue of Janis Joplin that she 'offered women the possibility of identifying with, rather than objectifying the star'. Clearly such an analysis of the female fan's viewing experience excludes the possibility of women experiencing conscious or repressed lesbian desire for their female idols. Nevertheless, on the whole we would argue that most of the fan behaviour we have described so far is primarily informed by deification: men enjoy this sort of worship as much as women. However, women's social subordination affects, perhaps even accommodates, their relationship to fandom.

Obviously there will always be exceptions, fans whose behaviour does not constitute anthropological fetishism. We would not wish to categorically state that the relationship of all fans to their idols is always about non-sexual worship. Our point is that this sexual behaviour is not the same as sexual fetishism. Clearly some fans would love to have sex with their idol and the erotic contemplation of the idol's image provides many opportunities for masturbation as well as scopophilic pleasure.[33] Female fans who throw knickers and keys on stage to male icons, from Bruce Springsteen to The Chippendales, are obviously motivated by powerful erotic desires. But we would argue that even some of this behaviour is not always as 'erotic' as it seems. Even when taken to absolute extremes, it appears to involve levels of 'anthropological' fetishism because of the deification involved in the behaviour. Often much of the behaviour of fans engages with, or cuts across, ideas about the Sacred.

So our point is that whilst some fan behaviour is sexual (and at these times the fan would prefer sex with the star rather than simply putting the star on a pedestal), yet this erotic behaviour, which appears to be fetishistic, is not the same as sexual fetishism. The star is rarely the only 'thing' that provides sexual stimulation for the fan; and the whole star not part of the star is what is sexually required by the fan.

This point is often confused because critics rarely measure or conceptualise the degree, nor the intensity, of the fan behaviour examined. Different contexts and different people will produce different extremes of anthropological fetishism, and at present there appears to be no conceptual model to measure this. Perhaps this is why some assume this behaviour to be about 'sexual fetishism'.[34] We would argue that erotic objectification, infatuation or even obsessive sexual interest in a person is unlikely to be the same thing as sexual fetishism.

Obsessive star stalking, as portrayed in popular films like *Play Misty For Me* (1971), on first sight may appear to be more relevant to ideas about 'sexual' than 'anthropological' fetishism. Though the women fans in these films are portrayed as almost 'religious' in terms of their obsession, it is sexual motivation that is shown to be at the root of the behaviour not 'religious' fervour. Moreover the behaviour looks 'fetishistic'. But this raises questions about the definition of fetishism - it is clearly not the same thing as deification or erotic fixation. We would argue that such films are not about fandom at all but instead reflect a more dangerous psychiatric condition known as erotomania;

and what's more, they give a sexist reading of it. Despite dominant Hollywood representations of deranged female erotomaniacs, more men than women suffer from erotomania. Indeed, in recent years as news reports reveal, more often than not it is male erotomaniacs who have threatened to, or actually attempted to, murder their chosen female idol/love interest.

'Erotomania' has been defined as: melancholy or madness arising from passionate love. Sometimes it is restricted to cases in which the imagination alone is affected.[35] Emily Apter suggests that erotomania is 'the theoretical predecessor of fetishism'.[36] Certainly, the theory of erotomania, elaborated in the 1880s by the doctors Moreau (de Tours) and Charcot, Magnan and Ball[37] did try to address ideas about 'fetishism' as a way of explaining how the individual fixations of erotomaniacs mean they fall in love with people they don't really know. But the concept of 'fixation' is different from the concept of 'fetishism' and research is inconclusive about the erotic behaviour involved. The work, which appeared before Freud elaborated his theory of sexual fetishism, is inconclusive because at the time of writing the authors were clearly using a very general category to mean fetishism, which did not seem to involve sexual disavowal through the substitution of a 'part' for the 'whole'. 'Erotomania' seems a far better description than 'fetishism' to describe the behaviour of some sexually disturbed individuals who suffer from obsessive fantasies or extreme erotic fixations. It should be pointed out that as a form of mental illness erotomania does not really offer the individual the same sort of 'coping strategy' (to allay anxiety) as is associated with fetishism. Additionally, sexual fetishists rarely seem to threaten or hurt other people; whereas the delusions of erotomaniacs may lead to violence. Monica Seles, for example, the tennis player, was recently attacked by a man obsessed with Stephi Graf, whom Ms Seles was beating. He stabbed her in the back of the neck when she appeared on the tennis court.

Stuart Cosgrove, in an article on erotomania, cites many actual cases observed in the late twentieth century. One female 'fan', Joni Penn, was sentenced to six years' imprisonment for locking herself into tv cop Sharon Gless's home after inundating Gless with hundreds of love-letters and phone calls and becoming generally obsessed with video recordings of *Cagney and Lacey*. Did this fan's behaviour involve 'anthropological' fetishism – had Sharon Gless become a sort of deity for Joni Penn – or was the behaviour entirely sexual? Cosgrove points to the difficulty of being precise about the nature of this sort of erotic behaviour, because 'star stalking, cinema's most deranged by-product, has not generated its own body of psychoanalytical knowledge'.[38]

So there is clearly a need for more research into the behaviour of female fans; our point is that when this behaviour is erotic, it does not conform to definitions of orthodox sexual fetishism. Often fan behaviour *is fetishistic* but it usually involves anthropological fetishism or commodity fetishism (as defined by Marx). Thus fetishism of objects by fans occurs in order to summon up the star's presence; this sort of fetishism appears to have much in common with religious worship and involves notions about the sacred, and is therefore 'anthropological' in type. Sexualised fan behaviour does involve the eroticisation of commodities, but this eroticisation of products or items of clothing associated with the star usually accommodates masturbatory fantasies rather than sexual fetishism. The fantasy is necessary because the fan doesn't really have access to the star: the object and the fantasy is not chosen in *preference* to the star in question (as the sexual fetishist chooses an object in preference to the person) but as compensation for lack of real opportunity.

The concept of 'anthropological fetishism', then, may only explain a limited range of behaviour by female and male fans, and other types of fetishism, such as commodity fetishism, often cut across it. This is because in the West we live in a social context determined by consumerism and commodity production. For this reason we think it is worth mentioning John Fiske's writings about the structures that underpin what he describes as 'the cultural economy of fandom'. This is because Fiske's analysis of fandom suggests that components of fan behaviour that are often mistaken for 'fetishism' perhaps can only be understood in relation to consumerism.

When talking about the way fans 'discriminate' Fiske draws on theoretical writing associated with the French philosopher Pierre Bourdieu to explain that fans make 'choices' about taste. He says fans should not be regarded as 'dupes' of capitalist marketing, which may try to address fans as a market by offering products connected with 'star' personalities. On the contrary, Fiske says the issue of 'taste' is crucial because fans do not simply buy anything or collect anything. Fans are extremely discerning about what they consume, and in terms of popular music, for example, are very fussy about who they are fans of. He argues that in selecting a personality or group (not any one would do) fans have already exercised discrimination, rather than fetishism. Indeed, fans often draw sharp and intolerant lines between what and who they are fans of. Fiske goes on to point out that when fans compile research about their idols, it is often obsessively comprehensive in its range and detail. This information has a social value and represents coherent knowledge which may give the fan a form of unofficial 'cultural capital' in certain contexts. Fiske suggests that for the fan this 'unofficial cultural capital' is gained not from being seen to know about things like 'art' or 'literature', which are located at the top of the official hierarchy about the meaning of culture, but from an alternative source. The function of knowledge about the star – 'unofficial' cultural capital – in the lives of fans, is to allow fans to differentiate themselves from other cultural groups, as well as to position them in a hierarchical relation to definitions about High Culture. So Fiske's point is that the process of 'collecting' commodities associated with fans seems to be doing other things as well as fetishising the star.

Fiske uses the term 'productivity' to explain what this behaviour might mean in social terms. Fans produce 'their own texts ... [like] bedrooms and the way they dress, their hairstyles, and makeup'.[39] In order to explain the significance of this point further it is necessary to explain the difference between Fiske's reading of 'productivity' and the term 'activity' used by other critics, like McRobbie and Garbar, who discuss fandom.

While the relationship of young women to pin-ups and pop stars has not yet been the subject of extensive feminist research, there are some early texts which address it and suggest it involves female 'activity'. Angela McRobbie and Jenny Garbar, writing from the Birmingham Centre for Contemporary Cultural Studies in the late 1970s, suggested that fan worship is structurally more likely to be accommodated by media aimed at young women, but conversely that female fandom is not a passive occupation. They argued that young women's magazines are based around an endless flow of myths and images of young male pop stars, and that this objectification of male pop stars, a long standing feature of post war girls' culture, interpellates the female gaze and involves active pleasure from looking. [40]

During their research McRobbie and Garbar noted that adolescent female readers of teenage mags often constructed elaborate fantasies around pop stars such as Donny Osmond or David Cassidy. While the idols may have changed, the location of fan behaviour as part of teenage 'girl subculture' makes the point that while female 'teeny boppers' may be more active than previously imagined, they engage in voyeurism as a consequence of social inequality, because:

> while boys can legitimately look at girls on the street and in school it is still not acceptable for girls to do the same. Hence the attraction of the long interrupted gaze at the life size Donny Osmond special.[41]

McRobbie and Garbar's point is that teenage magazines accommodate the female gaze in a state of erotic contemplation. They argue that – in the days before pop videos were available in the marketplace – young women's magazines catered to the erotic female gaze in a way that other forms of popular culture did not. We would argue that such objectification of the male body through what McRobbie and Garbar call the 'long gaze' may facilitate erotic pleasure from looking, but it also involves young women in summoning up notions of the deity and constructing ideas about the sacred and the profane. We suggest that this activity may often involve 'anthropological' fetishism, and warrant scrutiny on this score, a level of analysis missed by Fiske.

But what does Fiske mean by 'productivity' when describing such fan behaviour: how it is it conceptually different from McRobbie and Garbar's ideas about female 'activity'. To some extent McRobbie and Garbar were contrasting the activity of female fans with, for instance, the 'passivity' of consumers as conceptualised by the Frankfurt School, or the 'passivity' of female spectators, as conceptualised by feminist critics who argued that 'the male figure can't bear the burden of sexual objectification'.[42] But Fiske suggests that fans do more than 'actively contemplate' or 'renegotiate' the dominant meanings/ images of products associated with the chosen idol. He argues that his research shows that 'young girls ... find meanings of their own feminine sexuality that suit them, meanings that are [produced] *independently*' [our emphasis].[43]

As well as arguing that fans are involved in complex *independent* 'production of meaning' via their use of products associated with stars, Fiske also identifies that this fan behaviour is often characterised by excess. But the way some fans excessively consume products does not reinforce the logic of consumerism or position them as 'dupes' of capitalism; on the contrary, such excessive participation can perhaps offer challenge to it. This point about female fans as excessive readers/viewers can be conceptualised as a form of hysteria – and we would point out that 'excessive' fan behaviour is not confined to women but also relates to men.

While we agree that much fan behaviour seems to have a relationship to consumer production, we argue that theories of consumerism are not always appropriate to explain it. Fiske's account of 'discrimination' and 'productivity' cannot, for example, really explain the religious dimension to fan 'deification' and 'worship'. We would argue that not all aspects of 'fandom' can be contained within Fiske's cultural economy of fandom, because often fan behaviour appears to address ideas about the sacred. So the concept of 'anthropological' fetishism is as useful as the concept of 'commodity' fetishism to explain what fans are doing.

Male football fans, internationally renowned for hooliganism rather than anthropological fetishism, also often exhibit religious elements in their behaviour. They 'worship' or adore their team and talk about them in terms that invoke the sacred. This behaviour may often look tribal, and relate to nationalism and gender reaffirmation, or even 'resistance' of class oppression, as has been argued by many critics. But as far as we know it has not been discussed in relation to issues about worship or the mediated collectivity associated with fetishism in the anthropological sense.[44]

Anthropological fetishism may also explain the obsessive hoarding of a partner's effects by a widow or widower or the mother's collecting of her child's memorabilia. It is clear that behaviour associated with loss and grief crosses all types of sexual relationship as well as other social relations. People mourning lovers (heterosexual, bisexual or of the same sex), friends, parents, children or animals, have been known to develop fetishistic behaviour, in order to cope with this loss. We would argue that such behaviour is initiated by absence (not only death), and that some aspects of grief (though not all) may involve what we have termed anthropological fetishism. What the cherishing of objects associated with those we love has in common with the behaviour of fans is the desire to maintain a link to an absent person through a fetish object. The fetish itself – a photograph, a lock of hair, or whatever is chosen – becomes invested with presence, and so symbolically 'stands in' for absence or loss in the same way that the religious totem, for many people, represents a material presence of god. The relationship between anthropological, sexual and commodity fetishism in the analysis of the behaviour of fans is thus very complex. We feel that debate can only be helped by attempting to disentangle the threads. Certainly it needs to be recognised that the concept of anthropological fetishism is an important part of such analysis. We have also sketched out other areas in which this concept is useful in cultural criticism. We would like to add at this point that anthropological fetishism does seem to be gendered in our present culture. Women's social subordination may inspire them towards being practitioners of it as much, if not in greater numbers (as has been has suggested by Binet[45]), as men.

Commodity Fetishism

The bottom line in daily life is the commodity form.[46]

The history of the concept of fetishism has always been connected to commercial relations. In order to do business with the native populations, Pietz has argued, many European merchants arriving on the West Coast of Africa in the seventeenth century found themselves having to engage with forms of what we have described as anthropological fetishism. This may be why they were so anxious or intrigued by the idea of fetishism in the first place. In terms of the European experience, as well as the history of thought, the concept of the fetish emerged alongside that of the commodity form in the sixteenth and seventeenth centuries. It is accordingly not surprising that Karl Marx, writing virtually two hundred years later, should have connected them so literally.

The most significant discussion of commodity fetishism occurs in part one of *Capital* Volume One. Marx argued that when goods are produced for exchange in the market they come to be seen not only as articles of utility ('use values') but also as inherently valuable objects with special 'mystical' qualities. In commodity production, the value of products is displaced from the labour that produces it, and is thought to emanate from the product itself. Thus, in the commodity, the social relation between 'men' (ie, the social relations of production and exchange) assumes the 'fantastic form of a relation between things'.[47] Marx describes this as fetishism because, as in religion, a human product (in religion, an idea, or the invention of gods, in production, a product made by humans) acquires a life of its own, and enters into relations both with other things of its kind and with the human race.

The fetishism of the commodity is more than the attribution of magical powers to an inanimate object; it also involves what we would describe as a disavowal of human labour, a displacement of value from the people who produce things onto the things themselves. In the language of Marx, the commodity 'hides' the reality of human labour. In the passage on commodity fetishism, Marx continually describes the concept of value as 'hiding' the real social relations. For example, 'the determination of the magnitude of value of labour time is a secret hidden under the apparent movements in the relative value of commodities'[48]; the money form 'conceals' the social character of private labour and the social relations between the individual workers by making those relations appear as relations between objects. Thus, for Marx, the term commodity fetishism involved both an analogy with anthropological fetishism and an element of what we would describe as disavowal.

Marx developed commodity fetishism further in part two of *Capital* Volume One. Here he used it in order to refer to the exchange processes whereby alienation and dehumanization result from the the disavowal of the true significance of labour. Extrapolating from Marx's discussion, contemporary critic Michael Taussig writes that commodity fetishism involves:

> the attribution of life, autonomy, power and even dominance to otherwise inanimate objects and presupposes the draining of these qualities from the human actors who bestow the attribution.[49]

But the question must arise as to whether Marx's original metaphorical use of the term ever really becomes an autonomous, discrete, new kind of fetishism. Does it remain simply an infinitely extended metaphor from anthropological fetishism?

Marx did not concern himself in any detail with questions of distribution, the sort of consumer relations a commodity economy might institute.[50] Thorstein Veblen, however, in *The Theory of the Leisure Class*, first published in 1899, writing not long after Marx, began to examine the meaning of fetishised commodities for the individuals who consume them. Veblen, pessimistic about the way the people he calls the 'upper classes' abstained from productive work, took to examining their leisure patterns. He found mere idleness was not enough for the rich to demonstrate their wealth and that consumption patterns operated to reflect status:

> The quasi-peaceable gentleman of leisure, then, consumes of the staff of life beyond the minimum required for subsistence and physical efficiency, but his consumption also undergoes a specialization as regards the quality of the goods consumed. He consumes freely and of the best in food, drink, narcotics, shelter, services, ornaments, apparel, weapons and accoutrements, amusements, amulets, and idols or divinities. In the process of gradual amelioration which takes place in the articles of his consumption, the motive principle and the proximate aim of innovation is no doubt the higher efficiency of the improved and more elaborate products for personal comfort and well-being. But that does not remain the sole purpose of their consumption ... it now becomes incumbent on him to discriminate with some nicety between the noble and the ignoble in consumable goods. He becomes a connoisseur of incredible viands of various degrees of merit, in manly beverages and trinkets, in seemly apparel and architecture, in weapons, games, dances and the narcotics. This cultivation of the aesthetic faculty requires time and application, and the demands made upon the gentleman in this direction therefore tend to change his life of leisure into

a more or less arduous application to the business of learning how to live a life of ostensible leisure in a becoming way. Closely related to the requirement that the gentleman must consume freely and of the right kind of goods, there is the requirement that he must know how to consume them in a seemly manner. His life of leisure must be conducted in due form. Hence arise good manners ... High bred manners and ways of living are items of conformity to the norm of conspicuous leisure and conspicuous consumption. Conspicuous consumption of valuable goods is a means of reputability to the gentleman of leisure ...'[51]

Veblen's analysis of the way that commodities in the nineteenth century come to signify meanings unrelated to utility is linked to Marx's original use of commodity fetishism, but goes beyond it. The way in which the term commodity fetishism is most commonly used in contemporary criticism is closer to Veblen's usage than to that of Marx. Indeed, at the time of writing *Capital*, Marx had no inkling of the sort of 'conspicuous consumption' Veblen was later to describe, nor of the sort of conspicuous consumption that has since character-ised twentieth century Western society. The original explanation given by Marx locates 'fetishism' as a consequence of the *production* of commodities, rather than their *consumption*, as may be said to be implied in Veblen. Marx does not consider other possible magical attributions attaching to commodities. For instance the ability to confer status upon an owner (Veblen) or the ability to confer enhanced sexual attractiveness (current advertising claims for many products). It is only later commentators who have developed further analysis of other aspects of consumer fetishism as it relates to commodities.

The Hungarian Marxist intellectual, Georg Lukacs, writing some fifty years after Marx, used the concept of commodity fetishism to analyse the way that capitalism converts people and things into abstractions. He considered the way in which the commodity form 'invisibly' entered human lives, so that individuals could not begin to imagine or fully comprehend non-fetishised social relations, outside of capitalist logic. In capitalism, production is inseparable from com-modity production, and there can be no relationships of people outside the world of commodities. Lukacs defines this process as 'reification'. As Jhally, Kline and Leiss comment, 'Lukacs ... turned the undevel-oped notion of commodity fetishism into the concept of reification, which became subsequently – through its adoption by the Frankfurt School – one of the mainstays of social criticism in the twentieth century.'[52]

The significance of the concept of 'reification' is that it generalises

the concept of commodity fetishism to encompass the entire experience of life in capitalism:

> The transformation of the commodity relation into a thing of 'ghostly
> objectivity' cannot therefore content itself with the reduction of all objects
> for the gratification of human needs to commodities. It stamps its imprint
> upon the whole consciousness of man; his qualities and abilities are no
> longer an organic part of his personality, they are things which he can 'own'
> or 'dispose of' like the various objects of the external world. And there
> is no natural form in which human relations can be cast, no way in which
> man can bring his physical and psychic 'qualities' into play without their
> being subjected increasingly to this reifying process.[53]

What we have in the writing of Lukacs above is a definition that
posits commodity fetishism as both an objective process and a sub-
jective phenomenon. As Susan Willis comments:

> Objectively, there is a world of commodities and a market economy, whose
> laws we might apprehend, but which nevertheless seem to obey 'invisible
> forces that generate their own power' (Lukacs, 1971:87). Subjectively,
> people in commodity capitalism experience the estrangement of their
> activities as these too become commodities.[54]

The term 'commodity fetishism', whether associated with Marx's
original usage, or with the interpretation offered fifty years later by
Lukacs, figures as a metaphor, to explain cultural processes of mystification and reification. However, we would argue that these metaphoric interpretations would have to change in order to adequately
conceptualise the patterns of consumer culture that began to occur
from the later part of the nineteenth century. These changes were in
the area of packaging, marketing and advertising. Put simply, the
commodity form gradually began to be attributed with more and
more 'fetish' qualities. It was not simply the embodiment of value;
it could also contain many other 'magical' attributes. Once the separation from use value is made, the door opens to allcomers.

Increased urbanisation in the late nineteenth century produced a
shift in the way, for example, household food products and commodities were bought and sold. Richard Ohmann has identified that families
no longer had space to accommodate bulk buying: loose foodstuffs
like oats, previously bought in bulk, start to become available in 2lb
packages called 'Quaker Oats', subsequently advertised.[55] This change,
on a mass scale, produces two significant social consequences. First,
mass production and consumption create rationalisation of sales
formats and packaging of products (Taylorization). Second, marketing techniques are utilised to mediate between 'consumers' and 'com-

modities. This mediation involves, as Susan Willis has argued, 'packaging as a dimension of the commodity form itself' as well as advertising with its persuasive address to human desires as well as needs.[56]

What we are arguing then is that when society entered into an era of generalised mass production and consumption, the nature of the fetishism of commodities changed. The cause of this stems from both the revolution in packaging as well as the revolution in *communications* that occured in the nineteenth century, both of which contributed and led to the development of advertising. Through the medium of marketing and advertising techniques, central components of commodity production and consumption become expanded from Marx's original conceptualisation, to subsequently include metonymic processes of disavowal, as we go on explain.

While advertising may not have been a central feature of life in Europe in the seventeenth and eighteenth centuries, quack doctors as well as shop keepers, often promoted their wares. This genre of advertising continued and developed into the nineteenth century, but changed, as Raymond Williams has pointed out because modern advertising can now be 'traced, essentially, to certain characteristics of new monopoly [corporate] capitalism'.[57]

In the early twentieth century then, after the first world war, advertising developed and accelerated as a business, as a consequence of the recognition of consumer markets. It also benefitted from the development of motivational research and psychological techniques. Adverts started to feature objects, represented as associated with personal and social meanings.

Veblen had already hinted at this shift but does not explain how it will impact upon the workers' lives rather than those of the 'leisure class'. After the second world war, we find a shift in the way the working class is conceptualised (the embourgeoisement thesis) and a shift in the address of adverts aimed at the 'man in the street'. Beer for instance, is no longer represented as simply a drink but is represented as signifying true 'manliness'; metonymically the beer is now being associated with the 'Real Men' who drink it. A pint becomes a potent symbol of masculinity so that women are not expected to drink pints of beer. Raymond Williams call this metonymic transformation part of the 'magic of advertising'.

The fetishism at work in the adverts of the late twentieth century society not only disavows labour power, but often the 'use value' of the product. This is because advertising representations no longer attempt to connect products with their utility function, but set up a whole range of metonymic and metaphoric associations connected to other desires and aspirations.

Judith Williamson is one cultural critic who has written very astutely about this. Her perspective on commodity fetishism in advertising was one of the first to employ semiotics as well as an Althusserian model of ideology. By exploring the complex significations of advertising she is able to show how advertising moves commodity fetishism beyond the realm of metaphor, to become a discrete fetishism which 'is capable of transforming the language of objects to that of the people'.[58]

Williamson discusses how diamonds are marketed by likening them to eternal love, creating a symbolism whereby the mineral means something not in its own terms, as a rock, but in human terms as a sign. Here, she is identifying how advertising fetishises commodities. Not only through the process of mystification, but because the linguistic articulation involves metonymic or metaphoric substitution. Her work goes on to explain how people become identified with objects ('pepsi people' etc) through a process which sells us something else besides consumer goods: 'in providing us with a structure in which we, and those consumer goods are interchangeable, they [advertisers] are selling us ourselves.'[59]

Williamson's sophisticated utilisation of post-structuralist theories about encoding, to consider processes of mystification and reification as part and parcel of the fetishism of commodities, takes Veblen's reading of conspicuous consumption further. There has been an extension of the argument, even if it remains faithful to the logical structure of Marx's original conceptualisation of commodity fetishism. This 'extension' of the concept of commodity fetishism therefore necessitates a shift in explanation.

The original use of commodity fetishism associated with Marx we would describe as 'commodity fetishism: 1' encompassing ideas about disavowal of the labour process as well as mystification of objects. The emphasis taken up by Lukacs, on the other hand, which encompasses stage 1, generalising it as 'reification', we would describe as 'commodity fetishism: 2'. This is because there has been an extension of argument, an extension of the metaphor in fact. Williamson's usage goes further. Like other critics who have subsequently analysed advertising, she includes stages 1 and 2 commodity fetishism but extends her argument to include visual and linguistic representation which feature processes of disavowal. We would describe this usage as 'commodity fetishism: 3'. What Williamson describes in *Decoding Advertise-*

ments is not a substitution of a part (product) for the whole (capitalist relations), during the process of advertising, but rather a mystification of one thing into a more mystical other, achieved through metonymic and metaphoric use of signs. Fetishism, in this context, to requote Raymond Williams, goes beyond 'magic', because the goods being represented disavow not only production, but use value and also some levels of literal meaning. Clearly, there is an increase in the intensity of the fetishisation Williamson describes, compared to that originally conceptualised by Marx.[60]

Baudrillard's writing on commodity fetishism also seems to reinforce the idea that in post-industrial society fetishism of commodities is about more than just the disavowal of production. Indeed, Baudrillard offers a different perspective from that of Marx, Veblen, Lukacs and even Williamson in terms of his ideas about how commodity fetishism occurs at the level of the sign.

In *Decoding Advertisements* Williamson suggests that the fetishization of commodities, and mystification of the meaning of products, can be decoded through the application of semiotics to reveal the disavowal of production/real human desires. Williamson parts company with Lukacs in acknowledging the 'relative autonomy' of ideology (an effect of the Althusserian influence), though retains the idea of material/economic determination 'in the last instance'.[61] She does not believe that the logic of capitalism wholly determines the logic of meaning, which is why 'decoding' is possible in the first place. Baudrillard, in contrast, does seem to believe that the logic of capitalism is the logic of meaning. He denies the distinction between 'use value', which Marx saw as unmystified, and 'exchange value' which Marx saw as 'magical' and suggests:

> commodity fetishism ... is not a functioning of the commodity defined simultaneously as exchange value and use value, but of exchange value alone. Use value in this restrictive analysis of fetishism appears neither as a social relation nor hence as the locus of fetishism.[62]

Baudrillard argues that the autonomy of signs is not relative but absolute. Where Marx distinguished between 'false exchange value' and 'true' use value, Baudrillard overturns these definitions completely. He sees post-industrial society as having entered another stage in the mode of production, which he calls 'simulation'. For him the concept of 'use value' as a naturalisation of commodity relations is already fetishistic. This reading contradicts the orthodox reading of use value as unmystified. It further challenges the distinctions between subject/

object and production/consumption, contained in orthodox Marxism, which Baudrillard intended to 'implode'.[63]

Baudrillard contends that the concept of exchange value allows for
an anti-humanist understanding of the relationship between humans
and objects in post-industrial capitalist society. He argues that all production is fetishised into an abstract process in which, 'encompassed
by objects that function and serve, man is not so much himself as the
most beautiful of these functional and servile objects'.[64] He also argues
that 'use value' fetishism converts all human endeavours and desires
into a series of structurally equivalent 'needs' or signs of difference.
For Baudrillard it is this equivalence of linguistic structure that makes
the process of 'use value' identical to the process of 'fetishism'.

What is being sacrificed and therefore repudiated in Baudrillard's
work is real production of real commodities by real people in the real
world. This 'disavowal' occurs in Baudrillard's reformulation of 'use
values' as fetishised in order to suggest the complex status of the
commodity in post-modernity (ie, no economistic allusion to *need* can
account for the provision or existence of the commodity). Baudrillard's
work therefore represents a massive epistemological break with, rather
than an extension of, the logic of Marx's original conceptualisation
of commodity fetishism.

Baudrillard's arguments, which we posit as 'commodity fetishism
4', are contested by many intellectuals on the political left as contain-
ing inappropriate formulations of metropolitan capitalism. Judith
Williamson, for example, has criticised Baudrillard for his fatalism
and for not being able to 'recognise any world other than the world
of media signs'.[65] Christopher Norris has gone further and suggested
that Baudrillard is a 'purveyor of some of the silliest ideas yet to gain
a hearing among disciples of French intellectual fashion'.[66] Norris
cites Baudrillard's 1991 newspaper article on 'The Reality Gulf'
(published in *The Guardian*) which suggested that the Gulf War was
a 'hyperreal event' as evidence that Baudrillard has lost sense 'between truth and the various true seeming images, analogues and
fantasy-substitutes which currently claim that title'.[67]

It should be noted that none of the thinkers discussed in relation
to the concept of commodity fetishism, with the exception of Judith
Williamson, address how issues about gender impact on signs. The
notable male thinkers we have mentioned have in common with Karl
Marx, and orthodox Marxism, the idea that commodity fetishism is
ungendered in its definition.

This is because commodity fetishism is construed by orthodox

Marxism as an effect of capitalist relations of production *per se*, and the use of the concept of fetishism here is metaphoric. In Williamson's and Baudrillard's writing, however, their models are quite different; the concept of commodity fetishism is allocated a metonymic and metaphoric relationship to meaning as a consequence of the representations which are integral to post-industrial consumerism. This usage brings it in line, in terms of underlying structural components, with all the other types of fetishism described in this chapter; none of which readily engages with issues about sexual politics.

The analysis of commodity fetishism as something that is separate from gender seems problematic to us. This is because ungendered concepts of labour ignore the realm of the domestic and imply that 'work' usually takes place outside the home, and is therefore done by men. It should be noted that not only do women make up more than half of the world's population but most of them have traditionally done a double load of work, inside as well as outside the home. People use products to carve out identities for themselves, and in particular, to carve out gender identities for themselves (gender clearly means more than genital difference). We would argue that in post-industrial society it is impossible to free the analysis of gender from the commodity form, in the same way that it is impossible to distinguish between what have been described as 'real' needs and 'false' needs, without reference to psychoanalytic discourse. As Susan Willis has commented, to see gender as a process separate from commodities, is to imagine 'creating objects in terms of use value alone'.[68]

When analysing post-industrial capitalism, most critics generally accept that both women and men experience commmodity fetishism. Obviously, there are some gender variables that impinge on the concept as well as on the commodities produced in society. Research from Rosemary Scott's *The Female Consumer* [69] to Frank Mort's writings on 'Men and Shopping' [70] indicates that there are gender variables to take into consideration in terms of

1. how and what commodities are produced in the first place.
2. what commodities are preferred by each sex and
3. who does the shopping in households to secure the purchase of cheap or expensive objects.

Nevertheless, the orthodox labour theory of value, as it originated with Marx, is unable to conceptualise why women in households usually find themselves responsible for shopping for goods and services that facilitate the reproduction of labour power. Nor is it able to conceptualise why women, more often than men, are represented in popular culture as 'insatiable' consumers.

We feel therefore that the issue of sexual politics would make it more complicated, though not impossible, to remain faithful to the logic of argument about commodity fetishism originally made by Marx. In order to extend his ideas to explain life in post-industrial society, we would want to engage with the sexual politics underlying the production and consumption of commodities, and also to emphasise the visual as a component of the representation of commodities which, as Guy Debord has pointed out, gives use value to spectacle.[71] Indeed, the forms of post-industrial society such as the supermarket and the shopping mall demand analysis of the way spectacle impinges on ideas, and is integral to ideas about commodity fetishism. We take up this point about the visual aspect of commodities again when discussing gaze theory. In chapter six we analyse how codes of the sexual erotic have been commodified in the twentieth century, and how this 'consumer fetishism of the erotic' has permeated representation and has been mistakenly read as 'sexual fetishism' by some feminist critics. In particular, confusion arises because the accounts of sexual fetishism involved in the 'male gaze' have no model of the consumer context nor the intensity of sexual fetishism they discuss: we argue that such work is mistaken because it fails to acknowledge that orthodox sexual fetishism results in the *preference* for an object or sexual part above any other type of sexual stimulation.

Sexual Fetishism

Psychiatric or pathological fetishism is defined by Freud as occurring when an inanimate object or part of the body becomes the focus of arousal in preference to a person. Freud specifies:

> A certain degree of fetishism is thus habitually present in [normal] love ... The situation only becomes pathological when the longing for the fetish passes beyond the point of being merely a necessary condition attached to the sexual object and actually takes the place of the normal aim, and, further when the fetish becomes detached from a particular individual and becomes the sole sexual object.[72]

We feel that Freud's qualification that some 'degree of fetishism' is part of all human sexuality is perhaps the most important one. We would, however, disagree with his definition above (and in later writing) about what constitutes either 'pathological' or 'normal' love. This is why throughout this book we have chosen to use the phrase 'sexual fetishism' (originally associated with Binet's writing) rather than psychiatric fetishism. By doing this we hope to try to signal to the reader our discomfort with the use of the term pathological and with some of the prescriptions of psychoanalysis, while still examining the psychiatric literature.

Paul Gebhard is one of the few researchers we found who has addressed questions about the 'stages' of sexual fetishism mentioned by Freud in his earliest writings on fetishism. Gebhard attempts to refine Freud's perception about 'degrees' of fetishism. He suggests that sexual fetishism can be conceptualised along 'a continuum of intensities' as follows:

> Level 1: A slight preference exists for certain kinds of sex partners, sexual stimuli or sexual activity. The term 'fetish' should not be used at this level.
> Level 2: A strong preference exists for certain kinds of sex partners, sexual stimuli or sexual activity. (Lowest intensity of fetishism)
> Level 3: Specific stimuli are necessary for sexual arousal and sexual performance. (Moderate intensity of fetishism)
> Level 4: Specific stimuli *takes the place* of a sex partner. (High level fetishism)[73]

This model of three stages leading up to 'orthodox' sexual fetishism (ie, Freud's definition of it) we feel is helpful for two reasons. First, it enables critics to distinguish between those people who can only achieve orgasm from a fetish object (orthodox fetishism) and those who use fetish items, resulting in different degrees of sexual stimulation, within their sexual practice. Second, it allows us to discuss many sexual practices, involving levels of fetishism, without bringing back in those pathological connotations associated with Freud's 'orthodox' fetishists. This is important beause cultural critics often mistake sexual eroticism of body parts with sexual fetishism, and subsequently read a range of cultural forms as 'perverse'.

Throughout this book when we refer to 'orthodox sexual fetishism', we refer to Freud's version of it defined in the above which concurs with Gebhard's ideas about the 'fourth stage'.

But it isn't possible to take up Freud on fetishism and simply leave behind the pathological connotations associated with his writing. This is not only because, as Foucault has pointed out, '"fetishism" … served as the guiding thread for analyzing all the other deviations[74],' but because it is not easy to simply 'adapt' pyschoanalysis which has in fact itself operated as a discursive practice. We do our best in this book to try to write women into psychoanalytic accounts of fetishism but we are aware that psychoanalysis has constructed many repressive, prescriptive definitions about sexual 'normality' and 'perversity' which make it hard to conceptualise female desire as active.

In order to identify how ideas about fetishism have been central in constructing problematic definitions about perversity, we briefly look at the history of ideas associated with the original use of words to describe fetishism in the sexual sense, starting with the first discussion which appeared in 1886.

Krafft Ebing's *Psychopathesis Sexualis* (1886) looked at 'fetishism' in pathological terms by emphasising how it 'may become the cause of crime': he cited many cases of 'criminal fetishism', including those involving hair despoiling and robbery or theft of female linen, handkerchiefs, shoes and silks etc.[75] However, Ebing's criminological emphasis on fetishism, while acknowledging a sexual dimension, did not really include women, for he admitted that he had 'so far not succeeded in obtaining facts with regard to pathological fetishism in women'.[76]

Alfred Binet was the next to discuss sexual fetishism. In his 1887 'Le Fetichisme dans l'amour', he separated fetishism into 'sexual' and 'religious' types. He argued that in the sexual category, it becomes fetishism, as opposed to 'normal love', when 'love, instead of being excited by the whole person, is now excited only by a part. Here the part substitutes for the whole, the attribute becomes the quality.'[77]

Binet's 1887 discussion concentrates on male examples. He identifies how the part becomes totally separated from any individual person and 'the adoration is addressed solely to the material object'. He lists a whole range of things, parts of the body (large hands, mouth, hair) that have become the sole object of sexual desire, smell (body odours, perfume) sound (tenor of a voice, piano music) cloth (night caps, handkerchieves). Binet goes on to argue that the adoration of the fetishist develops for not just 'one object in particular, but for the whole genre'.[78] This latter point is reinforced in contemporary writing, such as that of sex researchers Masters and Johnson (1982) who argue that the fetishist will often go to great lengths to add 'just the "right" type of item' to their extensive collections of the preferred object. They cite Robert Stoller for their further suggestions that 'it is *preferred* to the owner because it is safe, silent, cooperative, tranquil and can be harmed or destroyed without consequence'.[79]

Freud's phallicising of fetishism comes about as a consequence of his explanation of the child's entry into sexuality. Taking the boy as the norm, Freud argues that the little boy moves towards heterosexu-

ality when castration anxiety disrupts the pre-Oedipal, dyadic relationship between the mother and baby. The child's realisation that
his mother does not possess a penis is translated as her having been
castrated by the powerful father (whom, within the oedipal conflict
he has wanted to eradicate from her desire, since it disrupts their
dyadic union). The boy fears the father will also take revenge on him
for his murderous wishes, and in rejection of the 'lacking' mother, he
'turns away' from her to identify with the potent father and takes up
a heterosexual orientation. The little boy's entry into 'normal' sexuality is thus the shock at the woman's lack of a penis. A fetishist's
development is arrested at this stage and he tries to deny sexual
difference by reasserting a penis-substitute onto the woman (the fetish).
The fetish object stands in for the mother's phallus. The little girl's
development is seen as only slightly different from the boy's norm.
The little girl, Freud argued, first becomes aware of her own 'inferior'
clitoris on seeing the father's penis, and this gives rise to 'penis envy'.
The little girl has three possible reactions: the first is that of frigidity
and neurosis; the second is a denial of her 'inferiority' and the adoption of an aggressive 'masculinity complex'; the third is the 'feminine'
oedipal move towards desiring the father, and disrupting the dyadic
union with the mother, who is also deficient. The turning to the father,
Freud asserts, takes the form of seeking a penis substitute: a baby by
the father.[80] Because Freud's analysis is based on castration anxiety
– the fear of losing the penis – it follows that fetishism must be a
purely male phenomenon. Girls have no penis so why should they
need to disavow the horror of its possible loss?

Freud's first discussion of fetishism didn't appear until 1905 and
his final commments were given in 1937. His explanation of the sexual
practice changes over the 32 year period and it is interesting to note
exactly how it does develop; and just when the denial of female agency
arises.

In Freud's first discussion of fetishism, in 'Three Essays on Sexuality'(1905), he explains fetishism as a process whereby a part of the
body or some inanimate object becomes the sexual object of desire.
His analogy is the anthropological fetish, believed to embody the deity's
presence. Freud stresses that this sexual activity is deemed 'pathological' only when the fetish 'becomes detached from a particular individual and becomes the *sole* sexual object'. Some degree of fetishism,
he accepts, also takes place in 'normal' love. [81] In this early essay, the
relationship of the individual to the fetish is argued to be symbolic:
'the foot for instance is an age-old sexual symbol which occurs even

in mythology; no doubt the part played by fur as a fetish owes its origin to its association with the hair of the *mons Veneris*'.[82]

In 1909, Freud read a paper 'On the Genesis of Fetishism', to the Vienna Psychoanalytic Society, as work in progress which did mention women fetishists.[83] Freud argues for fetishism as a perversion rather than a form of hysteria,[84] claiming that in the pathological form it is specifically due to unconscious anxieties. Ebing's argument that the fetish object originates from an association with the subject's first sexual excitation is accepted by Freud in order to explain the oddity of some of the object-choices of his patients. He specifically links fetishism to the repression of the drive to look, the scopic drive. His clothes fetishist, repressing the sight of his mother's 'castration', idealises the clothes that prevent him from seeing this awful truth. Fetishism is also linked to a love of odours and smells, and hence to the object-choice of feet. Almost as a joking aside, the paper goes on to state:

> half of humanity must be classed among the clothes fetishists. All women, that is, are clothes fetishists...It is a question again of the repression of the same drive, this time however in the passive form of allowing oneself to be seen, which is repressed by the clothes, and on account of which clothes are raised to a fetish.[85]

Here, Freud assigns to all women a form of fetishism as an explanation of why even intelligent women follow the demands of fashion and wear items of clothing which 'do not show them to their best advantage'. The element we need to draw out here is the passivity of the form and its universality to all women (whose role clearly is to make themselves as attractive as possible to the male gaze). Freud is not arguing that women actively practise the perversion, but that, repressing their desire to be looked at naked, they idealise the clothes that prevent this. Women are not being allowed a serious entry as practitioners of 'true' fetishism, but it is still interesting that at this stage they are brought into the debate.

Freud's main concern in the 1909 discussion of fetishism focusses on the splitting process, whereby one aspect of the object gets suppressed, while the rest is idealised into a fetish. The fetish is chosen for its metonymic nearness to the moment of repression, rather than for any metaphoric aspect. In the discussion that followed the delivery of the paper, two analysts (Steiner and Deutsch) suggested female analysands of their own who could be termed fetishists. Two of the ten analysts (Hitschmann and Bass) moreover, confess themselves to be shoe and hair fetishists respectively and thank Freud for explaining their predilections, which says rather a lot about Freud's inspiration.

In the 1927 article 'Fetishism' Freud moves away from documenting the practice in order to give it a psychoanalytic reading. He states categorically that the fetish stands in for the 'lost' phallus of the mother. The 'little boy' refuses to acknowledge the mother's castration (ie, sexual difference), since to do so would put his own possession of a penis under threat. Instead he makes the fetish stand in for his woman partner's (lost) penis, in order to allow him to perform the sexual act. To accept that the woman did not have one, would be to accept that he could lose his, and the consequent horror would prevent him being able to experience sexual arousal. The fetish acts as a protection from the horror (of female castration and lack).

Freud develops the splitting element and is careful to distinguish this as a 'disavowal' of castration, rather than simply a repression or denial: 'he has retained that belief, but he has also given it up.'[86] The subject oscillates between the opposing views that women have a penis (and hence his is safe) and that they do not (and hence need the penis substitute – the fetish). This oscillation, Freud argues, 'saves' the fetishist from denying the sexual difference and taking up the homosexual position. In this essay, the fetish is again chosen for its closeness to the trauma of seeing the female's 'lack'. The shoe, earlier argued as a symbol, is now chosen because of its nearness to the boy's inquisitive peering up a woman's legs.

Fur and velvet object choices, however, are explained as being because of fixations on the first sight of female pubic hair. As such, they still appear to be symbolic – no metonymic explanation is put forward. Underclothes, though, in this essay become object-choices because of their contiguity (nearness) to the moment of final undressing. The fetishist represses the denial of his mother's castration and fixates on the object seen just before that 'horrifying' revelation. Rather than standing in for a penis in the sense of an object pretending to be it, the fixation passes to the nearest safe thing to admit to having seen (the scopic drive) before the trauma. In the central case study in 'Fetishism', the fetish of a shine on the nose, ('glanz' in German, but the subject as a child learned English and had substituted 'glanz' for the curious 'glance' at the castrated absence) the metonymic dynamic is shown to be linguistic in origin. [87] Although the nose itself is argued to be a metaphor for the penis.

Ten years on, in 'An Outline of Psycho-Analysis', Freud is clear that the choice of the fetish can be either metonymic (contiguous to the revelation of female genitals) or metaphoric (stand as a symbolic representation of a penis). However, he admits that it is often impossible to assign the reason for the fixation. In this lecture, Freud's main interest is again the discussion of the splitting process, which he explains as the splitting of the ego. As a defence mechanism, disavowal is an *incomplete* attempt at detachment from reality – hence the oscillation between knowing and not knowing. A complete detachment would be a total repression or 'denial' of the reality. Because the repression is incomplete, it allows for real genital orgasm to occur, while safely protecting the fetishist from fully realising the threatening fact (of female castration). The fetish is therefore often described as 'doing-and-undoing' female castration.

Freud's phallicising of fetishism, which we have been tracing, probably developed from experiential evidence, as much as for theoretical reasons. In 1905 he was pathologising the practice without gendering it. In 1909, women were included in the discussion, although differentiated from proper fetishism by their passivity. In 1927, however, he opens 'Fetishism' with the statement, 'In the last few years I have had the opportunity of studying analytically a number of men whose object-choice was dominated by a fetish'.[88] The practitioner is now delineated as a man. The trauma is conceptualised as occurring to the little boy, and the practice is located as a denial of male castration anxiety for, 'probably no male human being is spared the fright of castration at the sight of a female genital'.[89] Women, having no penis to protect from this trauma, are therefore naturally eliminated from the account. By 1937, the genderisation has become overt, and fetishism is summarised as follows:

> This abnormality, which may be counted as one of the perversions, is, as is well known, based on the patient (who is almost always male).[90]

Juliet Mitchell, in *Psychoanalysis and Feminism*, tries to rescue Freud to some extent from his phallocentrism. She explains the privileging of castration anxiety as due to the patriarchal evaluation of society in the nineteenth century, rather than due to the psychic processes. Nevertheless Mitchell accepts Freud's account of fetishism as male in its orientation. Despite her more social alignment, she never questions that fetishism is a product of the anxiety to protect the penis. Nonetheless, she does include in her discussion of it a description of the process: 'in doing this fetishists have their cake and eat it'.[91] We find this a particularly interesting metaphor for the doing-and-undoing mechanism, and one to which we will return to in considerable detail in chapter four.

In chapter three,we question whether women do fetishize sexually, and what might be at stake in denying them an agency. At this point in the discussion, though, we hope it has become clear why the psychiatrist Robert Stoller could argue that a fetish is itself a highly compacted story:

> I have a hunch about the dynamics of erotic fetishises ... An object ... becomes a fetish when it stands for ... meanings that are wholly, or in crucial parts of the text, unconscious: a fetish is a story masquerading as an object.[92]

Three Types of Fetishism: Linguistic Implications

As we have shown in the foregoing discussion of anthropological, commodity and sexual fetishism, what the different types of fetishism have in *common* is the process of *disavowal*. In different ways, and as a consequence of different psychic and structural mechanisms, objects in our culture take on meanings that connect them to, or stand in for, other meanings and associations: but the connection is lost or partially denied as a consequence of the fetishism. How this 'disavowal' or object 'substitution' is accomplished in the first place depends not only on the type of fetishism examined but to a large extent on the explanation of it being offered. We have become increasingly aware that in most discussions of fetishism there is confusion, or at least linguistic slippage, in the figures of language used to describe fetishism. In particular there is confusion about:

1. *metaphor*: 'a figure of speech in which a name or descriptive term is transferred to some object different from, analogous to, that which it is properly applicable';[93]
2. *metonymy*: 'a figure of speech which consists in susbstituting for the name of a thing the name of an attribute of it or of something closely related';[94]
3. *synechdoche*: 'a figure in which a more comprehensive term is used ... as a whole for a part of the whole ... '.[95]

Jakobson, in 'Two Aspects of Language and Two Types of Aphasic Disturbances', argues that metaphor is a condensing of meaning; metonymy involves a displacement of meaning;[96] whereas a synecdoche is a form of metonymy, whose dynamic or association will be by definition metonymic. We would accept Jakobson's account, in accordance with the OED definitions above, and argue that the figure of fetishism is itself a synechdoche (a part for the whole substitution).

But we would point out that the process of fixing upon an individual, specific fetish is *either* metaphoric or metonymic. The latter occurs as a consequence of its nearness to the original object of desire: the fetish (eg, knickers) is often selected because of its contiguity to the original object of desire (the woman) and fear of her genitals.

Fetishism, we would argue, is by definition a displacement of meaning through the synechdoche, the displacement of the object of the desire onto something else through processes of disavowal.[97] The original object of desire is 'repressed' or 'hidden', and an item near it (in time or place) is selected as the fetish, thus allowing disavowal to take place. We would argue that the examples of sexual and anthropological fetishism we put forward share this synechodochal activity of substituting a part for the whole; though each uses that activity within a different discourse. Commodity fetishism, on the other hand, is slightly different, depending on which variant of commodity fetishism we are analysing. In the first sense of explanation, discussed by Marx, we would argue that the fetishism in question is actually metaphoric, adopted and adapted by Marx from the anthropological usage, to explain cultural processes of mystification; and subsequently adapted by Lukacs to include reification. Through the processes of 'conspicuous consumption', outlined originally by Veblen in the nineteenth century and expanded by many other critics in the twentieth century, commodity fetishism reaches another stage because of the development of mass production and mass markets. Here, objects are fetishised not only because they become separated from labour power (as Marx originally explained), but also because the intensity of the fetishism is increased by metaphoric and metonymic associations of meanings constructed by and through the salespitch. We would argue that, as with the other two types of fetishism, twentieth century commodity fetishism is involved in metonymic substitution processes. We acknowledge here, however, that we have had to expand Marx's original concept of commodity fetishism, in light of the work of other thinkers, in order to make this reading.

As we have mentioned above, all the types of fetishism share the act of disavowal. Disavowal, unlike displacement or sublimation, is not a total denial of the desire experienced, which is subsequently repressed into another sphere. Instead, through the mechanism of disavowal, the desire is granted a 'safe' expression and satiation in the external world, without having to accept the 'threatening' knowledge involved. Through the use of the fetish, the practitioner is able to continue to believe the false, while also knowing that it can not be true, since it does require a substitution. According to Freud, the fetishist both knows women do not have a penis (and hence he needs the phallic substitute – the fetish) and that they have one (the fetish object). The practitioner both knows and doesn't know simultaneously. This characteristic oscillation process is characterised in much of the literature on fetishism as 'doing and undoing'. This notion of doing-and-undoing, we believe, is relevant to all the types of fetishism. All uses of fetishism within their three distinct and separate discourses refuse to admit (whilst being simultaneously aware) that there is some sort of 'separation' taking place.

In what follows we clarify the nature of these separations, as they appear in clinical psychoanalytic writing about sexual fetishism. Our purpose is not to engage with linguistic complexity for the sake of it. We attempt to analyse some of the metonymic separations described in clinical writing on fetishism, amidst our broader discussion of the unusual fetishes of women, because we believe this will help us construct a theoretical underpinning for a new reading of the theory of sexual fetishism. This reading includes pre-Oedipal separations and metonymic substitutions as grounds for sexual fetishism. We believe this new reading, which locates fetishism as arising in a much earlier stage than in Freud's account and connects it to the oral phase, will accommodate and explain some of the experiences of women as sexual fetishists. Such a reading of fetishism also enables us to introduce food products, in a variety of ways, as objects of fetishism – usage of which we argue constitutes a fourth type of fetishism – in ways similar, if not exactly the same as, orthodox sexual fetishism.

Notes

1 W. Pietz, 'The Problem of the Fetish, II. The origins of the fetish', *Res* 13, Spring 87, p24.

2 H. de Oliveiria Marques, *Daily Life in Portugal in the Late Middle Ages*, University of Wisconsin Press, 1971, p227a.

3 Pietz, *op cit*, p34.

4 *Ibid*, p33.

5 *Oxford English Dictionary*, 2nd Ed., Vol 5, p857.

6 Cited in Pietz, *op cit*, p23.

7 Nicholas Villault, *Relatins de Costes d'Afrique, appelees Guinee*, Thiery, Paris 1669.

8 Charles de Brosses, *Due culte des dieux fetiches, ou Parallele degre l'ancienne Religio de 'Egypete' avec la Religion actuelle Nigritie*, Geneva, 1769.

9 *Ibid*.

10 Baron R von Krafft Ebing, *Psychpathesis Sexualis*, 10th Ed., translated by F.

J. Rebman, Rebman, London 1899.

11 Alfred Binet, 'Le fetichisme dans l'amour', in *Etudes de Psychologie Experimentale*, Octave Doin, Paris 1888, pp1–85.

12 W. Pietz, 'The Problem of the Fetish, I', *Res*, 9, 1985, p5–17; W. Pietz, 1987, *op cit*; W. Pietz, 'The Problem of the Fetish, IIIa. Bosman's Guinea and the Enlightenment Theory', *Res*, 16, 1988, p105–123.

13 Alisdair Pettinger, *New Formations*, Perversity Issue, Spring 1993.

14 Charles De Brosses,*op cit.*

15 E.B. Tylor, *Primitive Culture*, Volume 2, John Murray, Albermarle 1891, p145.

16 J.G. Frazer, *Totemism and Exogamy*, 4 vols, Macmillan & Co, London 1910.

17 Quoted in Sigmund Freud, *Totem and Taboo*, Routledge,London 1950, p103.

18 *Encyclopedia Americana*,International Edition, Americana, New York 1977, Vol 11, p137. See also *Dictionary of Philosophy and Psychology*, James Baldwin (ed), Peter Smith, New York 1940, Vol 1, p380, for the differentiation of 'anthropological' and 'pathological' fetishism.

19 For example, A. Lang says exogamy originated *before* totemism, in *The Secret of the Totem*, Longman, London 1905. Whereas E. Durkheim says exogamy *derives* from totemism, in *Les Forms Elementaires de la Vie Religieuse: Le systeme totemique en Australie*, Paris,1912.

20 Alfred Binet, *op cit.*

21 Lisa A. Lewis (ed), *The Adoring Audience: Fan Culture and Popular Media*, Routledge, London 1992, p1.

22 John Fiske, 'The Cultural Economy of Fandom', in Lewis, *op cit*, pp30–49.

23 *Ibid*, p32.

24 *Ibid*, p31.

25 Fred and Judy Vermorel, *Starlust: The Secret Fantasies of Fans,* W H Allen, London 1985.

26 *Ibid*, p122–3.

27 Suzanne Moore, 'Reach for the Stars', *Women's Review*, 21, 1986.

28 Vermorel, *op cit*, p128.

29 *Ibid,* p145.

30 Cheryl Cline, 'Essays from Bitch: The Woman's Rock Newsletter with Bite', in Lewis, *op cit*, p72.

31 B. Ehrenreich, E.Hess and G.Jacobs, 'Beatlemania: Girls Just Want to Have Fun', in Lewis, *op cit*, pp69–83.

32 Vermorel, *op cit*, p153.

33 Similar observations about there being an absence of appropriate theoretical work to explain the behaviour of, for instance, female fans who produce fanzines and create elaborate romantic and sexual fantasies depicting Star Trek characters have been made by other critics. We would not rule out some element of adoration or worship in this behaviour but suspect it is not the most dominant feature. These and other questions about erotic contemplation; about, for instance, why women meet regularly to create narratives and images which feature Spock and Kirk having a sexual relationship were considered by Constance Penley when she gave a talk at the ICA in 1989. Like Henry Jenkins, writing before her, Penley complained about lack of critical explanation of the sexual behaviour of some Sci-Fi fans.

34 See pp38–47 below.

35 Oxford English Dictionary, (2nd ed.) Clarendon, Oxford 1989, Vol 5, p374.

36 E. Apter, *Feminising the Fetish: Psychoanalysis and Narrative Obsession in Turn of the Century France*, Cornell, New York 1991.

37 *Ibid*, p56.

38 Stuart Cosgrove, 'Erotomania', *New Statesman*, 27 July 1990, pp31–2.

39 John Fiske, *Understanding Popular Culture*, Unwin Hyman, London 1989, p147.

40 Jenny Garber and Angela McRobbie , 'Girls and Subculture', in S. Hall (ed) *Resistance Through Ritual*, Hutchinson, London 1978.

41 *Ibid*.

42 Laura Mulvey, *Visual and Other Pleasures*, Macmillan, London 1989, p20.

43 Fiske, 1987, *op cit*, p274.

44 Fiske does, however, talk about the fact that fans acquire specialist knowledge about their object of interest, which he terms 'unofficial cultural capital'. Fiske argues that this unofficial cultural capital helps some young people, through their fandom, to differentiate themselves from other social groups.

45 Binet's argument, for example, appears to rest on the assumption that women are more spiritual than men in terms of their relationship to the Catholic church. We do not agree with any essentialist arguments that women innately have a stronger religious sense or are more 'spiritual', but would suggest that the cultural construction of femininity, as well as women's economic oppression, has often located women more firmly in the role of arbiters of spirituality, and thus often more firmly in the role of anthropological fetishists.

46 Susan Willis, *A Primer For Daily Life*, Routledge, London 1991.

47 Karl Marx, *Capital* Volume One, Pelican, London 1986, p164.

48 *Ibid*, p168.

49 Michael T. Taussig, *The Devil and Commodity Fetishism in South America*, University of Carolina Press, Chapel Hill 1983.

50 Marx does discuss circulation throughout Volume Two, but, except for the thesis of commodity fetishism and occasional remarks, the subjectivity of economic relations is not a major concern.

51 Thorstein Veblen, *The Theory of the Leisure Class,* Macmillan, New York 1899, pp63–4.

52 S. Jhalley, S. Kline, W. Leiss, 'Magic in the Marketplace: an empirical test for commodity fetishism', *Canadian Journal of Political and Social Theory*, 9, Fall 1985.

53 Georg Lukacs, *History and Class Consciousness*, MIT Press, Cambridge, Mass. 1971, p100.

54 S.Willis, *op cit*, p7.

55 Richard Ohmann, 'History and Literary History: The Case of Mass Culture', *Poetics Today*, Volume 9, 1988, pp357–75.

56 Willis, *op cit*, p3.

57 Raymond Williams, 'Advertising: the Magic System', *Problems in Materialism and Culture*, Verso, London 1980, pp170–195.

58 Judith Williamson, *Decoding Advertisements: Ideology and Meaning in Advertising*, Marion Boyars, London 1978.

59 *Ibid.*

60 Later in this chapter we outline Gebhard's models of intensities of sexual fetishism. Even though we have numbered our stages of commodity fetishism 1–4, we did not mean explicitly or implicitly to invite comparison between the stages

of commodity fetishism with those of sexual fetishism described by Gebhard. In forthcoming work we are writing outside of this book we may wish to make such a comparison in order to identify the problems with it.

61   Louis Althusser, *Lenin, Philosophy and Other Essays,* New Left Books, London 1970.

62   Mark Poster (ed), *Jean Baudrillard; Selected Writings*, Polity, Cambridge 1988.

63   Indeed, the notion of 'use value' legitimates what Baudrillard sees as an inappropriate idea about the specific historical individual who has specific needs in the world of objects.

64   Baudrillard, *op cit*, p69.

65   Judith Williamson, 'Lost in the Hypermarket', *City Limits,* December 1988.

66   Christopher Norris, *Uncritical Theory: Postmodern Intellectuals and the Gulf War,* Lawrence & Wishart, London 1992, p11.

67   *Ibid,* p15.

68   Willis, *op cit*, p24.

69   Rosemary Scott, *The Female Consumer,* Associated Business Progs., London 1976.

70   Frank Mort, 'Men and shopping', *New Socialist*, November 1986.

71   Guy Debord, *Comments on the Society of the Spectacle*, Translated by Malcolm Imrie, Verso, London 1988.

72   Sigmund Freud, 'Three Essays on the Theory of Sexuality', *The Standard Edition of The Complete Works,*translated by James Strachey, Hogarth, London 1953–64, Vol 7, p154. For a further discussion by Freud, see also 'Fetishism', *Standard Edition*, Vol 7, pp152–7.

73   P. Gebhard, 'Fetishism and Sado-masochism', *Science and Psychoanalysis*, Vol 25, pp71–80.

74   M. Foucault, *The History of Sexuality*, Vol I, Penguin, Harmondsworth 1979, p154. Parveen Adams also argues that 'the fetishism that produces the fetishist is also at the root of the other perversions. Fetishism is of the essence of the perversions', in 'Of Female Bondage', *Between Feminism and Psychoanalysis*, Teresa Brennan (ed), Routledge, London 1989, *op cit*, p251.

75   Baron R von Krafft Ebing, *Psychopathesis Sexualis, op cit*, p517.

76   *Ibid*, p25.

77   The translation is David Simpson's, from *Fetishism and the Imagination* , Johns Hopkins, Baltimore 1982, p132.

78   Binet, *op cit*, p71.

79   W.H.Masters, V.E.Johnson and R.C.Kolodny, *On Sex and Human Loving*, Macmillan, London 1982, p377.

80   'The Dissolution of the Oedipus Complex', *Standard Edition*, Vol 19.

81   *Standard Edition*, Vol 7, p154.

82   *Ibid*, p155.

83   Published in 1988, in 'Freud and Fetishism: Previously Unpublished Minutes of the Vienna Psychoanalytic Society', Louis Rose, *Psychoanalytic Quarterly* 57, 1988, pp147–160.

84   Perversions involve the active practice of the desire taking place in the real world, in relation to external objects. Because of their active nature they are seen as the preserve of men. Hysteric symptoms are suppressions of the desire into the more passive manifestations of delusions, obsessions and phobias, played out within the person's psyche. Because of this passive nature, they are seen as the

preserve of women more than of men.

85   *Ibid*, p156.

86   'Fetishism', *Standard Edition*, Vol 21, p152.

87   Lacan makes this point in 'The Agency of the Letter', *Ecrits*, A Shelston (ed), Routledge, London 1977, p170.

88   *Ibid*, p152.

89   'Fetishism', p54.

90   'Outline of Psycho-Analysis: chapter 8, the external world', *Standard Edition*, Vol 23, p202.

91   Juliet Mitchell, *Psychoanalysis and Feminism,* Allen Lane, London 1974, p85.

92   R.J. Stoller, *Observing the Erotic Imagination*, Yale University Press, New Haven 1985, p155.

93   *OED*, *op cit*, Vol 9, p676.

94   *Ibid*, p696.

95   *OED*, Vol 17, p478.

96   Roman Jakobson, *On Language*, Linda R Waugh & Monique Monville-Burston (eds), Harvard University Press, Cambridge, Mass 1990, p129.

97   Lacan has gone so far as to argue that the fixing of all desire is metonynic 'eternally stretching towards the desire of something else.' Hence, 'its "perverse" fixation at … the fascinating image of the fetish'.

2

Perverse Strategies: a Look at Women

When we started writing this book and let it be known that we were working on 'fetishism' this fact appeared to act as an unusual catalyst – one that inspired people we didn't know very well to have conversations with us about all the varieties of sexual behaviour they had experienced. Many people we spoke to about fetishism seemed to enjoy referring to themselves in slang as 'purves'[perverts].[2] The definition of perversion they were using, however, had little in common with ideas defined above about the corruption of religious belief. Instead it referred to ideas about sexual deviation and dominant perceptions of sexual normality. Or, as Mandy Merck has identified, the word 'perverse' was used to simply mean 'deviant from the broader opposition of what is expected or accepted (e.g. as in "you're just being perverse")'.[3]

We ended up having many weird and wonderful conversations about sex during the course of our research. These made it clear, very early on, that many people found ideas about sexual 'normality' old-fashioned and the product of censorious thinking about sexual pleasure. We found, consequently, that not only were orthodox definitions about perversity being redefined by many people, but also that some of them had some strange, or simply inappropriate, ideas about what exactly constitutes fetishism. Traditional shoe or leather obsessions were frequently cited as fetishism in the same breath as whipping, bondage, and genital mutilation. Often we found that people who thought they were talking to us about fetishism were really talking about sado-masochistic activities or the sort of cultural 'fixations' about objects that we would describe as 'commodity fetishism'.[4] In this chapter, as well as reviewing ideas about perversity, we distinguish between sexual fixations and sexual fetishism by defining fetishism in the orthodox sense as being the substitution of an object as the main focus of sexual arousal, in preference to the person themselves.

The confusions about the definition of sexual fetishism didn't surprise us because fetishism as a subject, and as a practice, is surrounded by many misconceptions. In the nineteenth century, for instance, Paul Garnier conflated fetishism and sado-masochism as being the same thing with his ideas about 'sadi-fetichism' and 'maso-fetichism'.[5] These conflations and confusions continue into the twentieth century and the voices of fetishists themselves are not always free of them. The word 'fetishism' itself, in contemporary usage, has virtually become a blanket term to characterise all erotic fixations or obsessions seen as 'perverse'. As we explained in chapter one, Freud points out that fetishism only becomes 'pathological' :

> when longing for the fetish passes beyond the point of being merely a necessary condition attached to the sexual object and *actually takes the place of the* [normal] aim ... when the fetish becomes ... the sole sexual object.[6]

Many of us may have a fixation about an object or a special part of someone's body at some time in our life but most of us see this as 'healthy' not pathological. This occurs not least because erotic visual images proliferating in the media fragment representations of the body and inform our subjectivity, by fragmenting how we see ourselves. For the majority of people however, inanimate objects or 'fragmented' body parts rarely become the sole sexual stimulus.

This point, about the common nature of some degree of fetishism, as part of all human sexuality, was taken up by sex researcher Paul Gebhard in 1969, who, as mentioned in chapter one, argues that fetishistic stimuli can be conceptualised 'along a continuum of intensities'.[7] He goes on to suggest, using behavioural definitions, that three levels of fetishistic behaviour are reached before the fourth stage of orthodox sexual fetishism.

This model of three stages leading up to orthodox sexual fetishism is helpful, as it allows us to discuss practices in contemporary subcultures, but enables us to leave behind the pathological connotations associated with Freud on fetishism. Sexual fetishism often entails a variety of behaviour which involves individuals becoming extremely attached to certain parts of the body or objects, but not as the sole sexual stimulus; some writers have used the word 'partialism' to describe this behaviour.[8]

Cultural fixations about sex, as well as some levels of sexual fetishism between the first three stages described by Gebhard, may be accommodated by fetish clothing or even magazines. But there is no recognition in the literature of the different stages (or intensities) of fetishism because the word itself is a blanket term that is supposed to include everything.

Sexual Subcultures

Skin Two, (see Illustration 2) describes itself as a 'fetish' magazine in the broadest of terms, and appears to address a wide readership of people who fetishise in the sexual sense, but does not exclude other sexual practices. It incorporates discussion of a whole range of sexual activities in its pages, from tattooing to scarification. Its publisher, Tim Woodward, says the magazine is 'produced by fetishists, for fetishists', although the strongest emphasis, in terms of content, is on sado-masochistic activities (like those involving master slave rituals as well as whipping and beating). And these do not necessarily involve high degrees of fetishism.

Skin Two has found a gap in the market and the magazine is able to acknowledge a diversity of 'sexual subcultures'[9] including heterosexual and homosexual/lesbian S&M practices. This is an important space (although not the only one) in the wider cultural context where fetishists are often constructed as 'perverts' in a negative sense. To celebrate fetishism, as *Skin Two* does, addressing both heterosexual and homosexual male and female readers, is also to acknowledge sexual diversity.

Women as practitioners, usually of S&M, are included in the magazine with its coverage of the 'international fetish scene'. Journalists like Michelle Olley and photographers like Grace Lau contribute to the magazine and try 'to make seemingly bizarre or even absurd fetish[es] into acceptable erotic image[s]'.[10] Some of the coverage includes stories and images by women for women but despite the best endeavours of all involved, it is still difficult to know exactly what women's relationship to sexual fetishism here might be.

Skin Two: Opening the closet for 'pervs'
Courtesy Skin Two magazine

Some individuals, including women, find leather and rubber objects, and outfits facilitating constriction, sexually exciting, both to handle and to wear. The colour black recurs frequently in fetish imagery associated with *Skin Two* magazine, as do tight bodices and thigh-length leather boots. These also have cultural connotations (wickedness, etc) which may give added sexual allure. But women too may find fetish objects, such as the thigh length boots or leather thongs shown in magazine spreads, sexually exciting and erotic in their own right. Other women who buy such objects, such as those working in the sex industry, may see this sort of clothing as simply part of the uniform, rather than something that personally turns them on.[11] But, it is not to true to say – as feminists like Andrea Dworkin appear to insist – that S&M outfits eroticise women's oppression, or accommodate subversion in dangerous fantasies of violence, and that only men get pleasure from women dressing up and objectifying their bodies. 'I have a leather fetish ... seeing, smelling or handling leather makes me cream', remarks Pat Califia, a non submissive lesbian sado-masochist who clearly does not wear leather for the pleasure of men.[12] Items of leather and rubber clothing or objects, produced by innovative designers such as Ectomorph, Kim West, Murray & Vern and Julian Latorre, and stocked by retail outfits like 'She and Me' (see Illustration 3) feature regularly as objects of fetishism for men and women. And this is in preference to other fabrics. But no one has adequately explained *why*.[13]

The media, it must be remembered, not only represent ideas but also regulate and legitimate them. Magazines like *Skin Two*, when representing images thought provocative or pleasurable, may not intentionally be laying down hard and fast rules to their readers about fetish 'codes'. Nevertheless, the recurrent focus on items like the stilletto, associated with male fetishism, might give some readers the impression that fetishism is primarily the sexual activity of men. Our research indicates this is not the case.

Women readers buy *Skin Two* magazine as well as fetish clothing. There are difficulties in trying to get enterprises specialising in fetishism to provide a gender breakdown of who buys what objects, but despite this we found that in many cases 40 per cent of all consumers are women. Many 'fetish' outfitters we approached suggested that women made up a significant proportion of their customers.[14] *Skin Two* also volunteered some views about women's relationship to fetishism. They estimate that as much as 38–40 per cent of their readership might be 'female', but it is impossible to know what the category

of London

| MISTRESS COSTUME | PLASTIC ZIP-SKIN OPEN | BOOTS - 6" HEELS | RUBBER CLOTHES |

| LEG SPREADERS | CHAIN SETS | STREET CLOTHES | PLASTIC RESTRAINTS |

| GIRDLES | STEEL BONED CORSETS | LEATHER BRAS EXT. | SHOES - 6" HEELS |

| SUSPENDER SETS | STREET CLOTHES | COSTUME - POP OPEN | RUBBER COLLECTION |

She an Me: Catering to the fetishist trade
Courtesy Skin Two magazine

'female' signifies. As Michelle Olley points out, 'we get a number of transvestites subscribing using their "femme name" so Miss H. Heels … may show up as a woman in our records but may in fact be a man.'[15] Additionally, Michelle Olley points out that some women readers engage with the magazine 'as part of a couple' while others appear to have a much more individualistic relationship to it (and perhaps to objects).

In what follows we go on to consider fetishism's relationship to a range of cultural practices and sexual subcultures in contemporary society: from women and sado-masochism, to areas that cut across fashion, including body decoration and modification, cross-dressing, vogueing, and homeovestism.

Women and S&M

Clearly women are customers of the fetish industries but this does not necessarily make women's relationship to fetishism that much clearer. Female consumers and readers may buy outfits or magazines to accommodate their own fetishistic desires. Or they may simply be trying out the fantasies found in the literature and/or accommodating the fetishistic desires of men who like their women to provide the right clothes. The issue of female agency, and the specific nature of female fetishism, highlights general problems about defining women's participation in sexual fetishism.

Some women, both heterosexual and lesbian, clearly do participate in S&M. On the whole S&M has little to do with real life violence against women, but is a cathartic game based on a whole gamut of fantasies about domination and subordination. Whether feminists politically agree with the idea of S&M or not, many researchers argue that relations involving domination and subordination are inevitably bound up with the evolution of sexuality. A degree of dominance and power 'play' can facilitate sexual orgasm for some individuals, whereas others are turned on by fear, threat and ultimately submission. Whatever the S&M scenario examined, it appears that in most cases partners agree upon the limits to the sexual psychodrama, in order to establish 'safe worlds' in which to act out their fantasies.

The sexual practices described by Pat Califia in the S&M stories found in her collection *Macho Sluts*[16], or the images of women having their 'clits' pierced in books like *Modern Primitives*[17], raise many questions about women's sexual pleasure, S&M and fetishism. Many women enjoy erotic practices like piercing, scarification and tattooing. The pleasures from these activities are clearly varied.

'Blood sports', involving consensual, and often public, piercings and scarifications, according to Della Grace, seem to be popular in some lesbian circles. At times these practices may push the parameters of the liberal model of S&M based on consent over the edge, as boundaries between pleasure and pain become blurred. But such cases are few and far between and not all body modifications or decorations hold such connotations. Paula P'Orridge, for instances, stresses the aesthetic pleasures of piercing: 'I've got five rings in my labia – all of them from different lovers. They are not exactly trophies – more like love talismans ... They are mainly aesthetic. I wouldn't say they make anything more sensitive.'[18]

Sheree Rose, on the other hand, commenting about body piercing suggests: 'Piercing in the S&M subculture is definitely the mark of submission. It is something a slave does to please the Master... I don't have rings in my labia: submissive women have rings which can be locked by their masters.'[19]

Many people involved in piercing, scarification and tattooing do talk about fetishism: 'he is a very skilled craftsman ... but his actual, certainly semi-skilled, sexual fetish was piercing and tattooing on himself'.[20] But we believe that the term fetishism, as used in this quote, can become an umbrella term for a whole range of 'perverse' practices. There seem to us to be clear links between piercing and sadomasochism. These practices, engaged in by men and women, seem to enhance, rather than replace, relationships and/or sex with actual people. Our understanding of orthodox sexual fetishism as replacing relationships (Gebhard's fourth degree) would not very often include S&M practices, including piercing.

Women certainly do attend a whole range of so-called 'fetish' clubs, London night spots such as 'Night of the Living Vixens', 'Fantastic Vox', 'Macho Sluts', 'Fruit', 'Kinky Disco', as well as 'Ciao Baby', the 'Cat House', 'Feet First', 'Sadie Masies' and the 'Clit Club'. These women enjoy dressing up in leather and rubber while some women get off on other appendages like dildos. We would want to argue that such women are fetishists in more ways than one. But it is impossible to assess this without more substantial empirical evidence, and without resorting to the use of psychoanalytic categories that have so far denied or ignored female agency. We look at these psychoanalytic categories in more detail in chapter three, when we discuss how clinical analysis of sexual fetishism, to date, has largely failed to conceptualise contemporary female sexual experience.

Fashion and Fetishism

The relationship between clothes and fetishism is diverse and complex. Fetishism of clothing may include 'orthodox' sexual fetishism, that is orgasm from an article of clothing which becomes the fetish object. But clothes can also function as icons of commodity fetishism, because consumerism uses sexuality, or more particularly, codes of the sexual erotic, to give fashion *meaning*. Pleasure from over-emphasising parts of the body through dress – be it breasts, waist, thighs, etc – may have a connection to visual pleasure, in that such images please the eye by fragmenting, sculpting or simply objectifying the body; but visual images are not always necessarily the same thing as fetish objects. As fetish objects, visual images rarely accommodate fourth degree sexual fetishism. Yet cultural practices that accommodate body modification – from corset-wearing to footbinding – are commonly interpreted by fashion historians, like Laver, as 'fetishism', even though such practices rarely accommodate orgasm in *preference* to some other sexual stimulation or contact. We would argue that such images and practices should be looked at as mild forms of fetishism, or, as in the case of tight lacing associated with corset wearing, perhaps as forms of S&M practice, depending on the context under scutiny.

There are so many myths about fashion and fetishism that it is no wonder that there is confusion. Fashion historians often use the term fetishism when they mean eroticism, and this slippage of terminology is very common to many discussions of fashion. Generally, fetishism of clothing is usually associated with men rather than women. Steretoypes of men being fascinated with women's clothes (for example, DH Lawrence's obsession with Gudrun's stockings in *Women in Love*[21]) have been with us for a long time, as have the stereotypes of men secretly dressing themselves up in women's clothes. Then there are the stereotypes of men, out of control around the fetish item, 'stealing' women's underwear. These too have been with us at least since the nineteenth century when writers like Krafft Ebing connected all sexual diversity with deviance and actual criminality.

The narratives that accompany such stereotypes in books by sexologists often represent men as extreme cases and as 'out of control'. Women are usually seen as victims of male sexuality and it is argued that fashions such as corsets, or even suspenders and stockings are just designed to 'please' men. Linda Gordon and Ellen Dubois go so far as to suggest that women in the nineteenth century, who campaigned against prostitution for the social purity movement, simultaneously colluded with ideologies that underplayed the existence and intensity of female sexual desire.[22] Even today these attitudes are still with us and can be found in the sort of feminist criticism that connects women wearing 'fetish-fashions' – from corsets to thigh-length leather boots – with their oppression. Feminists have argued that such items require women to manipulate their bodies and to be uncomfortable, or to be unrealistically thin, in order to resemble caricatures found in comic books where women look like the American tv 'Wonder Woman' stereotype. Such fashions are often dismissed as accommodating male objectification of women's bodies. We take up these arguments again in chapter six when we explain why the corset had many meanings, even for Victorian women, and that it would be inappropriate for feminists to simply dismiss such clothing as a metaphor of patriarchal oppression, which literally 'restrains' women from becoming fully emancipated.

Freud may have argued that 'all women are clothing fetishists'[23,] but most medical writers argue that orthodox clothing fetishism, for instance the fondling of undergarments leading to orgasm, is the province of 'deviant' men rather than women. But how can we avoid talking about clothing fetishism by women, when the fashion industry, one of the many homes of commodity fetishism, is aimed primarily at women rather than men? Even in the 1990s, when male narcissism is in evidence more than ever before, top fashion designers still design primarily for women because, overall, women still spend more money on fashion than men. All this activity of the female consumer cannot be explained in terms of women's desire to please men.

At the turn of the nineteenth century, Thorstein Veblen was one of the first to discuss women and clothing in relation to economic fetishism.[24] Writing after Marx he saw rich women in their corsets and finery as engaging in 'conspicuous consumption', a further development of the commodity fetishism which was originally described and defined by Marx.[25] Indeed, Veblen saw women's relationship to fashion as a sign of the fetishism of wealth. He saw women as decorative status symbols whose primary function, through the wearing of fashionable clothing, was to flaunt their men's accumulation of capital. Clearly in a context, as Ciciley Hamilton has pointed out, where many Victorian women viewed marriage as their 'trade'[26], there is validity in Veblen's thesis that women's bodies were often used as sites to flaunt their father's, husband's, or lover's wealth. In the Victorian period, more than ever before, both men and women used clothes, possessions and the other products they conspicuously consumed, to carve out class and gender identities for themselves.

This process of using clothes as fetish objects to differentiate changing social roles between the sexes was also examined by J C Flugel, who in the 1930s wrote a ground-breaking book on the subject called *The Psychology of Clothes*.[27] Flugel tried to explain the nineteenth century masculine renunciation of fashion in terms of economic shifts in the mode of production as well as changing psychology and social attitudes.[28] He argued that in the Victorian period women became constructed as *beautiful* 'Angels at the Hearth' while men renounced beauty to become *useful* 'Providers'. This was a shift from the eighteenth century when many Regency bucks wore make-up and fully enjoyed the pleasures of adornment and narcissism. It is only since the second half of the twentieth century that critics have really attempted to think about why in the Victorian period women's bodies became more eroticised than men's; explanations often point to the ramifications of the development of photography in the same period.

The objectification of women's appearance is now so central in Western culture that the relationship of women to fashion appears in itself to be fetishistic, or at least fixated on certain parts of the female body. Modern women often see themselves in fragments – a good pair of legs, tits or eyes, etc. Some women get fixated on emphasising their lips (by constantly putting on lipstick) or maintaining impractical ultra-long varnished nails at the expense of free movement. This behaviour appears to be linked to the overall effect of objectification of the female form. As John Berger has pointed out, to understand why women may enjoy commodifying themselves it is necessary to understand the effect of representation upon cultural definitions of masculinity and femininity. In essence Berger argues that women objectify themselves as a consequence of having internalised male ways of seeing the world. He says, 'from earliest childhood she has been persuaded to survey herself continually' and this surveillance is commodified by capitalism. In other words he locates the objectification of female appearance as a product of consumerism; commodity, not sexual, fetishism.

Across the cultures and the centuries fetishism has often been associated with perverse cultural codes which promote fashions that celebrate women 'suffering' to achieve beauty. Footbinding, or the wearing of corsets by women, are traditionally cited as evidence of masochism by vain or unthinking women. These fashions have also been seen as fetishistic in the sense of erotically over-emphasising parts of the female anatomy – a tiny foot or waist – to accommodate male pleasure. Strictly speaking, fashions which fragment the body constitute cultural eroticism or cultural fixation, not sexual fetishism in the orthodox sense. Fragmentation is related to objectification (and to fetishism), but over-emphasis of parts of the body is not the same thing as not wanting physical contact with the body at all. Fetishism involves the substitution of a part (the woman's handbag) for the whole (body of a woman) in order to achieve orgasm, as explained by Freud in his readings of orthodox sexual fetishism.

Representations of women in corsets or high-heeled shoes may look fetishistic to some feminists, but whose is the fetishism under scrutiny, and what degree of fetishism are we talking about? For example, discussion of images of powerful women which uses terms like 'phallic replacement' to describe how these images work, in our view confuses commodity fetishism of the erotic with orthodox sexual fetishism. This school of feminist criticism tends to describe 'women as spectacle' of the 'male gaze', and this has been equated with 'scopophilic' fetishism (ie, visual images become the fetish object of the voyeur). Because of the anxieties of the male unconscious, such discussion implies, these 'fetishised' images of powerful or fashionable women will never change, because men 'need' phallic replacement when they see representations of women, to cope with their castration anxiety. This is a 'universal' view we disagree with because we believe men *can* change. Over the last twenty years images of women (and men) have changed quite a lot. Indeed, we would find the concept of a commodity fetishism of masculinity (ie, powerful women are constructed as masculine) more helpful an analysis of phallic replacement issues. (We discuss this in more detail in chapter 6.)

One of the reasons we find the 'woman as fetish' argument so misleading is because, as Caroline Evans and Minna Thornton have pointed out before us, 'fashion … is difficult to discuss … because its essence lies in its transitoriness.'[29] In the fashion system, bondage apparel or even cross-dressing (which have intrigued researchers on fetishism for so many years) may be worn as nothing more than as part of a season's 'new look'. The new look is, of course, an economic necessity for the fashion industry, an integral device used in order to persuade people to keep buying clothes; the proliferation of visual images of women is part of that marketing strategy, rather than a direct consequence of castration anxiety.

Female Crossdressers

Another element of the 'season's new look' which may need to be addressed is the perennial woman in a man's suit. This is because for many years now the medical profession have connected dressing up in the clothes of the opposite sex with fetishism. Certain questions about female 'cross-dressing' should be re-considered, because male 'transvestism' is recognised as sometimes involving levels of fetishism, whereas women are rarely imagined to be clothing fetishists by the theoreticians on the subject.

When writing about transvestism, critics like Peter Ackroyd have found that some transvestite men achieve sexual gratification from wearing women's clothes: 'when I dress up it feels as if I have a continual orgasm'.[30] Most medical writers agree with the view that fetishism and transvestism are often (but not always) connected.[31] Explanations vary and there is no consensus about the motivation of either homosexual or heterosexual transvestites who achieve erotic pleasure from wearing clothes of the opposite sex. Nevertheless, the idea that some male transvestites may go on to have fetishistic relationships with women's clothes, rather than with sexual partners, is repeated throughout the medical literature on transvestism.[32]

Ackroyd is unsure exactly how to quantify this fetishistic behaviour. He points out, speculatively, that 'many transvestites, out of embarrassment or genuine disinterest, minimize the fetishistic elements of their cross dressing.'[33] He goes on to concur with the orthodox view that female transvestites are 'rare' and unlikely to become fetishists. Ackroyd suggests that this is because in our culture men's clothes are not emphasised as erotic as much as women's. Other critics have pointed out that 'men's clothing when worn by women only enhances the spectacle of femininity'.[34] But this latter point may be appropriate only to contemporary culture. Historically, women cross-dressers may have simply been wearing the uniform for the job – like the black female slaves who in the early nineteenth century adopted trousers and other male attire because it helped them perform hard labour when doing work like digging trenches or even stage-coach driving.[35]

Since women have had easy access to wearing men's costume, perhaps it is logical to assume that it would be unlikely for them to find male garments dangerous or erotic. Some male transvestites (though clearly not all of them) seem to associate women's attire with illicit connotations that men's clothes, even undergarments, do not appear to offer to women.[36] Despite this gender gap, Ackroyd has speculated that 'men's clothes could become fetishes for women on the basis of the infantile female's belief in their own castration ... on this basis it would be possible to construct a plausible etiology for female transvestism'.[37]

The American psychiatrist Robert Stoller, well-known for his writings on 'perversion', would not agree with Ackroyd. He makes a clear distinction between cross-dressing and transvestism. He argues these terms should *not* be used as interchangeable concepts. He comments, 'the term transvestism should only be used to describe fetishistic cross-dressing, that is erotic excitement induced by garments of the opposite sex'.[38] He goes on to point out that female transvestism is 'rare', whereas female cross-dressing can be explained in terms of social factors.

This argument that female transvestism, and female fetishism associated with it, are rare, is further legitimated by feminist writing on the subject. Julie Wheelwright locates female cross-dressing as being primarily about social disguise.[39] For instance, in the past male disguise was often adopted by women who wanted to join the army, as a form of resistance to the social ideologies about femininity that said they could not be soldiers. Male attire gave women access to the greater social freedoms enjoyed by men.

Dutch writers Rudolf M. Dekker and Lotte C. van de Pol agree with this view. Despite their book title, which uses the words 'female transvestism', the authors say that evidence from the seventeenth and eighteenth centuries, when 119 cases of female cross-dressing were documented, shows that the cross-dressing was primarily about gender 'disguise'. They point out: 'We do not think the modern notion of transvestism contributes much to explain why women in the seventeenth and eighteenth centuries decided to cross dress'.[40]

Similarly, Annie Woodhouse, writing on the subject of female transvestism, concurs with the orthodox view and points out:

> there is no evidence, then or now, of fetishistic cross-dressing by women, the derivation of sexual pleasure from wearing certain garments or fabrics. Male dress was adopted for practical reasons ... As Stoller (1982) points out female transvestism is largely a non issue as it is extremely rare'.[41]

Woodhouse goes on to align herself with Stoller and argue that 'the term transvestite should be taken to refer to men dressing as women'.[42]

We are sceptical about the certainty of the above comment, which writes women out of the entire account. We must confess, in addition, that despite the gender issue we haven't been completely persuaded by the dismantling of psychological distinctions between 'cross-dressing' and 'transvestism'. Cross-dressing appears to mean simply dressing up as a person of the opposite sex, whereas 'transvestism' implies there is an erotic charge connected with this behaviour (even though previously this has only been connected to male experience). In a recent book, Majorie Garber presents many new case studies of both men and women who have 'cross dressed'.[43] This material is exciting because so much of it documents new historical evidence about female activity. But again, it is difficult to know whether many of these cases involved fetishism because she uses the terms 'transvestism' and 'cross-dressing' interchangeably, ignoring the sexual distinction used by medical writers. This is because Garber reads cross-dressing as 'sign', as well as social behaviour. Her point in emphasising cross-dressing as sign is to argue that as a sign it is one that articulates a 'category crisis'.[44]

While we agree with Garber that in certain contexts (though not all), the figure of the transvestite or cross-dresser may destabilise gender boundaries, we are not convinced that this would always be so, or would necessarily articulate 'a crisis of category itself'. Underlying Garber's assertion about the radical potential of cross-dressing as sign is her idea that cross-dressing destabilises all social hierarchies:

> not only male and female but also gay and straight and sex and gender. This is the sense – the radical sense – in which transvestism is a third.[45]

Here, Garber suggests that cross-dressing is always a transgressive act. This is why she hints that the figure of the cross-dresser 'marks the space of desire'[46] and of a 'third' trans-gender term.[47]

But how is cross-dressing transgressive, and what is it a third term of? While we can see that in some contexts the figure of the cross-dresser might be a transgressive one, we feel the transgression depends upon *context*. For example, at London nightclubs at the moment, such as 'Kinky Gerlinky, wearing drag is not about transgression or being risky, but is *de rigueur*. Additionally, as a sign it may serve to generate containment of sexual categories, by reinforcing sexual binary oppositions. This line of argument about the issue of 'containment' is one that Garber does not address or answer in her book, but 'containment' theorists such as Michel Foucault, who have written so eloquently about sexuality, would probably demand such an analysis.

Garber's most important contribution to this chapter is that she locates cross-dressing as something that women engage in in large numbers.[48] We were frustrated however, by her concurrence with the idea that women rarely fetishise. Garber discusses female theatrical performers, for example, who dress up as men and wear codpieces. Her analysis concerns only the public meaning of these events, in terms of the theatre of spectacle. She doesn't take the analysis of women any further to consider the differences of meaning provided by different contexts; for instance, differences between the public and private realms. She therefore doesn't discuss the question of female fetishism as an erotic reality for women, but instead dismisses feminist interest in this as another form of penis envy, which she calls 'fetish envy'.[49] (We discuss this point further in chapter six when we look at the way literary feminists have conceptualised women and fetishism.) Yet wearing a codpiece by a woman, and/or cross-dressing when she isn't being paid to do so, or being asked to do so, may involve unconscious or complex sexual desires and fantasies; Garber doesn't pay much attention to the female unconscious at all when discussing the question of fetishism in relationship to women. As Louise Kaplan, has commented about the erotic potential of cross-dressing: 'what distinguishes a female transvestite from other women who cross dress are her unconscious motives and the fantasy life that reveals these motives.'[50]

In the psychoanalytic literature there are case studies that analyse the female unconscious in more detail and reveal women engaging in cross-dressing for sexual pleasure. However, these cases of female transvestism involving fetishism in the orthodox sense are usually viewed as 'exceptional'. E. Guthiel writing in 1930, for instance, says his patient is a rarity when he describes a 34 year old female excited by wearing clothes of the opposite sex.

> I may say that simply putting on men's clothing gives me pleasure. The whole procedure is comparable to that tense anticipation of pleasure which subsides into relief and gratification as soon as the transvestism is complete. I even experience lustful satisfaction in dreams of this act.[51]

Clearly, the above comments locate Guthiel's case study as a 'transvestite' in the sense of Robert Stoller's definition of the term.

Stoller, himself, despite his contention that women are less likely to engage with the sexual perversions than men, cites three case studies of female transvestites who were all turned on by wearing male attire. He includes discussion of a 'divorced woman' who became aroused by Levi jeans. He quotes her as saying:

> when putting on the Levi's, I feel very excited immediately. I feel the texture, roughness of the material as I pull them over my feet, over the

calves of my legs, onto my thighs ... clitoris. It's a marvellous sensation but becomes close to painful if I am unable to relieve sexual tension.[32]

There are also case studies of women called 'transvestites' (in our view inappropriately) which turn up in the newspapers every now and again. In 1991 the *Sun* reported the case of eighteen year old Jennifer Saunders, who was prosecuted for her 'transvestism' and sentenced to six years imprisonment (she was released in 1992 after winning her appeal against her sentence). Evidently, this young woman dressed like a man, and like the fictional seventeenth century pick-pocket Moll Cutpurse, passed herself off as a boy in order to date girls.[53] The court alleged that Saunders seduced two seventeen year old girls whose parents said their daughters did not know about the disguise until it was 'too late'; other commentators have alleged that the girls did know Saunders was a girl but lied because they hadn't 'come out' as lesbians to their parents.

Although the above case of cross-dressing appears to have involved disguise rather than sexual fetishism, it does highlight, as does Garber's book, the importance of clothes in constructing sexual identities.[54] Today, women are allowed to wear trousers with less comment than a man would provoke in a skirt; nevertheless it is still not acceptable for women to look too 'butch' or too 'mannish'.

Lesbian Cross-dressers

Lesbians are well aware of the taboos surrounding female identity, particularly lesbian identity. Lesbians who play with style, or dress up as men, may have a different relationship to the attire of the opposite sex than other women. In some subcultural lesbian circles[55], it is now fashionable for women to base their look on the archetypal 'mannish' figure made by Radclyffe Hall in the 1920s, or earlier literary figures like George Sand, who was known to enjoy cross-dressing in men's clothes. The tuxedo, the monocle, short hair and the elongated cigarette-holder were recognisable dress codes of lesbian Paris of the 1920s.[56] This look has come back and in contemporary London co-exists with the lesbian 'boy' look which often features razored hair and Doc Martens, as well as other lesbian dress codes.

Some lesbian dress-styles owe as much to ideas about 'resistance' and 'protest' as to ideas about sexual fetishism. Most subcultures are involved in renegotiation of dominant values and attitudes. And lesbians who have embraced the 1920s Paris look or the more criticised lesbian butch look (rather than adopting the style of what has been dubbed the terrain of the 'lipstick lesbian'[57]), may have done so precisely because it offends the homophobic and celebrates female strength as well as lesbian desire. Other lesbians, recognising the potential of playing with identity, have more than one image of themselves as 'queer'.[58] Lesbian photographer, Della Grace, for instance, was featured in the *Guardian* newspaper in 1992 playing around with her personal image and presenting two contrasting portraits of herself, one as 'Della Butch' and the other as 'Della Glam'.

Most discussions about the recurrence of the mannish figure in lesbian self portraits,[59] and about the pleasure achieved by lesbians from wearing male attire,[60] have been informed by social rather than psychological explanations. Our research has found that in a few cases at least something like sexual fetishism was involved in a woman dressing as a man, lesbian, heterosexual or bisexual. It is difficult to be more positive or direct about this behaviour, because the question that is impossible to answer, without more extensive research, concerns the degree of female sexual fetishism under scrutiny.

Get Up and Vogue

Madonna's *Vogue* video makes reference to the monocled dyke and to the practice of 'Vogueing' – dressing up as somebody else, engaged in by some lesbians and other women. Vogueing features prominently in many sexual subcultures and needs to be looked at in relation to questions about fetishism. Vogueing can involve both male and female cross-dressing. Some New York gay subcultures, for instance, feature vogueing as part of an elaborate ceremony, where poor black and Hispanic drag queens dress up and mimic rich society white women and magazine fashion models. Vogueing, however, not only features transvestism but also accommodates 'homeovestism', which we defined as dressing up in the clothes of the same sex person.[61]

On the New York scene poor black boys are found to dress up as rich white boys as well as girls. This vogueing 'masquerade' is enacted through the commodity fetishism of clothing, which articulates class, gender and racial stereotypes. Individuals accentuate stereotypical ways of behaving – be it 'upper class' or 'masculine' or 'feminine', and often emphasise shape as well as sexual parts of the body to accomplish the masquerade. But the question 'homeovestism' raises, concerns the nature of the fetishism involved. The idea of achieving orgasm from clothing, as associated with male transvestism, may not be relevant to homeovestism specifically; nor does it provide an adequate model to talk about all the levels of fetishism involved in homeovestite masquerade achieved when men vogue as men or women vogue as women.

Writers on vogueing such as Becquer and Gatti would certainly agree that it would be inappropriate to talk about vogueing simply as either transvestism or homeovestism. For they have argued that 'vogueing is a site of intersection for the categories of race, class, gender as well as sexuality'.[62] They point out that vogueing can often be read as involving a critique, or a least a restructuring, of some of the social and sexual identities on offer in post-industrial society.

Vogueing cuts across many social categories. Ethnicity, class, sexual orientation as well as gender boundaries are played around with and this 'playful' behaviour often provides an astute commentary about the artificial nature of identity. It would be inappropriate to discuss vogueing in terms of any single concept of homeovestism or trans-vestism, because not all voguers cross- dress, and because the fetishistic pleasures from vogueing cut across a range of types of fetishism, not just sexual fetishism.

In some recent films – primarily about homosexual subcultures – vogueing is shown to be a dominant leisure activity. For example, in *Paris is Burning* [63] and *Tongues Untied* [64], fetishism of clothing as an erotic commodity (particularly 'sexy' items belonging to the opposite sex) is ostentatiously celebrated. But fetishism is not the most signifi-cant aspect of the clothing or of the behaviour under scrutiny. Some voguers are 'fans' who clearly see their copying of their idol's look as a sort of triumphant celebration. We discussed the meaning of some types of fan fetishism in more detail in chapter one when we looked at the behaviour of fans in relation to ideas about 'anthropo-logical fetishism'.

Becquer and Gatti comment that vogueing involves issues about 'disguise' and 'renegotiation of reality'. They point out that 'at balls Voguers compete for realness'. What could be more challenging to definitions of social reality or sexual normality than individuals who start to renegotiate the framework of social and sexual identities, albeit in a playful postmodern way?

So how can we assess the pleasures on offer to the women who vogue? There are so many cultural, as well as psychological, factors to take into account when looking at this practice, that to focus solely upon the psychoanalytic framework appears inadequate. Vogueing may well engage with complex narcissistic social and sexual fantasies, it may well involve 'inappropriate' identifications with objects and images; but vogueing by its very nature radically reveals the instability of identity in post-modern culture. It also reveals the perverse masquerade inherent in taken-for-granted cultural ideas about masculinity and femininity.

Femininity as Perversion

So far in this chapter we have discussed the question of fashion and fetishism primarily in relation to women cross-dressing as men. We have hinted that fashions of previous generations which have been central to the regulation of ideas about femininity, from footbinding to the wearing of corsets, can be construed as perverse. However, we would like to take this analysis of fashion and fetishism a step further. As Caroline Evans has pointed out, 'fashion is important in revealing the perverse masquerade of gender itself, in particular the perverse masquerade of femininity.'[65] This analysis of 'femininity as perversion' is also discussed by Louise Kaplan who reintroduces the notion of homeovestism to the debate.[66] Kaplan's concept of the female homeovestite involved in a feminine masquerade is based on two main sources. The term itself was first used by George Zavitzianos in 1969 when he discussed and extended Joan Riviere's writing about masquerade which had appeared some forty years earlier, and Kaplan quotes both articles.

As we have mentioned, a female homeovestite is a woman who dresses up as a woman, one who masquerades as a quintessential feminine type. We have suggested that Dolly Parton or even Barbara Cartland could fall into this category. But we would point to any bride on the day of her 'white wedding'. Some critics, like tv presenter and drag queen Rupert Charles, take the argument about masquerade even further and remind us that 'every time you put on clothes you put on drag'.[67]

This idea of clothing being essential to gender masquerade, as we have mentioned, was originally identified by the psychoanalyst Joan Riviere writing in 1929.[68] Her work provided case studies of women working in jobs previously considered 'masculine' occupations. She found that the new social order expected women to express 'masculine ambition' while remaining 'feminine' in appearance and in accord with all the other cultural codes associated with femininity. Riviere was deeply suspicious of the 'scientific professors and business [women] who seem to fulfil every criterion of complete feminine development'.[69]

Her case studies of such 'feminine' women revealed many underlying anxieties about femininity. Riviere argued that their elaborately feminine attitudes were used like a mask to hide the more masculine traits.

Riviere used this idea of 'masquerade' to explain why some of her female case studies found it necessary to hide their intellectual powers behind a facade of self-demeaning femininity. Nevertheless, she was careful to insist that there was no simple distinction between the 'masquerade of femininity' and 'real' womanliness. Instead, she suggested that the masquerade was used as a sort of fetishistic device to avoid anxiety by women from the perceived threat of punishment for being too much like men.

But what sort of fetishism are both Riviere and Kaplan hinting at in relation to masquerade or homeovestism? Surely, these terms operate only to pathologise the behaviour of all women who wear feminine clothes? Louise Kaplan explains that, although 'any person dressing in the clothes of his or her own sex could be a homeovestite', this does not mean that everyone is. The important qualification for Kaplan is that a homeovestite women is 'a woman who is unsure of her femininity, a woman who is afraid to openly acknowledge her masculine strivings'. She suggests, 'the crucial motive of a woman who colludes in the fetishization of her own body is ... dread of annhilation.'[70]

A homeovestite woman, according to Kaplan, perceives that she lacks 'natural femininity'. Kaplan argues such a woman 'learned long ago that the best she could do was to dress up as a woman. In the way she dresses, styles her hair ... [she] imagines that she is decorating femininity onto the outside of her body, which she thinks of as a container tool'.[71]

The explanation offered by Kaplan for this masquerade of femininity stems from her idea that 'the crucial motive of a woman who colludes in the fetishisation of her own body is sexual anxiety ... These fetishized Olympias [the name of a centrefold] and Marilyns [Monroe] are the most obvious victims of a commodity fetishism that infiltrates the whole social order.'[72]

The fetishism inherent in the masquerade of homeovestism is thus located by Kaplan as a fetishism of commodities which confer femininity. Some female images inspire individual women in their everyday life to buy things to 'produce' some exaggerated types of femininity, and they often commodify themselves to conform to male definitions of what is 'sexy' or 'feminine'. This is clearly not fetishism in the sexual sense (the clothes being the primary object of orgasm). So we can rule out homeovestism as a practice that intrinsically accommo-dates sexual fetishism by women, in the sense of Gebhard's 'fourth degree'. However, homeovestism can involve fragmentation and exhibitionism. Kaplan found that some women appear to experience sexual pleasure from dressing up to be looked at, and this behaviour is fetishistic; but she doesn't suggest that this exhibitionism is more pleasurable for them than having sex with partners.

We would argue that the concept of masquerade and homeovestism relates to both women who vogue as women and men who vogue as men. But we would point out that men find it much more difficult to be feminine than women do to be masculine because our culture reifies masculinity. Looking across the popular arena at images of 'macho' men found there, it seems to us that nowadays men are more aware than ever before of the need to dress up as men, and to self-consciously construct gender images and engage in a degree of fet-ishism. But this commodification of gender, which is at the root of homeovestism, is not the same thing as sexual fetishism; rather it constitutes commodity fetishism of the gendered erotic. It must be remembered that consumer objects and style, from haircuts to jew-ellery, are used by society to identify gender differences in Western culture. It is, therefore, at the level of consumer choice about the meaning of gender that we find fetishism at the heart of homeovestism. This level of consumer fetishism is an integral part of all forms of 'dressing up', like transvestism or vogueing. Some of these cultural practices may indeed involve individuals who fetishise in the sexual sense to the stage that Gebhard has described as the fourth degree. But it is our view that female homeovestism, unlike some male trans-vestite practices, rarely, if at all, accommodates fully fledged fourth degree sexual fetishism.

Fetishism as Lifestyle

Certainly fashion itself, as a discourse as well as a design practice, has confused definitions of fetishism and eroticism. Bondage fashions for women, which emerged with Vivienne Westwood's punk collection of 1976/7, challenged any simple reading of women as objects of fetishism. 'Sex is the thing that bugs English people more than anything else. So that's where I attack' commented Westwood[73]. She subse-quently inspired many punk women to reinvent the meaning of sexual fetish codes for themselves through their relationships to leather and rubber.

Women have used fashion and the consumer objects associated with fetishism to carve out identities for themselves within many subcultures across Europe and America. Since this happened, and since punk went mainstream, the iconography of traditional sexual fetishism has also started to be reappropriated.

In the 1990s, when 'authentic' subcultural activity seems to change more quickly than ever before, youth style (incorporating fetish codes) appears to have more in common with lifestyle marketing. Subcultural clothing styles no longer form part of the 'crack' in national consensus. Nor do they represent a 'countercultural' space outside of dominant culture, as postulated by some subcultural theorists writing from the Birmingham Centre for Contemporary Cultural Studies. Vivienne Westwood designs, for instance, are an integral part of the fashion system, rather than being in resistance to it. Female punks in bondage gear are humorously recreated in order to promote the National Westminster Bank and Abbey National; and in so doing these advertisements covertly and perhaps unintentionally legitimate fetish style. In the 1990s Madonna and various Hollywood films stars like Kim Basinger, Sharon Stone and Michelle Pfeiffer seem to have incorporated this shift, and have appeared both in public and in films wearing fetish fashions, thus seeming to promote kinky sex. This is not to say there is not still a separate subcultural fetish scene, apart from Hollywood reappropriation, that has its own ideas about how to regulate fetishism, but things are changing. As one reader to *Skin Two* magazine commented, perhaps the subcultural fetish scene is not as underground as it once was, because

> rubber, leather and S&M are going through the same stage now that the condom went through ... it was an illicit object, but now any one can buy a pack virtually anywhere. I look forward to the day when I can walk into Burtons and ask for a rubber suit. The press exposure fetishism is getting is bringing that day closer.[74]

Even the quintessential British home, that terrain of the private and 'personal', has been invaded by fetish iconography, which seems to have lost many of its illicit significations. Some home furnishings have utilised associated textiles, like leather, rubber, studs and spikes, to decorate items usually covered in softer fabrics. Many items, from Craig Morrison's spiky leather sofa (see Illustration 4) to high fashion rubber holdall bags have been given the 'fetish' treatment.

Social renegotiations of traditional fetish codes can also be observed not only in the media but on the London Club scene in the

1980s and 1990s. Most of the clubs cited in the style journals, or listed in magazines like *Time Out*, do not regard fetish behaviour as rare or extraordinary (although it is often posited as 'exciting'). Many fashion magazines have reflected these shifts in fetish style. *Elle* magazine as well as style journals like *The Face* and *ID* have frequently included features of highly stylised bondage costume, and other leather or rubber objects, in their fashion spreads of women's and men's underwear. These days it seems S&M fetish fashions have even arrived at the underwear counter of M&S (Marks and Spencer).

These 'fetish' items and images make their way into the youth culture market because they are associated with sex, and sex is used to sell everything. The intention of magazine spreads that feature rubber dresses (see Illustration 5) or leather outfits is probably not to say anything deeply significant about fetishism. Instead the fetish items are there as superficial 'sexy' fashions, new 'lifestyle' designs to be worn after buying the up-to-the-minute rubber home furnishing which are also featured.

These current levels of representation of fetishism, we would argue, have created a different social context. For example, the easing of censure towards rubber and leather has allowed women to explore their relationship to them. Nowadays even fetish parties like those organised by *Skin Two* magazine or London clubs like 'Submissions' are regularly frequented by female 'clubbers' as well as hard core sado-masochists. Similarly 'Kinky Weekend' breaks are a central component of the sexual travel tours that are offered to Europeans flying to Bangkok or Thailand, who may never before have thought of fetishism, bondage or S&M.

In this changing cultural context is it not surprising that concrete visual evidence of women's fetish activity – recorded by photographers like Della Grace (see Illustration 6) and Grace Lau (see Illustration 7) has not provoked wider discussion? From these images as well as the brief survey of material we have covered here, it is clear that women are actively involved in a range of fetishistic activities some of which may be closely related to the orthodox definition of sexual fetishism. On the Left there has been some attempt to reconceptualise the female erotic but even allegedly serious intellectual magazines like the *New Statesman and Society* still haven't got a clue about what's going on for some feminists. The patronising patriarchal tone echoed in a recent article entitled 'Sex Rampages of the Feminist Porn Queens' reveals this. We found fetishistic behaviour by women

Craig Morrison Sofa
Courtesy Skin Two magazine. Photograph Peter Ashworth

Fetishism as life style: Rubber dresses hit the fashion spreads

Della Grace: Female fetishist art

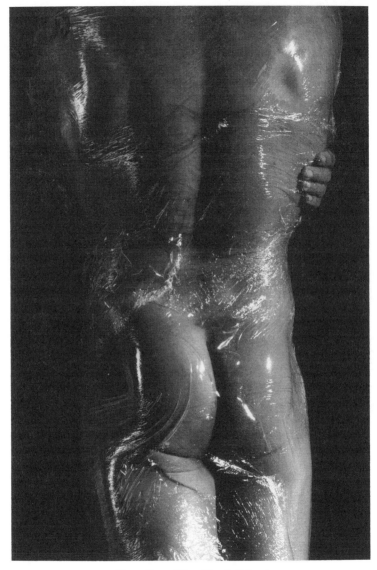

Grace Lau: Cling film fetish art

Food fetishism: The Haagen-Dazs experience
Sophia Chauchard-Stuart

still being framed by the same tired old questions – 'does it constitute pornography'?[75]

The activity of women in sexual subcultures – as clubbers and consumers of fetish items, as readers of fetish magazines, as female transvestites and homeovestites – is evidence of the occurrence of female fetishism in contemporary society. Although our discussion about the level of sexual fetishism involved in these practices is inconclusive, in terms of presenting evidence about what Gebhard describes as the 'fourth degree' of sexual fetishism, nevertheless we believe that our documentation of activities of women in social and sexual subcultures challenges many of the assumptions of previous research. We feel that the activity of women we have discussed in this chapter should at least undermine the certainty of previous accounts which do not connect women with fetishism, or when they do, do not recognise women as sexual fetishists and continue to describe such behaviour as 'rare'.

More substantial research is clearly needed into these areas of female sexuality. In the meantime, in this book we aim to establish the existence of certain types of behaviour which constitute sexual fetishism by women. We feel that this argument about women and fetishism is important, not for its own sake, but because it challenges the binary oppositions (male active, female passive) within the dominant readings of sexuality, on which many of the aspects of social order are based.

The Problem with Perverts

Can this recognition of female sexual activity ever be liberatory? If fetishism is seen as the province of perverse men, then surely female fetishism (if recognised) will probably only be seen as twice as bad! Although this is a possible response we believe that our reading of sexual fetishism as an activity of women leads to some useful insights. For example, it does force some redefinition of the concept of perversion pioneered by sexologists and psychiatrists in the nineteenth century.[76] This process of redefinition has important theoretical implications, as writers on sexual politics like Jeffrey Weeks and Jonathan Dollimore have pointed out before us.[77] Our contribution to the debate we hope will further dismantle certainties about what constitutes perversity, and therefore help us undermine authoritarian discourses of sexual regulation.

In the 1960s Britain saw a liberalising of laws on sexuality, influ-

enced by the Wolfenden Report, which led to changes to the Sexual
Offences Act of 1967 so that homosexual acts between consenting
adults were finally decriminalised.

Yet it would be inappropriate to say that attitudes towards homosexuality or other diverse sexual practices completely changed after
the 1960s. It is not simply that in the 1980s the AIDS epidemic has
reinforced old prejudices, it is also clear that the older legal and medical
definitions of perversity never entirely went away. These still construct our sexual practices within an implicitly moral framework as
either 'normal' or 'deviant'.

Such ideas about what is normal and what is deviant have permeated what Gramsci defines as 'common sense',[78] as medical definitions have established themselves as orthodox terminology for the
discussion of all diverse sexual practices. But since changing attitudes
have meant that sexual practice does not necessarily conform to the
expectations of previous generations, these nineteenth century formulations are problematic in twentieth century society. It's not simply
that the post 1960s generation expect more from sex than reproduction (the usual nineteenth century designation of the 'normal aim' of
sex). But in today's environment, the high risk associated with unprotected penetrative sex means that people have begun to become much
more imaginative about sex. 'Fetishism is a way of expressing your
sexuality without putting your health at risk' commented Michelle
Olley of *Skin Two* magazine, at the conference on Perversity at the
ICA. Such attitudes may also mean that in subsequent years our whole
attitude to a number of sexual practices now considered to be 'deviant' will have to be turned completely around. As Lynne Segal has
pointed out, 'Aids could serve as a spur, not for more of the same
evasions and hypocrisy around sex, but for ... the recognition of sexual
diversity.'[79]

Cultural historians continue to remind us that today's definitions
of sexuality should be approached with caution. Definitions often say
more about the period than the behaviour in question, and are
constructed rather than described by the discourses through which
they are spoken. 'To explore the history of perversion is to see not
only how culture is formed but consolidated, destabilised and re-
formed,' comments Jonathan Dollimore.[80]

Michel Foucault, in *The History of Sexuality: Volume One*, was one of
the first to make a full critique of the Freudian psychoanalysis that
had been central in laying down the law about perversity. Foucault
argued that psychoanalysis has been involved in the 'implantation' of

a discourse which is both the product and the vehicle of an almost invisible exercise of power. He goes on to assert that the tone of authority in discourses about 'perversity' operates not only to explain but also to regulate and therefore determine human sexual behaviour.[81]

Women are by and large excluded from the traditional psychoanalytic accounts of perversity. For example, female 'homosexuality' is either not seen at all or not defined as a perversion; whereas male homosexuality was originally categorised as perverse.[82] Other practices analysed as 'perverse' are: voyeurism, sadomasochism, exhibitionism, genital mutilation, and of course fetishism.[83] These activities have been seen, from the earliest thinkers to those of the present day, as being:

1. deviant from 'normal' heterosexual practices.
2. requiring a male agent.
3. something abnormal (fetishism is rarely constructed as one of a range of sexual practices).

We argue that writing women into the action in discussions of perversity has the effect of beginning to deconstruct the whole discourse. This is a slow process because female activity is ignored by those who regularise and enforce medical concepts of normal and abnormal mental phenomena. In 1952, for example, the American Psychiatric Association published the *Diagnostic Statistical Manual of Mental Disorders* known as DSM, and the sexual deviations were grouped in this manual with the psychopathic personality disorders. This helped to legitimate the perversions being cited as legal offences, lending authority to the prevailing belief that 'perversions' were engaged in by persons with anti-social and criminal tendencies, usually men, who are found to be more criminal than women.[84]

Some psychiatrists have continued the line of argument in which the perversions are seen as endemic to male 'pathology' and 'criminality'. They have mobilised crime statistics which show that women are proportionately less 'criminal' as well as less 'perverse' than men. Many have argued that less than 1 per cent of cases of perversity are female and that even studies of sexual masochism show that 'the ratio of cases is approximately 20 males to one female'.[85] Whilst we do not wish to claim that women are inherently more perverse or masochistic than men, we would question all this statistical evidence and argue that female activity has been overlooked because official definitions have often meant that female behaviour has been interpreted inappropriately. The 'perversion gap' has meant, as Marjorie Garber has pointed out before us, 'that women are thought to have neuroses (like hysteria) and only men have psychoses, perversions and 'paraphilias' (like fetishism and transvestism)'.[86] Indeed, to reclaim fetishism for women is to undermine many major assumptions of perversity theory.

Many critics would object to our assertion that female behaviour has been 'overlooked'. Stoller, a notable example, has argued that:

> Perversion is far more common in men than in women. I do not think this is merely a counting error and that women's perversions are hidden from researchers. I also do not believe that women are less perverse only because they do not dare and that when, society treats women the same as men, women ... will be as perverse as men.[87]

Despite what he says, we feel that Stoller himself has overlooked many aspects of female behaviour which could be labelled perverse. For example, erotic vomiting by women, as we will explain in chapter four, is a form of behaviour that Stoller confesses he could not understand, but which we interpret as possible evidence of fetishism by women.

To make the case for female agency on the pathologised subject of perversity could be understood as the assertion of women's rights to be constructed as sexually active. But it could also be politically compromising, to associate sexual activity by women with 'perversion'. This situation highlights one of the difficulties of trying to engage with problematic psychoanalytic terms in our discussions. The very concept of fetishism brings with it the idea of perversion because psychoanalysis has historically operated to pathologise all diverse sexual activity. Worse, it has operated to pathologise sexual behaviour between *consenting* adults. (Homosexuality, for example, is still viewed by some as a perversion.) This creates a problem for anyone trying to engage with radical sexual politics in order to welcome the reception of ideas about sexual diversity; any level of diverse sexual experimentation is constructed as aberrant.

To construct commonly occurring sexual practices as 'perverse' is inimical to a radical sexual politics. However, our model of sexual diversity certainly does not align us with any simple libertarian position. Although we have problems with a lot of the behaviour deemed 'perverse' by psychoanalysis, we would not want to rule out the appropriateness of all definitions. Our model of 'perverse' sexual practice would be one which takes place without the consent of adult participants. Conversely, any sexual practice which involves consent by all individuals over sixteen years of age, and does not lead to extreme physical damage, we would not classify as perverse. Indeed, we are not unhappy that paedophilia and bestiality are pathologised as perverse practices, because they do not involve mutual consent between adults and are often demonstrably harmful to the individuals concerned, both physically and emotionally. Using this model, rape clearly would be defined as perverse. The model of consent has its limitations, but arguably it could be incorporated into the law, as the civil rights group Liberty are arguing, to contrast it with non-consensual sexual acts. Such a strategy might stop responsible sexual practice being constructed as perverse and criminal.

Sex Today

The psychoanalytic model does not utilise the idea of consent as a criterion of normal sexual behaviour. We think this is a problem. In the 1990s – especially in a culture where unprotected penetrative sex again, as in the nineteenth century, carries with it the risk of infection and death – we would argue that a significant proportion of the population will find it necessary to experiment with non penetrative sexual practices, and so many official definitions of perverse behaviour will become even more inappropriate than they are now. Or to put it more bluntly: for many people 'kinky sex' nowadays is part of 'normal' experimentation and/or practice and so old definitions of perversity no longer apply. Dr. Glen Wilson of the Institute of Psychiatry and co-author of research into so-called 'sexual deviancy' concurs with this view. His research has shown that at least 30 per cent of people use S&M games as a form of sexual enhancement in the bedroom. An even higher proportion of them report fantasies including some element of dominance and subordination.[88] Such statistics indicate that old definitions of perversity no longer apply. This fact is recognised by many people including newspaper agony aunt, Deidre Saunders who writes for the *Sun*. This paper's editorials may be outraged by Frank Bough's alleged bondage sex escapades, but Dear Deidre's 1992 phoneline about *What Counts As Kinky Sex* tells listeners:

> no form of sharing physical passion is wrong as long as you don't damage each other either physically or emotionally ... What one finds erotic another may find degrading, so you need to negotiate. Be firm ... be open minded ... but don't do anything you consider inside to be very wrong.[89]

From anecdotal evidence we have gathered about sexual behaviour we find similar views repeated. We need, however, to be cautious about making sweeping statements without more corroborating statistical evidence from separate sources. We note that even after 24 years of gay liberation, a poll carried out in the 1980s[90], revealed that 75 per cent of young people surveyed (aged between 15 to 25) 'found homosexuality an unacceptable lifestyle'.[91] Still, as a measure of popular opinion, Dr. Wilson's survey and tolerant tabloid agony columns about sex appear to suggest sexual variations are more common in the average bedroom than was imagined in the nineteenth century.

The popstar Madonna, who has been outspoken about 'Kinky Sex' and who has recommended sexual diversity to the masses, has been more reticent about her alleged bisexuality. She made headlines with her book *Sex* by admitting to bisexual fantasies, and later, after much criticism for her reticence on the subject, acknowledging that she had really experienced actual lesbian sexual affairs. Nevertheless, despite the sensationalism and 'moral panics' that surround Madonna's videos and performances she has done much to promote the image of a sexually active women. As well as vying for interviews with Madonna, women's magazines seem to be competing with each other to promote female sexual activity and independence, and to tackle sexual subjects. In one month alone *She* argued 'Quickie sex is the Bees Knees' and *Marie Claire*, explained to readers 'why we want you to grab him'.[92] The editor of *Company* magazine, Mandi Norwood, went so far to argue that 'the sex supplement promotes monogamy in the Age of AIDS by helping couples to make their sex lives more interesting'.[93]

Women talking about sex are becoming quite common. For example, the series 'Rude Women' challenged myths that women don't like sex or experimenting.[94] After one programme in the series was shown, some British supermarkets claimed they had sold out of clingfilm as women were alleged to be rushing out to buy it after watching photographer Grace Lau wrap up her male model in cling film for an erotic shot (see Illustration 7). All this activity is evidence that women now have a higher profile as sexually active and independent sexual beings than ever before. Meanwhile, of course, violence against women continues and women workers in the sex industry – prostitutes, exotic dancers, nude models, escorts, porn actresses and workers in massage parlours – reveal that the men who go to them for 'deviant' sex can't imagine their wives enjoying the same acts; these men evidently continue to exhibit the sexist attitudes that divide women into Madonnas v Whores.[95]

We certainly can't afford to be blase about sexual 'liberation' in the 1990s, when we are still witnessing the continued Clause 29 backlash against homosexuality. Recently, there have also been some worrying legal judgments about sexual practice, and a number of sado-masochists, mostly middle aged homosexual men, have been convicted at the Old Bailey. These trials constitute part of what has become known as the Operation Spanner case, which dates back to December 1990. Those arrested for their offending acts (which included whipping, scratching, piercing and cutting of genital organs among other things) were consenting adults who carried out their activities in the privacy of their own homes. But the lynchpin of the case for the prosecution concerned the fact that some of these acts were recorded on videos made for private (and therefore non-commercial) use. This is how Scotland Yard's Obscene Publications Squad were brought in. The acts in question did not constitute GBH or require hospitalisation but nevertheless Judge Rant was persuaded to sentence at least 11 men to up to four a half years for assault; 26 other individuals were cautioned.

As a consequence of the injustice of the situation, the Operation Spanner case has provoked a civil liberties issue because, as Jeffrey Weeks, historian of sexuality, has observed, 'what makes the Spanner case so interesting is that it has become a filter for almost all the essential issues in today discussions of sexuality'.[96] Judge Rant may not believe it is OK for men to go around sandpapering each other's scrotums or afixing each other's genitals to bits of wood via chains[97], but his judgment has resulted in the ludicrous situation whereby lovebites, according to legal precedent (sustained by the House of Lords), now constitute acts of violence! At the time of writing this judgment is being taken to the European Court.

The Spanner case clearly raises issues about 'taste' as well as personal morality. It is difficult in today's political climate not to view Operation Spanner as part of an anti-gay backlash, rather than as a backlash against fetishism. As Angus Hamilton, a defence solicitor on the case has pointed out:

> I'm not saying heterosexual S&M behaviour won't be attacked, not at all. But I found it difficult to believe quite the same interest, manpower or money would have gone into an operation involving married couples.

Clearly, the legal cases brought to court by Operation Spanner have serious implications for all heterosexuals involved in S&M activities, particularly those who wish to document or film their personal behaviour, or that of others involved in sexual subcultures. Some critics have suggested when discussing Operation Spanner that there is a censorship issue involved at the heart of it all, and that 'it's as if people validate their response through their disgust at the activities under scrutiny'. [98]

Perhaps it was disgust rather than criminal activity that legitimated Scotland Yard's costly involvement in the biggest investigation into S&M that Britain has ever seen. In such a context, where individual sexual practice and sexual identity is, despite the efforts of the Wolfenden Report of over thirty years ago, still being policed by the state, how can we argue for female fetishism as part of a positive image of sexual diversity? Especially when, as Pat Califia has pointed out, 'if you are publicly identifiable as a perve, you face job discrimination, street violence and the loss of custody of your children. That's a lot to deal with …'[99]

One familiar strategy is to say that the fetish films being made are 'artistic', or for individuals to regard their body modifications as art. But this sort of thinking won't persuade the psychiatrists that fetishism is creative or even 'positive' in its social implication. As if it was not bad enough to connect fetishism with 'deviance' and with actual 'criminality', Freud also went on to connect fetishistic behaviour with the inability of individuals to transform perverse desires into 'civilised' achievements.[100] Many institutions which regulate psychoanalysis – like the Tavistock and Portman Clinics in London – seem to still concur with this way of thinking and are rather slow, to say the very least, in reformulating theories to take account of cultural shifts in sexual and social behaviour, or to comprehend the purely aesthetic value of fetish art.

Some critics would argue that those interested in art should just get on with it; those interested in civil liberties should campaign for a Bill of Rights; and those interested in sexual politics should abandon psychoanalysis. We would go along with the first two but have problems with the idea of abandoning psychoanalysis. The model on which the perversions are built clearly contains some outmoded ideas about what constitutes 'normal' sexual behaviour in contemporary society. And by engaging with clinical definitions of sexual fetishism (and the existing psychoanalytic framework) in order to identify active female sexual behaviour we recognise that we have come up against some extremely problematic definitions about 'pathology', about which we have many worries and reservations. But we still wouldn't jettison psychoanalysis. To explain our position about the use of psychoanaly-

sis within this book we would align ourselves with Jonathan Dollimore
and echo his observation:

> to recover the lost histories of perversion ... is to recognise the inadequacies
> of ... psychoanalytic accounts ... yet ... to deploy psychoanalytic catego-
> ries ... [is to] concede inconsistency without regarding it as an insuperable
> methodological problem [and] ... welcome the theoretical tension be-
> tween psychoanalysis and materialism (which is what this inconsistency
> amounts to), finding in it the impetus to recover the historical and political
> dimensions which more theoretically self-consistent critiques often gesture
> towards but rather more rarely engage with, and none more so than
> psychoanalysis.[101]

It may be true, as Louise Kaplan has argued, that 'every text on
perversion bears some features of a perverse scenario because the
author's perverse fantasies are stirred up by what he or she is writing
about'. She goes on to advise that 'anyone who writes about perversion has to be wary of falling prey to the perverse strategy'.[102] Reading
the case studies of fetishism we tend to agree with her, because the
descriptions by some psychiatrists of the behaviour of their patients
seems far more perverse to us than the behaviour itself. Nevertheless,
despite its problems, we believe that psychoanalysis contains so many
valuable insights as a body of theory that it would be foolish to abandon
it. We hope that the stalwarts in the institutions will open up their
minds and try to re-evaluate new evidence about the female sexual
behaviour we, and so many others, have uncovered. Freud admitted
he didn't completely understand the 'dark continent' of female sexuality, and we think it is about time psychoanalysis improved its ability
to discuss this subject. We therefore hope our findings about female
fetishism might have ramifications, not only for the study of female
'perversity', but also for the whole subject of female sexuality.

The debate about female perversity has already been initiated by
many feminist writers and activists[103], who have been worried about
the sexual essentialism of some of anti-pornography debates.[104] Recently Louise Kaplan has drawn attention to massive clinical and
theoretical neglect of research amongst women on the subject of
perversity. She argues that one problem is that there is a 'tendency
to cast about for females with the fetishistic perversions that are typical
of men, the exceptions of the rule'. However, Kaplan is able to side-
step the political problems attached to the official definitions of
perversity by redefining virtually all diverse sexual activities as 'perverse strategies' : 'perversion is a psychological strategy. It differs from

other psychological strategies in that it demands a performance'. Kaplan qualifies her descriptions of the 'perverse strategy' by saying that all perverse activities involve deception as part of their psychological activity. [105]

Whilst we welcome Kaplan's attempt to address the issue of women and perversity, and to try to redefine the concept of perversity itself, we have problems with some of her analysis. Firstly, it seems inappropriate to apply the idea of 'deception' to our understanding of sexual fetishism – we feel the concept of disavowal is far more appropriate. Second, Kaplan talks about challenging ideas about male agency which are endemic to psychoanalysis, but unfortunately her research has been criticised for not saying exactly what she means by femininity and masculinity, 'the very myths of primary gender that she is trying to undermine'.[106] Third, she seems to view much female behaviour, from female anorexia to women wearing punk outfits as a product of individual pathology rather than of culture. She fails to see in these activities the possible 'resistance' by women in context of inappropriate definitions of their lives: whereas psychologists such as Liam Hudson would view this behaviour, by punk females, for example, as very specific to the female condition. Hudson has argued that this sort of behaviour can be understood through the insight that women 'create perverse situations' whereas men 'tend to act out, especially aggressively, their perverse needs'.[107]

It is our contention, based on Foucault's reading of fetishism as 'the foundation perversion'[108] – and our reading of it as an activity engaged in by women – that all the so-called 'perversions' have been inappropriately formulated on the assumption of male agency. This may have happened, in part, as a consequence of all the old-fashioned myths that female sexual drive is more passive than men's.[109] We would argue that cultural factors mean that women experience sexual desire differently from men, and that accounts of female sexuality need to analyse the inscription and decoding of female sexuality.

We hope our own interpretation of women as active practitioners of fetishism may further develop the debate about the active elements of female desire. We believe our approach is different from that of others, such as Louise Kaplan, who talk about female 'perversions'. This is because throughout the book, unlike Kaplan, we try to offer some deconstruction of the psychoanalytic discourse through which perversion is spoken. To paraphrase Foucault, fetishism is the foundation model perversion on which nineteenth century psychiatry has been built.[110]

This means that our analysis of women as practitioners of fetishism undermines this very foundation by calling for a change of thinking in at least four areas:

1. we reject the notion that sexual fetishism generally requires a male agent.
2. we also dispute that all the other perversions require male agency.
3. we argue that fetishism, and other sexual deviations, are not uncommon as was previously thought by nineteenth century writers.
4. we argue that the pathological categories currently employed to describe fetishistic behaviour are often simply inappropriate as an explanation of wider cultural shifts concerning today's sexual practice.

Notes

1 *Oxford English Dictionary* Vol 11, 2nd Ed., Clarendon, Oxford 1989, p618–9.

2 Comment by Michelle Olley of *Skin Two* at the *Preaching to the Perverted Conference* at the ICA on July 11, 1992.

3 Mandy Merck, *Perversions: Deviant Readings*, Virago, London 1993, p2.

4 See full definition and discussion of commodity fetishism on pp29–38.

5 E. Apter, *Feminizing the Fetish: Psychoanalysis and Narrative Obsession in Turn of the Century France*, Cornell University Press, 1991, p127. Original source given as: Paul Garnier, *Les Fetichistes pervertis et invertis sexuels*, J-B. Bailliere et Fils, 1896.

6 Sigmund Freud, 'Three Essays on the Theory of Sexuality', *The Standard Edition of the Complete Works*, translated by James Strachey, Hogarth, London 1953–64, Vol 7, pp135–243.

7 P. Gebhard, 'Fetishism and Sado-Masochism' in *Science & Psychoanalysis*, Vol 25, 1969, pp71–80.

8 W.A. Ross has argued 'partialism is a form of fetishism, though not quite the same thing. In partialism the individual is attached to a particular point of a woman's body – a selective fixation on some feature such as bosom, legs, thigh, hair … .By contrast, fetishism is partialism carried to extremes, where it becomes a sexual obsession.' *The Sex Life of the Foot and Shoe* Routledge, London 1977, p172–3. Such distinctions reinforce ideas about the differences between 'normal' and 'pathological' sexuality (ie, partialism and fetishism) and therefore we believe is less useful than Gebhard's continuum of 'degrees' of fetishism.

9 Clarke defines 'subculture' as 'first relating to the parent culture of which the subculture is a subset', S. Hall (ed), *Resistance Through Ritual*, Hutchinson, London 1978. Gay and lesbian communities are often referred to as 'sexual subcultures' as are other communities, such as the readership and members of various publications and clubs.

10 Grace Lau, 'The Voyeuristic Camera', *Skin Two*, Issue 2, 1984.

11 F. Delacoste and P. Alexandra (eds), *Sex Work: Writings by Women in the Sex Industry*, Cleis Press, USA 1987.

12 Pat Califia, 'The Power Exchange', *Skin Two Retro*, Tim Woodward Publishing Ltd, London 1991, p91.

13 There have been rather strange theories about it including one in which, extrapolating from an article by Gillespie in the *Skin Two Retro*, we found the suggestion that rubber fetishism might be activated by the memories of rubber teats of bottle fed babies: those who prefer leather are imagined as remembering the leathery feel of the mother's own breast.

14 We surveyed all the retail shops and manufacturers listed in the back of *Skin Two*, 1991.

15 Michelle Olley of *Skin Two* Magazines, Tim Woodward Publishing Ltd, confirmed this figure in her letter (8.4.91) in reply to ours asking about female readership. She said 'we spend a long time figuring out the gender of our readers but it is impossible to tell precisely ... our female readership is approximately 38–40% – that's a guestimate based on many factors. It is also based on the telephone enquiries we get – about 2 calls in every 5 are from women.

16 Pat Califia, *Macho Sluts*, Allyson Press, Boston, Mass. 1988.

17 V. Vale and A. Juno (eds), *Modern Primitives: An Investigation of Contemporary Adornment & Ritual*, Re/Search Publications, USA 1989.

18 V. Vale and A. Juno (eds), *op cit.*

19 *Ibid*, p110.

20 Genesis P'Orridge talking about Mr. Sebastian, V. Vale and A. Juno (eds), *op cit*, p165.

21 See 'Lorenzo as Closet Queen' in A. Carter, *Nothing Sacred*, Virago, London 1982.

22 Linda Gordon and Ellen Dubois, 'Seeking Ecstasy on the Battlefield: Danger and Pleasure in Nineteenth Century Feminist Sexual Thought', *Feminist Review* 13, Spring 1983, pp42–54.

23 Louise Rose, 'Freud and Fetishism: Previously Unpublished Minutes of the Vienna Psychoanalytic Society', *Psychoanalytic Quarterly*, 57, 1988, pp147–160 (p156).

24 Thorstein Bunde Veblen, *The Theory of the Leisure Class: An Economic Study in the Evolution of Institutions*, Macmillan Co, New York 1899.

25 See definition of 'Commodity Fetishism', pp29–38.

26 C. Hamilton, *Marriage as Trade*, Women's Press, London 1981.

27 J. Flugel, *The Psychology of Clothes*, L. & V. Woolf, Institute of Psychoanalysis, London 1930.

28 *Ibid*.

29 Caroline Evans and Minna Thornton, *Women and Fashion: A New Look*, Quartet, London 1989, p81.

30 Peter Ackroyd, *Dressing Up: Transvestism and Drag: the History of an Obsession*, Thames & Hudson, London 1979, p21.

31 Some medical writers note, however, that 'in a purely behavioural sense transvestism and fetishism are independent patterns'. Some qualification of this distinction is made by the comment that 'difficulty arises when we attempt to *interpret* these patterns'. H. Brierley, *Transvestism: A Handbook with Case Studies for Psychologists, Psychiatrists and Counsellors*, Pergamon, Oxford 1979, p224.

32 Many critics qualify that married male transvestites are able to have 'fulfilling' relationships with women. See Y. Sinclair's *Transvestism Within A Partnership of Marriage and Families*, The TV/TS Group, London 1984. The author stresses

this point using case studies and quotes from wives.

33　P. Ackroyd, *op cit*, 1979.

34　E. Apter, *op cit*, 1991.

35　Lillian Faderman, *Odd Girls and Twilight Lovers: A History of Lesbian Life in 20th Century America*, Penguin, Harmondsworth 1992. An illustration opposite p86 shows a photograph 'of Mary Fields born a slave who often wore men's clothes as a stage coach driver'.

36　We should qualify this point again by saying that not all male transvestites consciously find clothes erotic. When interviewed on ITV's 'Good Morning Britain' slot in 1990, some tvs invited on as guests said they didn't find wearing women's clothes erotic but it just made them feel good and/or that they enjoyed the element of disguise in passing as 'female'.

37　P. Ackroyd, *op cit*, 1979.

38　Robert Stoller, *Observing The Erotic Imagination*, Yale University Press, New Haven, London 1985, p176.

39　J. Wheelwright, *Amazons and Military Maids: women who dressed as men in the pursuit of life, liberty and happiness*, Pandora, London 1989.

40　*The Tradition of Female Transvestism in Early Modern Europe*, Rudolf M. Dekker and Lotte C. van de Pol, Macmillan, London 1989, p55.

41　Annie Woodhouse, *Fantastic Women: Sex, Gender and Transvestism*, Macmillan, London 1989, p18.

42　*Ibid*, p18–20.

43　Marjorie Garber, *Vested Interests: Cross-Dressing and Cultural Anxiety*, Routledge, London 1991.

44　*Ibid*, p16.

45　*Ibid*, p133.

46　*Ibid*, p133.

48　Margorie Garber, p44, cites references we hadn't heard of before like the 1985 publication, *Information for the Female to Male Crossdress or Transsexual*, in a way we haven't been able to find in British books.

49　M. Garber, *op cit*, p118, does talk about 'fetish envy' but this relates only to her analysis of the wearing of cod pieces by female performers in the theatre, discussion of which is critically assessed in chapter six of this book.

50　L. Kaplan, *op cit*, 1991, p244.

51　E. Guthiel, 1930, 'Analysis of a Case of Female Transvestism', in W. Stekel, *Sexual Aberrations*, Vision, London 1953.

52　R. Stoller, *op cit*, p143.

53　By feminist novelist Ellen Galford, *Moll Cutpurse*, Virago, London 1992.

54　Shaman, in anthropological literature, are described as wearing the garb of the opposite sex in order to create ambiguous categories around themselves and thus to distinguish themselves from other villagers.

55　It is not entirely accurate to speak of 'a' lesbian subculture. As Lillian Faderman has pointed out: 'Despite heterosexuals' single stereotyping of "the lesbian", lesbian subcultures based on class and age [differences], not only had little in common with each other but their members often distrusted and even disliked one another'. *Odd Girls and Twilight Lovers*, p160.

56　M. Garber, *op cit*, p153.

57　M. Garber, *op cit*, p160.

58　Defined by Cherry Smyth in *Queer Notions*, Scarlet Press, London 1992.

59 'These photographs show us only this ... that the lesbian self portrait is as persistent as it is impossible...', Mandy Merck, 'Transforming the Suit: A Century of Lesbian Self Portraits', in Tessa Boffin and Jean Fraser (eds), *Stolen Glances: Lesbians Take Photographs*, Pandora, London 1991, p21.

60 K. Rolley, *Feminist Review*, No. 35, Summer 1990, p54–66.

61 See discussion in Louise J. Kaplan, *Female Perversions*, p237–283, 'The Temptation of Madame Bovary'. Kaplan's concept of the female homeovestite involved in a feminine masquerade was based two main sources. The term itself was first used by George Zavitzianos in 1972 ('Homeovestism: Perverse Forms of Behaviour Involving the Wearing of Clothes of the Same Sex') when he discussed and extended Joan Riviere's 1929 piece ('Womanliness As Masquerade') about the feminine masquerade.

62 'Elements of Vogue' by Marcos Becquer and Jose Gatti, in *Third Text*, 16/17, Autumn/Winter 1991.

63 *Paris is Burning*, Paramount: 1990, Director Jenny Livingston.

64 *Tongues Untied*, PBS, USA, distributed by Framelines: Director Marlon Riggs.

65 Talk, '*Preaching to the Perverted Conference: Are Fetishistic Practices Radical*', Institute of Contemporary Arts, London, July 11th, 1992.

66 See discussion in Louise J. Kaplan, *Female Perversions*, p237–283.

67 *Elle* magazine, 1992.

68 J. Riviere 'Womanliness as Masquerade', *International Journal of Psychoanalysis*, Vol 10. pp303–13.

69 L. Kaplan, *op cit*, 1991.

70 *Ibid*, p258.

71 *Ibid*, p259.

72 *Ibid*, p262.

73 Vivienne Westwood interviewed in 'Sex is Fashion, Fashion is Sex', *Z/G*, 1980.

74 Alex Crewkerne, *Skin Two*, Issue 12, 1992, p57.

75 The tone echoed in Roy Kerridge's article *Sex Rampages of the Feminist Porn Queens*, in *New Statesman & Society*, 23. 2. 92.

76 Havelock Ellis and John Addington Symonds, *Studies in the Psychology of Sex*, Vol 1, Sexual Inversion, Wilson and Macmillan, London 1897.

77 Jeffrey Weeks, *Sex, Politics and Society: the Regulation of Sexuality Since 1800*, Longman, London, 1989; Jonathan Dollimore, *Sexual Dissidence: Augustine to Wilde, Freud to Foucault*, Clarendon Press, Oxford 1991.

78 Antonio Gramsci, *Selections from the Prison Notebooks*, edited and translated by Quintin Hoare and Geoffrey Nowell Smith, Lawrence and Wishart, London 1971, p325.

79 Lynne Segal, 'Lessons from the Past', in E. Carter and S. Watney, *Taking Liberties: Aids and Cultural Politics*, Serpent's Tail/ICA, London 1989.

80 J. Dollimore, 1991, *op cit*, p104.

81 M. Foucault, *The History of Sexuality, Volume One*, Penguin, Harmondsworth 1979, p156.

82 At first Freud did not classify male homosexuality as perverse because he found it to be so pervasive in human psychology. See discussion, J. Dollimore, 1991, *op cit*, pp169–204.

83 These definitions are discussed on pp7–8 of Louise Kaplan, *op cit*.

84   Frances Heidensohn, in *Women and Crime*, Macmillan, London 1985, argues the reason why women are more law abiding than men is not biological but a consequence of complex ideologies of femininity which 'produce conformity' p108.

85   L. Kaplan, *op cit*, p78.

86   M. Garber, *op cit*, p98.

87   R. Stoller, *op cit*, p34.

88   Dr. Glen Wilson,'The Limits of Liberty' interview with Alex Kershaw, *The Guardian Weekend*, 28.11.92.,

89   Phoneline advertised in 'Dear Deidre' column of the *Sun*, Friday 17.4.92.

90   M. Bronski ,*Culture Clash: the Making of a Gay Sensibility*, South End Press, Boston Mass.1984.

91   This evidence seemed to be contradicted by more positive recent survey findings about homosexuality compiled by *The Guardian* newspaper in 1992 when covering Ian McKellen's visit to Downing Street to meet the prime minister, John Major.

92   'Sweet Smell of Sexccess', *The Guardian*, 27.7.92

93   *Ibid.*

94   Belinda Allen, Producer, A Middlemarch Film, Channel 4, 6.5.92.

95   From the case studies identified in Frédérique Delacoste and Priscilla Alexander (eds), 1987, *op cit.*

96   Jeffrey Weeks, quoted in Alex Kershaw's *The Limits of Liberty*, *op cit.*

97   'Deviant Laws', Suzanne Moore, in *Looking For Trouble*, Serpent's Tail, London 1992, pp151–54.

98   Adam Mars Jones quoted in Alex Kershaw, *op cit.*

99   Pat Califia, 'Love and the Perfect Sadist, *Skin Two*, Issue 12, 1992.

100   Freud suggests that repression of the perversions produces 'civilisation'. See S. Freud *Three Essays on Sexuality*, as well as discussion in J. Dollimore, 1991, pp174–218.

101   J. Dollimore, 1991, *op cit*, p170.

102   L. Kaplan, *op cit*, p10.

103   See 'Perverse Politics: Lesbian Issues', *Feminist Review*, No 34, Spring 1990, for instance.

104   Andrea Dworkin and other radical feminists have been accused of essentialism by British anti-censorship campaigners amongst others.

105   L. Kaplan, *op cit*, p10.

106   Wendy Steiner 'Politically Correct Kinks', *Independent on Sunday*, 13.10.92, p33.

107   Liam Hudson, in David Thomas, *Not Guilty: Men the Case for the Defence* , Weidenfeld, London 1993, p39.

108   M. Foucault, *op cit*, 1979, p154.

109   These stem from the idea that because the female egg waits for the male sperm to swim up to it and fertilise it, that women are not as sexually active; such myths may also derive from sight. Male erection is visible whereas female desire is not always visible and so is imagined to be less intense.

110   M. Foucault, 1979, *op cit*, p154.

3

Women and Sexual Fetishism

'Is that "lack" or a million dollar pussy?'   *Village Voice* film critic on Sharon Stone's famous 'flash' in *Basic Instinct*, 1991.

Over the years feminists have been identifying the many limitations of the passive construction of female sexuality in psychoanalysis, and redressing some of the absences. We believe that clinical discussion about 'fetishism' to date has been guilty of 'repression' and wish to argue for a more active status for women within it. Our aim is not to achieve 'perversion theft'[1] but to forge a new understanding of the term fetishism based on female experience. And we would argue, with Carol Gilligan, that 'the inclusion of women ... implies a change in the entire account'. [2] In this chapter we want to question psychoanalysis's denial of women's fetishism, and to ask what is at stake behind such a denial. Our aim is to begin to tease out an alternative psychoanalytic model that enables women to have space as practitioners.

Freud claimed that women rarely, if ever, fetishize, because fetishism arises from the little boy's horror at first seeing the female genitals. The fetishism is an attempt to cope with the castration complex through a simultaneous acceptance and denial of what *he* has seen. The fetish object stands in place of the maternal phallus.

Since little girls do not have a penis to protect, they do not undergo the same fear of deprivation. Girls do not undergo a horror at the sight of female genitals, because that is what they are accustomed to. Women, therefore, do not need to deny any anxiety about losing the penis, since they have no penis to lose; and so, according to Freud, they do not need a fetish.

Since Freud's seminal essays on fetishism,[3] the idea that women fetishise only rarely has dominated thought on the subject. Freud's assumption that women do not have fetishes has now become the accepted view of female sexuality, as evidenced by Edward Norbeck's entry for 'Psychiatric Fetishism' in *Encyclopedia Americana (1977)*:

> Psychiatric fetishism has been reported almost entirely in Western societies, where the neurosis is confined principally to males.[4]

Is Female Fetishism Rare?

At least a third of the psychoanalytic literature we have looked at contains detailed references to women who fetishise. Havelock Ellis agreed that women did, though he claimed that it was primarily lesbians; Stekel identified a woman kleptomaniac who, 'following the theft would rub the silk against her genitals', as well as a woman with a jewellery fetish and a woman who fetishised dolls;[5] many of Clerambault's case studies were women who fetishised silk.[6] G. A. Dudley identified a seventeen year old female mackintosh fetishist who said that once a week she 'undressed and slipped on her mackintosh' for sexual excitement, commenting that 'ordinary levels of intercourse just don't appeal to me'.[7] And the list continues: Ilse Brande's 'Un case de phobie d'impulsion et de comportement fetichiste chez une femme' identified a woman fetishist;[8] as did Spiegel's discussion of Nora and her string fetish;[9] Zavitzianos identified a woman who described masturbating while holding a non erotic book (the book is her fetish because 'the book then played a role comparable to a transitional object') and a car ('in the transference neurosis, the father's car also became a fetish');[10] Nancy Friday identified a urologenic woman, Faith, who said she derived pleasure, 'by seeing, thinking, or hearing about uncontrollable urination';[11] G. Bonnet identified a woman fetishist in 'Fetichisme et exhibitionnisme chez un sujet feminin':[12] as did Gosselin and Wilson, whose survey identified a woman rubber fetishist who placed rubber 'in direct contact with her body ... and orgasm occurred frequently as a result'.[13]

This is not the only evidence. Early surveys, like Gilbert Hamilton's 1929 research into marriage, indicated that women, in significant numbers, fetishise. Hamilton's survey asked many detailed questions about human sexuality, including some appertaining to fetishism.[14] For example, Table 415[15] showed that 9 per cent of women compared to nought per cent of men found that the sight of a sexual object gave them pleasant sexual feelings: whereas Table 416[16] showed that 15 per cent of men compared to 2 per cent of women, said they would find it thrilling to possess an undergarment or similar object belonging to their partner. Though the intensity of this sexual fetishism may not constitute fetishism in the sense of Gebhard's 'fourth degree'(outlined in chapter one) it does give evidence of active eroticism by women. There were other contradictory variables that were hard to make sense of in Hamilton's survey and perhaps this is the reason why his 1929 research findings were not followed up in the 1953 Kinsey Report, which briefly made reference to him.[17] Indeed, despite the minor acknowledgement of Hamilton's work, the Kinsey report went on to produce similar denials to the other clinicians: 'it has been known for some time, and our own data confirms it, that fetishism is an almost exclusively male phenomenon'.[18]

The French psychiatrist and contemporary of Freud, Clerambault, diagnosed women fetishists in 1908 (the year before Freud's paper on fetishism to the Vienna Society, where he claimed all women were clothes fetishists). Clerambault accepted that his female patients masturbated with silk, but argued that the silk was not a true fetish because women lacked the imagination to transform it into a vehicle of 'homage to the opposite sex'.[19]

Only men were allowed the requisite imagination to be true fetishists and use their shoe or piece of cloth as part of a fantasy sexual union with a woman. Female fetishists valued their silk, he claimed, for its tactile quality alone and as such were 'selfish'. Clearly Clerambault was at pains to prevent women being 'true' perverts, ascribing this to their lack of the powers of the imagination. In fact, however, what he seems to be describing are men whose fetishism involves fantasies about having sex with a partner, whereas it is the women who fetishise in the 'fourth degree', and have a relationship solely with the object.

Early sexologists and psychiatrists such as Havelock Ellis had admitted that fetishism, along with sadism and masochism, is found in 'woman inverts' (ie, lesbians), but, like other writers on the subject, Ellis takes this as one more sign of the abnormality and unwomanliness of 'inverts'[20] In *Sexual Aberrations*, Wilhelm Stekel begins by saying that he has observed 'a few cases of female fetishism',[21] and he includes their case studies in his discussions. But he argues that such occurrences 'are much more seldom, or at least appear to be so because the personal love conditions of women ... operate at a deeper level and come to the surface much less frequently.'[22]

G.A. Dudley wrote that, 'even though female fetishism is not entirely unknown, as some investigators think, we are prepared to admit it must be extremely rare'.[23] This sentiment is repeated by Ilse Barande, who agreed that fetishism in women was rare, and by G. Zavitzianos.[24] Nancy Friday's investigation of female sexual fantasies in 1975 put forward similar conclusions about the rarity of female fetishism: 'Faith's is the only fetishist fantasy among all that I've collected. This correlates with standard psychoanalytic findings that female fetishism is rare'.[25] G. Bonnet, writing in 1977, made similar observations.

Yet these analysts who are arguing theoretically that women rarely fetishise, are doing so in the face of their own case studies of women who are fetishists. Each analyst says their own case study is one in isolation, 'a rarity'. Having viewed the literature, we would argue that women fetishists, even in the limited arena of psychoanalytic case studies, are not as 'rare' as is imagined.

The case study literature we have examined is evidence that women are not a rarity, but constitute a sizeable minority of fetishisers. Further, it is possible or even likely that more examples of female fetishists have gone undetected. This is because, on the whole, fetishists do not see their problem as abnormal; case studies tend to arise when a fetishist enters analysis because of some other personal problem. And when it is borne in mind that both the analysand and the analysts are not expecting to consider female fetishism, the surprise is, surely, that so many women practitioners have actually been documented.

The question must arise, why do all the surveys and psychoanalytic case studies claim that female fetishism is rare, in the face of much persuasive evidence to the contrary? The answer, we believe, lies in phallocentricism. The primacy Freudian theory gives to the fear of castration and the phallic mother has, we feel, created a blindspot that prevents the analysts and psychologists from seeing the evidence in front of their eyes. So we come, through our narrow focus on fetishism, to support the French Feminists's view that the law of castration and sexual difference have been unchanging organizing principles of Western patriarchy. Our attempt to refute their analysis of fetishism is a parallel attempt to question the underpinning phallocentricism of psychoanalysis.

Models of the Castration Complex in Relation to Fetishism

Freud pins the very existence of his castration complex on the 'proof' of fetishism. In the 'Fetishism' essay he states bluntly:

> an investigation of fetishism is strongly recommended to anyone who still doubts the existence of the castration complex.[26]

In both 'Three Essays on Sexuality' and '"Civilized" Sexual Morality and Modern Nervous Illness', Freud further argues that while men become perverts, women under the same psychic stress become hysterics, because women hold weaker, more passive sexual instincts and are more prone to repression. He goes so far as to imagine dysfunctional families where the same stimuli would affect the sexes differently. Freud says that the brothers in such a family would develop into perverts, whereas the sisters would become hysterics.[27] So castration anxiety *defines* his model of fetishism, which is always seen as a male perversion, just as fetishism *proves* the castration complex.

Since Freud's original formulation of the castration complex there have been two main developments of it taken up by the psychiatric profession. These come from Melanie Klein, (writing from the 1920s to the 1940s) and Jacques Lacan (writing from 1953 to 1981). They need to be assessed briefly, in relation to the question of whether or not they allow space for women to fetishise sexually.

Melanie Klein: Klein's work with young children led her to emphasise the pre-oedipal first year of the baby's life, and hence the mother-child relationship.[28] During this first phase feelings of love and aggression (which Freud situated in the Oedipal triad) are fantasised onto parts (part objects) of the mother's body, primarily the breast. It is the vicissitudes of the baby in relation to the part, and then the whole, mother that are central to the developing psyche. Prior to the oedipal phase, Klein posited a 'feminine' phase in which both sexes identify with the all powerful mother (whose body also incorporates the desired father's phallus within it). However, after the Oedipal stage, which she posits much earlier than Freud, Klein reverts to concurring with the castration complex in boys and penis envy in girls.

Although Klein still endorses penis envy in girls, she does move away from Freud's emphasis on the importance of the phallus. She does this by shifting the stress back to an earlier, pre-Oedipal stage of the baby's relation to the breast and then to the whole mother, during what she calls the 'feminine' phase. Such a model might enable some clearer explanation of female fetishism, but it is not a significance that Klein's followers have been quick to grasp. Most of the analysts which we cited at the beginning of this chapter, claiming that their female patients are the exceptions that prove the rule that female fetishism is rare, are, in fact, from the object-relations school.

However, despite this school's *own* reluctance to include women as practitioners of fetishism, we do in the final section of this chapter, consider the implications of their revisions for the analysis of fetishism. This is because, almost despite themselves, Kleinian-based analysts have made some important distinctions about fetishism. Their emphasis on 'orality' and 'individuation' argue for a shift towards highlighting an earlier phase in the baby's life, prior to the castration complex. Individuation, or differentiation, is the point at which the baby perceives a demarcation between itself and the object world, the point at which it makes a separation between self and other (the me/not-me distinction). An emphasis on this earlier phase allows entry for girls as well as boys to develop into sexual fetishists, since it focusses on differentiation rather than the later sexual difference.

Jacques Lacan: As mentioned in our earlier chapters, the Lacanian model of psychoanalysis which developed in France now permeates academic departments as well as consulting rooms around the world. Lacan, returning to Freud via structuralist and post-structuralist concepts of signification, develops the theory of the castration complex in relation to the baby's subjection into language.

Initially the baby exists in the Imaginary (pre-Oedipal) perceiving itself as part of the mother. Between six and eighteen months, the baby enters the Mirror Stage, identifying with the image of itself reflected to it by others (a mirror, its mother, an 'other'). It thus becomes aware of the dual, dyadic relationship with its mother. 'In the Imaginary there is no difference and no absence, only identity and presence'.[29] The Oedipal entry of the father ruptures this dyadic unity and represses the Imaginary to form the unconscious.

In Lacan's model it is the phallus that ruptures the baby's dyadic relationship of plenitude, and wounds its precarious narcissistic image of self, when it realises that the mother desires something 'other'. As such, the phallus exists as a symbol of what the mother desires, rather than as an actual penis. With the rupture of the Imaginary, the baby begins to take up its 'identity' within the symbolic order, within language, and also with reference to the phallus:

> Sexual difference is then assigned according to whether individual subjects do or do not possess the phallus, which means ... that anatomical difference comes to *figure* sexual difference, that is becomes the sole representative of what that difference is allowed to be.[30]

The little boy's final separation from the mother arises because of her 'lack' and he aligns himself instead with the paternal metaphor, the phallus.

Lacan returns to the concept of castration as central to the construction of sexuality, and for all that the phallus is a symbol (the ultimate signifier of unity and authority within the patriarchal code), the woman is still defined by the absence of any such signifier. Girls, being figured as lacking, have nothing to lose. And Lacan, following Freud, links fetishism to the protection of the signifier (the actual penis, as signifier of the phallus).

In 1956, in 'Fetishism: The Symbolic, the Imaginary and the Real', Lacan and Granoff endorse Freud's castration theory as the explanation for fetishism. They explain how fetishism ocurs within the Lacanian model in the Imaginary, since the patient denies the symbolic value of what he is doing.[31] It is taken for granted throughout that the patient will be male.

In his 1958 essay, 'Guiding remarks for a Congress on Feminine Sexuality', woman's 'lack' still, in Lacanian thought, removed her from the discussion of fetishism as a practitioner.

> Since it has been effectively demonstrated that the imaginary motive for most male perversions is the desire to preserve the phallus which involved the subject in the mother, then the absence in women of fetishism, which represents the virtually manifest case of this desire, leads us to suspect that this desire has a different fate in the perversions which she presents. For to assume that the woman herself takes on the role of fetish, only raises the question of the difference of her position in relation to desire and to the object.[32]

For Lacan, the signifier of desire (the desire of the Other) is the phallus. He argues that since woman does not possess one of her own, she 'becomes the phallus', ie, the thing her mother desires (a Lacanian effect of the mother's penis envy). All children desire to be the phallus for the mother, but the boy, having a penis is able to move on to 'having the phallus' and stop 'being' it. The girl, having no part of the body to construct the phallic signifier onto, is not able to move from 'being' to 'having', and so can not move into the symbolic code. She remains with her body as phallus, as the core of her femininity. Further, she invests her lover's penis with this signification of desire – 'she finds the signifier of her own desire in the body of the one to whom she addresses her demand for love.'[33] Lacan goes on to state, in the subsequent sentence, 'certainly we should not forget that the organ actually invested with this signifying function takes on the value of a fetish'.[34] But in spite of this, we believe that Lacan is not arguing that women engage in fetishism in our use of the term, because here it carries more of a Marxist sense. Lacan's 'fetishisation' is not being analysed as a synechdochal disavowal, but as the reification of the penis's importance as a phallus.

Gerard Bonnet, in 1977, used the Lacanian framework to analyse his ('rare') female analysand's bathrobe fetish.[35] His initial sugestion is that the bathrobe signifies her possession of the paternal phallus (reading 'robe de chambre' as signifying 'femme de chambre'). He then goes on to develop the French term for 'plank of wood' (bord de branche) from 'robe de chambre' and argues that his patient wishes to be her mother's missing phallus. He concludes that she oscillates continually between the maternal phallus and the paternal phallus, and hedging, declares she 'is not *not* a fetishist'

In 1990 in Paris followers of the Lacanian model held a conference on perversions, subsequently published as *Traits de Perversion dans Les Structures Cliniques*.[36] The paper given by the psychoanalytic study group from Paraguay was entitled 'Do Women have Fetishes?'.[37] Beginning with the orthodox claim that female fetishism is rare, the paper goes on to argue that psychoanalytic practice does demonstrate that women do have fetishes, in a neurotic form. It cites the case study of a bulimic who revealed a fetish for feet in plaster:

> She could not look at a foot in plaster without getting aroused and masturbating ... 'When I am alone at home, I stand in front of the mirror, I get out some stockings, which must always be white and have the toe piece cut out, I put them on and look at them until I am aroused, I become 'another' and then I masturbate.'[38]

They explain this fetish as allowing her to establish a phallic identity, citing Lacan's 'it is the woman herself who assumes the role of the fetish'. However, they argue that the analysand, fixated on her identity with the castrated mother and with penis envy, needs the phallic mediation of the fetish to be able to climax (so that she oscillates between having a phallus and being the phallus). She therefore has an erotic relationship to an object outside of her own body, and hence is practising a perversion, but they still argue, only in a neurotic (ie, hysterical) form.

> Why can the man, faced with the same discovery [of maternal castration], put a halt to this fetish? One must approach this point structurally. From the point of view of the woman, who does not have a penis, and is not attached to the phallus like a man, there is another encounter with the reality of the climax, different from the phallic climax of the man. The Name-of-the-Father as imperative phallic attributes the climax to the phallus, and man's name is inscribed there, while the woman, with regard to the climax in a state beyond the phallus, would find herself beyond castration (is she the superego, or is she very near?)[39]

Mary Ann Doane explains this notion of being 'near': for Lacan, since they lack the phallus 'women are deprived of the distance required by language – femininity is closeness, nearness, "wrapped in its own contiguity"'.[40]

The Paraguayan study group thus argues for a woman fetishist and yet questions exactly how a woman can relate to the loss of the phallus. The paper ends by questioning 'can perversion exist in women?'.

The Lacanians, as the Kleinians and Freudians, are unwilling to admit that women do fetishise in a perverse form. This is because women, denied the symbolic code, are argued to be hysterics and are asserted to hystericize the phallus on their own bodies. We think these positions say more about the theories being employed by the analysts than about the women being observed and described.

Women as Fetishists: a Critique of Phallocentrism

From Freud to Lacan to Foucault, fetishism has been held up as the signifier of all the other perversions:

> No other variation of the sexual instinct that borders on the pathological can lay so much claim to our interest as this one (*Freud*).
>
> The very nucleus of perversion, that is, fetishism (*Lacan*).
>
> The model perversion which ... served as the guiding thread for analyzing all the other deviations (*Foucault*).[41]

Could the importance that is attributed to fetishism be because it is located so firmly on the protection and valorization of the phallus? We could almost argue that fetishism as a male preserve is itself a signifying concept of psychoanalysis's phallocentric discourse. Psychoanalysis must deny women as practitioners of fetishism because to admit that they are questions the importance of the phallus as *the* signifier of desire (and hence value?).

Freud was writing in late nineteenth century Vienna, when the dominant view of women was of someone 'other', passive, and emotional. Women's lives in practically all of late twentieth century Western Europe are very different. The concept of women and their abilities has changed radically, yet the same nineteenth-century model of their psyche, especially their psychosexual makeup, is still being used.

Arguing that women can and do practise fetishism thus becomes a way of challenging the psychoanalytic model of female sexuality. It is also a way of showing how this existing model is in fact simply a way of reinforcing phallocentric value.

Luce Irigaray was expelled from l'Ecole Freudienne for challenging Lacan's phallocentrism. Her work deliberately conflates commodity
and sexual fetishism in her analysis of women's role within a patriarchal system. In *Speculum of the Other Woman*, she argues that Freud,
in order to identify with the law-giving father, had to construct women
as 'fetishised objects, merchandise of whose value he stands surety'.[42]
She goes on to unpack this whole economy of desire, to free women
from the passivity Freud allocates. She never goes so far as to allow
women to fetishise (since for her too fetishism is linked to castration
anxiety) but she succeeds in destabilising many of the axioms underpinning psychoanalysis.

She is useful to us in particular in reviewing Freud's 'need' to
construct women as having 'penis envy'. Irigaray argues that it is only
the male gaze that sees woman's genitalia as 'lacking', since for little
girls their clitoral stimulation has perfectly satisfied their autoerotic
desires. Little girls thus have to 'become women' through a painful
and cultural feminisation process that internalises a phallocentric view
of their 'flaw'. Freud's horror in women's 'castration' is specifically
'a hole in *man's* signifying economy'(our emphasis). Why, she argues,
does Freud choose the term penis *envy* to explain the little girl's
experience? 'Envy, jealousy, greed are all correlated to lack, default,
absence. All these terms describe female sexuality as merely the *other
side* or even the *wrong side* of male sexualism'.[43] Freud's invention of
female 'penis envy' is, according to this logic, a sublimation of the
masculine discourse's own castration anxiety.

> For the 'penis-envy' alleged against woman is – let us repeat – a remedy
> for man's fear of losing one. If *she* envies it, then *he* must have it. If *she* envies
> what *he* has, then it must be valuable. The only thing valuable enough to
> be envied? The very standard of all value. Woman's fetishisation of the
> male organ must indeed be an indispensable support of its price on the
> sexual market.[44]

Irigaray argues that the concept of penis envy is an attempt by
men to deny the possibility that women might have another form of
desire.

Sara Kofman, another feminist critic working within a psychoanalytic framework, takes the issue of 'penis envy' and fetishism and neatly
turns the tables on Freud and his analysis in *The Enigma of Woman:
Woman in Freud's Writings*.[45] Kofman focuses her concept of fetishism
on the doing-and-undoing compromise: 'the split between denial and
affirmation of castration.'[46] Using Derrida to stress the 'undecidability'
of the fetish, she goes on to argue that, in fact, 'penis envy' as a

concept is *itself* a compromise solution. The concept is a 'screen solution' serving to cover up or mask Freud's real fear of incest (uncovering the mother) that would be involved in revealing female sexuality.

> To respond 'truly' to the riddle of female sexuality would have been in one way or another to dis-cover the Mother, to commit incest ... that is why the only responses he himself gives are false solutions that camouflage the mother's sex, conceal what he has always known as in a dream, mask the dreamed-of relations with the mother. 'Penis envy' is one of these 'screen solutions' that serve as a cover-up ... the very mask of blindness.[47]

And Freud himself pointed to the similarity of the mechanisms at work in 'screen solutions' and in 'fetishism'.[48]

A woman-centred analysis of Freudian theory, then, could argue, via Irigaray and Kofman, that the concept of 'penis envy' could itself be described as a fetish to safeguard the value of phallocentrism within a patriarchal medical discourse: the male's obsessive fixation on his own signifying value cannot allow a denial of its importance (or the unimportance of a 'lack' within the feminine). Such a discourse *must* reflect the 'other' in a 'back-end' of male sexualism. Could this be why psychoanalytic and psychological discourse has wilfully refused to see women as practitioners of fetishism? Because an acceptance of female fetishism challenges the very signifier of desire, in a way that none of the other perversions do?

Towards a Feminised Model of the Erotic

As we have seen, arguing that women fetishize in itself challenges the phallocentric dominance of the castration complex within psychoanalytic theory. Further, it argues for the need for a new formulation of the female erotic. If women are allowed to fetishize, then the castration complex cannot be the only explanation – something else must be occurring as well, or instead. In trying to conceptualize this 'something else', a new and positive construction of female sexuality must come into play.

During the 1970s and 1980s, many feminist theoreticians challenged the phallocentricism of Freud and Lacan, lead by Cixous, Irigaray and, to some extent, Kristeva. In their search to encapsulate a feminine erotic, they return to the pre-oedipal to formulate sensations of pleasure before castration occurs. Women's eroticism is then allied to this sensation anterior to the mark of the phallus. But such a strategy, though liberating the pleasure from the symbolic phallus, does leave women in a regressive and psychotic space. What prevents the French feminists from sufficiently evolving a feminine route for erotic desire, is that, for them, the phallus constructs both desire and language. The symbolic code (language) is marked by the phallus and so the feminine is barred from it. In other words, a feminine erotic can not be expressed by language. Each of them have, in their various ways, tried to break or deconstruct the language they use, to allow entry for a view of the feminine, but that has made their work often difficult. Perhaps this is one reason why, while they have been taken up by feminist theoreticians, they have not on the whole been adopted by practising psychotherapists.

Cixous, Irigaray and Kristeva: French Feminists and the Pre-Oedipal

Hélène Cixous rejects the masculine libidinal economy resulting from the fear of castration. In 'Castration or Decapitation', she argues that the masculine focus on the castration complex leads to women being denied (decapitated) within society. Allowing women to 'speak of her pleasure', she argues, would 'dephallocentrize the body, relieve man of his phallus, return him to an erogenous field and a libido that isn't stupidly organized round that monument, but appears shifting, diffused, taking on all the others of oneself'.[49] However, she agrees that women have no place within the symbolic code and so one can only gesture towards a female libidinous economy which she sees as being endless, without closure (naming, by definition involves closure). In 'The Laugh of the Medusa', she argues for a female libidinal economy for women that she calls 'the realm of the gift', stemming from a woman's ability to bear a child.[50] This representation is constructed not from a 'lack' but from a positive *generosity*; an ability to embrace difference and the other. The woman can encompass having a child within her own body and yet allow it its own existence. Unlike the man, she feels no need to incorporate and dominate. The ability to sustain this diversity contradicts the phallic desire for unity and appropriation and stems from woman's closer links to the pre-oedipal Imaginary, where difference between mother and child has not yet been established. The woman, not having experienced castration anxiety, has not so fully undergone the rupture from this state, and the Imaginary plenitude is therefore more available to her.

> For her joyous benefit she is erogenous; she is the erotogeneity of the heterogeneous: airborne swimmer, in flight she does not cling to herself; she is dispersible, prodigious, stunning, desirous and capable of others, of

the other woman that she will be, of the other woman she isn't, of him, of you.[51]

Luce Irigaray, too goes back to early pre-Oedipal mother-daughter relationship as a key to the female libido. In 'And one does not stir without the other', she challenges the castration model by arguing that the daughter turns from the mother to the father because of the surfeit of mothering, rather than any perception of 'lack'.

> I want no more of this stuffed, sealed up, immobilised body. No, I want air ... I'll turn to my father. I'll leave you for someone who doesn't prepare anything for me to eat. For someone who leaves me empty of him, mouth gaping for his truth.[52]

Like Cixous, Irigaray suggests a female libidinal economy as fluid and multiple in opposition to the phallus being unified, concrete and defined. In 'When our lips speak together'[53] she argues that the female libidinal economy is open, endless, always in movement, the body as a limitless realm. However, since women are excluded from the symbolic code, she agrees that there is no symbolism for this feminine libido apart from the 'two lips', both oral and vaginal, that auto-erotically challenge the unity of the phallus.

Julia Kristeva redefines Lacan's Imaginary as the *semiotic* undifferentiated pre-language pulsions (predominately anal and oral) articulated within the dyadic *chora* of mother and child.[54] This semiotic *chora* is ruptured by the baby's access to the symbolic order of language and the splitting (or individuation) is consolidated by the Oedipal threat of castration. With its access to the symbolic phase, the baby represses the semiotic, but this continues to make itself felt by its disruptions of the signifying process (contradictions, meaninglessness, ecstasy etc). Like Cixous, Kristeva valorises this pre-oedipal phase that disrupts the phallic symbolic order. However, Kristeva does not so much challenge the Lacanian centrality of the phallus in the construction of sexuality, as argue that girls suffer a form of 'castration' through 'the process of learning the symbolic function' they enter into.[55] She sees women as negatively defined and marginalised, once they place themselves within the symbolic order.

Specifically in relation to fetishism, we also refocus on the pre-Oedipal and we feel that it is important not only to challenge the concept of penis envy but also the phallus as the only signifier of desire. If a rupture, an absence, is necessary to construct desire, is the phallus the only signifier that could make such a break? Might there not be some other, as yet unsymbolised, signifier that would allow girls access to desire and to the symbolic code? In a sense, the french feminists' acceptance that women are excluded from the symbolic code, and that a feminine libidinal economy cannot be defined, allows psychoanalytic practioners to largely ignore it.

Two feminist psychoanalysts, however, have striven to extend the analysis through looking at women's relation to the perversions. And they too gesture towards a woman-centred alternative to the phallus as a signifier of desire. The arguments of Estella Welldon, in the United States, and Parveen Adams, in Britain, have proved useful to us in their attempt to challenge the theoretical gender-weighting of perversions as active and male, and hysteria as passive and female. Though not directly arguing on behalf of all female fetishists, by introducing discussion about mothers as sexual abusers of children (Welldon) and about lesbian sado-masochists (Adams), they call for an explanation which is beyond the realms of present psychoanalytic theory.

Mothers as Perverts: Estella Welldon

Estella Welldon's *Mother, Madonna, Whore* denounces the construction of women's psychosexuality as the back end of male sexuality. Welldon calls for a symmetrical view of the two sexes, which will take full account of the 'important, complex, and uniquely feminine physical, physiological, and symbolic characteristics'.[56] She argues that anxiety about separation from the mother is the most important element in perverse formation, rather than castration anxiety. She further suggests that psychoanalytic theory places the stress on penis envy in order to deny, unconsciously, the power of the pre-Oedipal mother.

The core of her book is an attack on Western society's denial of the existence of maternal perversion, because of the cultural idealisation of motherhood. When she turns briefly to female fetishism, citing Zavitzianos's case study of a woman fetishising books and her father's car, she gives a convincing re-reading of the car as being more about the symbolic re-entry to the womb (because of its enclosed space) than about penis envy.

However, her focus on maternal abuse means that some of the potential insights are passed over. She briskly dismisses any attempt to make an equivalence between the male and female perversions (because of the difference in psychosexuality) and concentrates on how the patient pinches the children in her care. Welldon suggests that the patient could be repeating the abuse instigated by her mother on her when she was a child. Welldon thus hijacks a discussion of fetishism to focus on her thesis. In passing over the fetishism, Welldon's important work has failed to address properly the fact that her patient, a woman, does find sexual satisfaction in her engagement with objects (the car and the book).

Much more problematic though, is that in her attempt to theorise from maternal abuse, Welldon links her model of female sexuality inextricably to motherhood. She posits the womb, as the counterpart to the male penis, as the part of the body used to pursue perverse sexual goals. Choosing the womb, rather than the clitoris or a polymorphous sexuality, obviously shuts off any libidinal pathway for women removed from the desire to procreate.

To ask for a new psychodynamics that takes into account women's distinctiveness is one thing, but to argue, as she goes on to do, that the difference is so wide that no real equivalence can be made, is to insist on a 'separatist' psychopathology. Such a reaction overprivileges both the phallus and the womb, demonising and idealising their importance in a way that reinforces and mirrors the very phallocentricism that we wish to challenge. Despite these caveats, Welldon's book usefully points to the need to try to define a female psychosexuality outside of the field of the phallus.

Lesbian S&M : Parveen Adams

Parveen Adams, in her discussion of lesbian sado-masochism, posits a female desire detached from the phallic reference. In her essay 'On Female Bondage', she argues that she is searching for a new phenomenon – sexuality organised in a different relation to the phallus – within a psychoanalytic framework.[57] She goes on to argue that lesbian sado-masochists should be seen as enacting a perverse scenario, but one in which desire is 'freed from the penile representation of the phallus.'[58] She cites Bersani and Dutoit, who distinguish between two types of fetishists: neurotics who use the fetish to disavow the absent phallus; and perverts who accept that mother does not have a penis and for whom therefore, 'since the mediating substitute is missing, desire is "cut off" from the phallus; henceforth anything can come to be the object of desire.'[59] Pathological fetishists, the first type, are locked into a rigid compulsion in their relation to the fetish. Adams argues that pathological masochists are also locked into such a process and have regressed from genital pleasure to an anal excitation in being beaten. However, lesbian sado-masochists differ from such cases in both experiencing genital pleasure and in having an erotic plasticity of desire. It therefore follows for Adams that, though perverse, lesbian S&M cannot be pathological:

> which is to say that she has succeeded in detaching herself from the phallic reference and in orientating her sexuality outside the phallic field; which in turn suggests that the question of sexuality has finally been divorced from the question of gender.[60]

Unfortunately, Adams claims that only lesbian sado-masochists inhabit this new sexuality. Both heterosexual women and traditional lesbians have the phallus as their signifier of desire, 'and nothing changes this'. So she does not here look for a new representation of female desire distinct from 'penis envy' for all women. But she does use lesbian sado-masochism as a phenomenon that can transgress all that is 'proper' about the Lacanian phallic order.

Grosz and Lesbian Fetishism

Elizabeth Grosz is another critic who has argued for lesbian practice as challenging conventional theory.[61] She suggests that all lesbians are able to fetishise, like men. Lesbians who have a 'masculinity complex,' as outlined by Freud, have not given up the clitoris as the main genital organ, and so in fact disavow their *own* 'castration' (rather than their mother's). The lesbian fetishist then either turns her own body into the unrelinquished phallus, or takes a phallic woman (ie, another with a masculinity complex) as her desired object.

Although interesting in its theoretical argument that women can be fetishists, Grosz's argument clearly still privileges the phallus as the signifier of desire. It concurs with Parveen Adams' view of 'non-perverse lesbians' in still locating female desire on a structure of penis envy.

Revisions to Theory of Fetishism:
Clinical Case Studies

In what follows, we investigate some of the case studies of fetishism in order to argue for a revision to the theory, which would create the theoretical space for the recognition of women as practitioners of fetishism.

The majority of available case studies on fetishism (as on eating disorders) are written by object-relations theorists, so the psychoanalytic model of this section is predominantly Kleinian in origin. This is not to say that we endorse the Kleinian psychoanalytic model in its entirety, or over and above the Lacanian. We certainly would not wish to throw out the notion of the uncertainties and the unattainability of desire given in the Lacanian model – especially since fetishism, by its very nature, maps this oscillating uncertainty so closely.[62] And we also agree with Jacqueline Rose's explanation of Lacan's polemic against the Kleinian focus on the mother-child relationship, as justified in so far as the Kleinian model evades the issue of *desire* (signified for Lacan by the father).[63] Desire is clearly something that no discussion of sexual fetishism can leave out of the account.

Our motive for concentrating on the material in such detail is that some of the object-related findings can be utilized towards a new definition of feminine psychopathology in relation to fetishism. Further, we argue that the model used to discuss fetishism in the British and American journals is astonishingly similar to the way the same theories discuss eating disorders, in particular bulimia.

In the next section we present, in chronological order, summaries of the more important revisions, from our point of view, to the theory of fetishism. We believe that the case studies put forward by Sylvia Payne (1939), W. H. Gillespie (1940), Bak (1953), Winnicott (1958), Melitta Sperling (1963) and Masud Khan (1979) reveal that some of the problems with the Freudian theory of fetishism have been addressed within the psychiatric profession. Taken overall, these revisions will be seen to point strongly towards another model of fetishism that runs alongside the orthodox Freudian one: a model that, focusing on the earlier individuation process, and separation anxiety, opens up a space to include women as both sexual fetishists and fetishists of food. Within object-relations clinical writing it has already been revealed – though it is often ignored:

1. that fetishism is as much about the disavowal of *individuation* [separation from the mother] as it is about sexual difference
2. that fetishism carries a strong oral component
3. that a narcissistic blow to the body image of either sex can develop the fetish at puberty
4. that fetishism is in fact a highly creative compromise which, through its doing-and-undoing oscillation, enables the subject to cope with unconscious menace, while still allowing the gratification of pleasure on the plane of the real (not denied or repressed as in sublimation or hysteria).

In the final, fourth point, we do not wish to deny that the fetishist, so obsessed with gaining a particular shoe that she feels compelled to steal it from the person sitting next to her on the bus, feels out of control. Or that being out of control in itself is often deeply disturbing. Nevertheless, the masturbation over the gained object *is* a sexual, genital gratification of pleasure, without consequent psychic damage. As we have mentioned, fetishists rarely seek psychiatric help for their fetishism. Although they realise their sexual practice would be looked upon as odd, they are on the whole perfectly well satisfied with it.

Payne: As early as 1939, Sylvia Payne's discussion of fetishism centred on a Kleinian model of early ego development and internal objects. In 'Some Observations on the Ego Development of the Fetishist', Payne moves the discussion from the 'phallic' stage back to the much earlier phase of ego development, when 'part objects' of the mother and father are introjected into the baby's internal world. In her case study, Mr. A's mackintosh fetish 'stood for the father's penis or the woman's genital, nipple, body, anal tract.'[64] The mackintosh, she stresses, is also a defensive mechanism against the fetishist's aggression towards the loved object.

Gillespie: In 1940, the Freudian W. H. Gillespie discusses Payne's theory in a paper to the British Psycho-Analytic Society and agrees on taking the fetish formation back to the earlier stage of development. While he does not contradict the classic castration anxiety, he too focuses on the oral features: 'it is clear that these phantasies were motivated only partially by castration anxiety – another important factor was the phantasy of the penis as a source of food'.[65]

This oral element clearly causes Gillespie some unease, since he sees it as going against the Freudian hypothesis. He initially rejects Payne's conclusions, arguing that the oral component is not necessarily 'deeper' than the phallic, but rather a 'disguise' for it. His reason for arguing this is that (and one can almost hear the exasperation) 'it is castration anxiety we are dealing with, not the trauma of weaning or something of that sort'.[66] However, he capitulates in the face of the evidence, decides he is unable to privilege the phallic over the oral, and tries for a compromise solution:

> May it not be that we have actually to deal with neither the one thing or the other, but a combination of the two?[67]

This is an important shift: if fetishism's development is moved back from phallic castration anxiety to an early stage of ego development, then clearly the way is open for the inclusion of girls as well as boys. *Bak:* In 1953, Bak's paper to the American Psychoanalytic Association situated fetish fixation as part of separation anxiety. Freud's thesis is that during the castration complex the little boy detaches himself from the mother and turns towards the father. Bak disentangles the processes, so that the fear of castration *and* the separation from the mother are seen as two distinct elements (not part of the same process). He then concentrates on the anxiety involved in the individuation process: 'the fetish undoes the separation from the mother through clinging to the symbolic substitute'.[68] The mother that the child strives to cling on to is a pre-phallic mother who is thus seen as unthreatening to the little penis, so that 'both phases of danger, ie, separation and castration, are defended by the fetishistic compromise.'[69] This shift of emphasis on the causal mechanism of fetish fixation is again important for allowing a space for women as potential practitioners. However, the new developements are still constructed around the castration theory, without thinking to challenge it, in its entirety.

Winnicott: D. W. Winnicott, whose representation of object relations theory has been a major influence of the British school, in 1958 turned his attention briefly to fetishism, when outlining the theory of the 'transitional object'.[70] The infant develops from a sensation of being magically a part of the maternal breast, through to an awareness of itself within an outside environment, via the safety or comfort of a transitional object. In unusual cases, Winnicott argues, the transitional object may develop into a fetish.

Sperling: Melitta Sperling, in New York, took exception to Winnicott's view that the transitional object was universal and not pathological. She argues, on the contrary, that if a child becomes attached to an inanimate object before the age of two, then they have become fixated on object relations as a denial of the weaning process. For Sperling, the mother coerces the child into this fixation because of her own ambivalence to the separation process, and the fetish is seen as allowing the two of them to separate in reality, 'by magically undoing the separation'.[71] This allows a facade of normality for both mother and child. In her paper Sperling puts forward the fundamental point that the fetishist gains 'gratification in reality' (whereas the neurotic experiences it only in fantasy, or through symptoms). Sexual release is 'immediate, unmodified and instinctual'.

When making these points, Sperling uses the term 'he', but of her six case studies, four are women. Two seem to us problematic as sexual fetishists, since no libidinous gratification is involved, but her third case study is clearly a fetishist. The woman plucks her pubic hair, burns it and orgasms to the smell. The fourth woman eats her plucked hair and Sperling explains her uncertainty about categorising her as a fetishist; however she mentions in passing that she is also anorexic and was referred due to her 'pernicious vomiting'.[72]

Greenacre: Phyllis Greenacre's article, 'Perversions: General Considerations regarding their Genetic and Dynamic background', written in 1968, consolidates many of these views.[73] Welldon cites both Payne and Greenacre as being among the female analysts trying to offer a more complex model of feminine psychopathology, who were ignored by the phallocentric psychoanalytic movement. Most of them were only published in little known journals.

Greenacre argues for a pathological ego development. The subject fears disintegration during the individuation process, because of a disturbed mother-child development. While she includes both sexes in her discussion, and focuses on the individuation process, all her case studies are male. She begins by arguing strongly that it is a disturbance in the separation process during the first two years which forms the potential for a later fetish fixation. During the later castration complex, Greenacre suggests, the potential fetishist regresses to the feeling/thought of the mother's breast as both a direct comfort and a substitute for the castrated penis. This links the oral component, mentioned by Gillespie and acknowledged by Greenacre as an important characteristic, to the Winnicott transitional object. She sees the breast as being the model for the transitional object used by the child to bridge the gap between the 'I' and the external world. Like Winnicott, she sees the use of a transitional object as 'universal' and non-pathological. But unlike him, she insists on designating it a prephallic 'fetish':

> Occasionally this early fetish continues on into a later form, but more frequently it is given up spontaneously with the phallic-oedipal period. It seems about as frequent in girl as in boy babies.[74]

However, where there has been a 'severe impairment of object relationships' between mother and infant, the anxiety during the castration phase becomes acute, because of the child's weak body image. The fetish then develops 'almost literally as a stop-gap' to enable sexual performance, despite the low body-image. Greenacre thus consolidates many of object-related theories in:

1. relating the early fetishising of objects to the 'transitional object' relations evidenced in both genders;
2. reinforcing the oral characteristics; and
3. seeing it in relation to narcissistic questions of body image (prima-

rily, but not only, genital size) in the later, phallic stage of development.

One of the case studies cited by Greenacre is of a woman, 'Nora', in Nancy Tow Spiegel's 'An Infantile Fetish and its persistence into young Womanhood'. Greenacre uses Nora to illustrate her thesis of the faulty development through all the various phases, which stands as another obvious example of the fact that women *do* fetishise.

Soon after weaning at 8 months (ie, early object loss of the mother's breast), Nora was observed twisting a string of beads and staring at it unblinkingly. During the masturbatory phase, this staring and twisting of the string became elaborated upon. Masturbating without the string (which must not become contaminated) made Nora feel 'bad' and so she would resort to the string ritual to make herself feel 'good and pure' again. In both the 'doing' and the 'undoing' rituals, she would suck with her lips and tongue. Nora stole her first shoe-string from her mother's shoe at the time of her brother's birth, when she was experiencing even further rejection from the mother. She became obsessed with fantasies of large breasts and with her own lack of breast development. The narcissistic body-image blow, for which the string compensates, is thus clearly applicable to girls as much as boys. Between the ages of 15 and 18, Nora began to steal sweaters from full-breasted girls. The excitement thus experienced impelled her to steal the same girls' shoe laces, at which point the excitement developed into sexual arousal. These shoe strings then became the object of Nora's fully developed 'doing and undoing' masturbatory ritual.

Spiegel does not challenge the assumption that women fetishists are rare and sees Nora as rather the exception that proves the rule. *Masud Khan*: Masud Khan's 1979 book *Alienation in Perversion* is still being used as a textbook for training analysts on the perversions in Britain. With nods to Greenacre, he argues that with excessive impingement by the mother, the infant ego creates a 'collated internal object' instead of developing via the transitional object. This collated internal object can only be experienced and activated by the adult subject through specific sexual practices. Masud Khan posits the view that ' perverse-formations are much nearer to cultural artifacts than disease syndromes as such'.[75] He differentiates this early, infantile dissociation from the later defensive splitting of the object discussed by Payne and Gillespie.

Although the discussion is of a generalised 'he', when he goes on to look at case histories, he does refer to a fetish/bondage practitioner who is a woman. However, we do have serious problems with Masud Khan's designating as a 'fetish' an artificial penis worn by his patient's female lover. A sexual fetish object is one that is surprising in its choice. A piece of string or a plaster caste are, on the surface, surprising choices for sexual arousal. Their very oddness points to the workings of the unconscious. A penetrative sex toy is not a surprising choice. We would not therefore designate it a fetish object, and suggests that the analyst's concept of 'normal' has been clouded by the lesbian aspect.[76] When he discusses the case study of a 'true' fetishist he reverts to a male case study and cites fear of losing the penis as the explanation.

Nevertheless, his conclusions allow space to separation anxiety and fear of abandonment as primary anxiety affects. He says that these components subsequently overload onto castration anxiety in the phallic phase. Khan also argues that the protective and libidinous elements in fetishism prevent any real submergence into pathology. 'I am inclined to say that in the capacity to create a fetish we see the inherent strength of the infant-child ego and its capacity to save itself from total collapse and disintegration'.[77] He therefore focusses on the compensatory strengths of the practice. Going on to discuss the primacy of Freud's castration complex/phallic mother, he argues for another reading of the 'phallic mother' construct that we find intensely interesting. He argues that the phallic mother is not a construct to deny sexual difference, but to satisfy the desire to merge with/possess the mother (ie, to deny individuation):

> My case material suggests that the phallic mother imago upon which the fetishist is fixated is composed from sensations derived from the self-phallus in the excited states and the maternal object towards whom they are directed. Also involved are passive longings for the father's penis.[78]

This imago of the self *and* object of desire, is clearly open to the little girl (whose signifier of self-desire would be something other than a penis). What is also being silently rejected here is the 'trauma' of seeing the female genitals, in classic male castration anxiety. Instead, the image of the phallic mother is more an excited fixation on desire and fear of annihilation through individuation (rather than loss of penis). Our reading of Masud Khan does not equate with his own conclusion. Unfortunately he goes on to move the fear of annhilation back onto the penis and fear of castration and superimposes it back to the Freudian phallic mother image as 'protection' of the penis.

Towards a New Theory of Fetishism

In the past, Freudian and Lacanian theories have taken centre stage in the analysis of sexual fetishism. Although Kleinian and French Feminist insights have to some extent been visible in academies and consulting rooms, the dominance of Freudian ideas about castration anxiety, the phallic mother and penis envy have obscured the impact and importance of other feminist insights about autonomous female sexuality – and consequently about female fetishism. In this chapter, then, we have found it necessary to review and describe clinical writings about fetishism which we found among the psychoanalytic journals, but which contradict orthodox Freudian accounts of fetishism, and Freudian ideas about the behaviour of women.

We have reviewed the revisions to Freud's theory of fetishism. We have done our best to move away from a phallocentric analysis of fetishism, which has a blind spot about female desire – and to the female gaze at the erotic. And we hope that the ideas about autonomous female desire we have discussed show how and why women might become fetishists. In addition, by foregrounding those studies (often Kleinian) that explain fetishism by focussing on the oral stage (instead of Freud's emphasis upon the genital stage) we have been able to include a new dimension to discussions of fetishism: that fetishism occurs also as a consequence of separation anxiety. What we are gesturing towards, then, is a different explanation of the causal mechanisms of 'perversity' in adult life. This does not mean we reject out of hand the idea that fetishism may also arise as a consequence of castration anxiety. All we are saying here is that at this genital stage of the fixation, a new positive theoretical model of female sexuality needs to be designed, to be able to account for the development of female fetishists.

We realise that such an attack on the signification of the phallus, for women, could in itself be seen as yet another form of penis envy. (As Naomi Schor's account of 'perversion theft' and Marjorie Garber's of 'fetish envy' indicate). But any criticism of inequality necessarily leaves itself open to the claims of 'envy' by its detractors.

Clearly there are gender differentials that are significant to many types of human behaviour, and we have not been able to fully assess the structural differences which may cause men and women to fetishise differently, or in different numbers. It could be that repressed behaviour is often triggered by cultural events. For example, whilst we would be cautious about making general arguments, we can point out that

there already exists cultural evidence that has challenged Freud's idea
that women are invariably hysterics and that men are perverts. Male
hysterics were diagnosed after the first world war, in the cases of shell
shock, as Elaine Showalter has identified. [79] Changing cultural formations can act as triggers to releasing repressed behaviour that may
not have been seen in large numbers before. Conversely, certain types
of behaviour can remain 'hidden from history'. Perverse behaviour
by women, and by female fetishists in particular, may not have been
seen before because their behaviour was not 'recognised' as such.
Thus the Freudian fixation on protecting the penis has obscured
recognition of female fetishism.

Notes

1   Naomi Schor, 'Female Fetishism: The Case of George Sand', in *The Female
Body in Western Culture: Contemporary Perspectives*, Susan Suleiman (ed), Harvard
University Press, Harvard 1968, pp363–372. On p371 Schor discusses the problems of trying to address female fetishism and jokes that 'perversion theft' could
be read as a form of 'penis envy'. She rejects this Freudian formulation arguing
for a need within psychoanalytic discourse to find some other way of talking about
female experience, in particular of fetishism.

2   Carol Gilligan, *In a Different Voice: Psychological Theory and Women's Developement*,
Harvard, Cambridge, Mass. 1982, p25.

3   Freud, 1905, 1927,*op cit.*

4   *Encyclopedia Americana*, Americana, New York 1977, Vol 11, p137. *Encyclopedia Britannia* maintains its reputation for reserve by not admitting any kind of
fetishism other than the anthropological kind.

5   Wilhelm Stekel, *Sexual Aberrations*, John Lane, London 1934, Vol 1, p363
and p34.

6   Joan Copjec's essay, 'The Sartorial Superego', *October* 50, Fall 1989, p56-
95, discusses Clerambault's interest in fetishism and argues that the 40,000
photographs of draped figures, and his lectures on drapery, point to Clerambault
himself being a cloth fetishist (particularly of stiff silk). Further discussion of
Clerambault and fetishism can be found in Emily Apter, *Feminizing the Fetish*,
Cornell, Ithaca 1991, pp106–7, and her entry on 'Perversion' in *Feminism and
Psychoanalysis*, E Wright (ed), Blackwells, Oxford 1992, p312.

7   G.A. Dudley, 'A Rare Case of Female Fetishism', *International Journal of
Sexology*, 8, 1954, p33.

8   Ilse Brande, 'Perette et son gai (d'un cas de phobie d'impulsion et de
comportment fetichiste chez une femme)'. Memoir de candidature au titre de
Membre adherent a la Societe Psychoanalytic de Paris, 1962.

9   Nancy Tow Spiegel, 'An Infantile Fetish and its Persistence into Young
Womanhood', *Psychoanalytic Study of the Child*, *The International Journal of Psychoanalysis*, 22, 1967, pp402–425.

10   G. Zavitzianos, 'Fetishism and Exhibitionism in the Female and their
Relationship to Psychopathology and Kleptomania', *International Journal of Psychoanalysis*, 52, 1971.

11 Nancy Friday, *My Secret Garden: Women's Sexual Fantasies*, Virago/Quartet, London 1975, p172.

12 G. Bonnet, 'Fetichisme et exhibitionnisme chez un sujet feminin', [Fetishism and exhibitionism in a female subject] *Psychoanalyse a l'Universite*, 2, 1977, pp231–257. Reprinted in *Voir, etre vu: Etudes cliniques sur l'exhibionnisme* ,Presses Universitaires de France, Paris 1981, Vol 1, pp93–4.

13 C. Gosselin and G. Wilson, *Sexual Variations: Fetishism, Sado-Masochism and Transvestism*, Faber, London 1980, p49.

14 Gilbert Hamilton, *A Research into Marriage* , Boni, New York 1929, pp463–4.

15 *Ibid*, p463.

16 *Ibid*, p464.

17 Kinsey Institute for Sex Research, *Sexual Behaviour in the Human Female* , Indiana University Press, Bloomington 1953, p679.

18 *Ibid*, p679.

19 From *Passion erotique des etoffes chez la femme* ,1908, quoted in Copjec, *op cit*, p87.

20 Havelock Ellis, *Studies in the Psychology of Sex*, [36], Random House, New York 1910, Vol 2, part 2, p482.

21 Stekel, *op cit*, p3.

22 *Ibid*, p6.

23 Dudley, *op cit*.

24 Brande, *op cit*, and Zavitzianos, *op cit*.

25 Nancy Friday, *op cit*, p171.

26 'Fetishism', p155.

27 '"Civilised" Sexual Morality and Modern Nervous Illness', Standard Edition, Vol 9.

28 *The Selected Melanie Klein*, Juliet Mitchell (ed), Penguin, Harmondsworth 1986.

29 Toril Moi, *Sexual/Textual Politics*, Methuen, London 1985, p99.

30 Jacqueline Rose, 'Introduction II' in *Feminine Sexuality:Jacques Lacan and the Ecole Freudienne*, Juliet Mitchell and Jacqueline Rose (eds), Macmillan, London 1982, p42.

31 J. Lacan & V. Granoff, 'Fetishism:the symbolic, the imaginary and the real', in *Perversions: psychodynamics and therapy* , Sandor Lorand (ed), Ortolan, London 1965, pp265–276.

32 Lacan, 'Guiding remarks for a Congress on Female Sexuality: IX Female homosexuality and Ideal love', in *Feminine Sexuality*, *op cit*, p96.

33 Lacan,'The Meaning of the Phallus', in *Feminine Sexuality*, *op cit*, p84.

34 *Ibid*, p84.

35 Bonnet, *op cit*.

36 *Traits de Perversion dans Les Structures Cliniques*, Rapports de la Recontre internationale 1990 du Champ freudien a Paris, Navarin 1990.

37 *Ibid*, pp432–5.

38 *Ibid*, p433, our translation.

39 *Ibid*, p435, our translation.

40 Mary Ann Doane, 'Masquerade Reconsidered: Further Thoughts on the Female Spectator', *Discourse*, 11, Fall/Winter 1988–89, pp44–5.

41 Foucault does not explain why he makes this claim, but it is commonly made amongst those discussing the perversions.

42   Luce Irigaray, *Speculum of the Other Woman*, Transl. Gillian Gill, ; Cornell , Ithaca 1985.

43   *Ibid*, p51.

44   *Ibid*, p53.

45   Sarah Kofman, *The Enigma of Woman: Woman in Freud's Writings*, transl. Catherine Porter, Cornell, Ithica 1985.

46   *Ibid*, p86.Her discussion in this early essay still locates fetishism in the castration complex, but in the later 'Ca Cloche' in *Les fins de l'homme: A partir du travail de Jacques Derrida*, Galilee, Paris 1981, Kofman argues for a fetishism shorn of all sexual difference, a perverse oscillation that refuses to anchor *either* gender to castration anxiety and thus becomes a mark of deconstructive undecidability. As such, it has moved outside the field of what we would call sexual fetishism and become a deconstructive oscillation that we consider in our concluding chapter on the post-modern.'A generalised fetishism, defined as a generalised oscillation, does not exclude a female fetishism, since it implies the generalisation of the feminine and the end of the privileging of the phallus, which ceases to be a fetish.'(Sarah Kofman) from Schor, *op cit*, p173. Emily Apter sees Kofman as arguing for a demasculinized fetishism. 'Regardless of sex, the fetish is generated as a guarantee against the disappearance of an idealised phallus,' itself a representation. 'As the representation of a representation', and itself signifying 'radical undecidability', Kofman's fetish is 'recast as the foundation for an ironic, gender-free metaphysics, '*Feminizing the Fetish*, p110.

47   Kofman, *op cit*, p94–5.

48   See Freud on 'Screen Memories,' *Standard Edition*, Vol 3, pp301–22. He argues that screen memories are a process of denial that does not sufficiently bury the affect of horror or significance, and hence have a more repressive form of disavowal; though in footnote 2, p154 of 'Fetishism', added in 1920, he specifically allies fetishism to screen memories in representing the submerged infantile phase of sexual development.

49   Hélène Cixous, 'Castration or Decapitation?', transl. Annette Kuhn, *Signs* 7 (1), Autumn 1981, p51.

50   'The Laugh of the Medusa', in *New French Feminisms: An Anthology*, Elaine Marks and Isabelle de Courtivron (eds), Harvester, London 1981, pp243–264; see also, *The Newly Born Woman*, Hélène Cixous and Catherine Clement, transl. Betsy Wing, Manchester University Press, Manchester 1986.

51   'The Laugh of the Medusa', p260.

52   Luce Irigaray, 'And one does not stir without the other', transl. Helene Wenzel, *Signs* 7 (1), Autumn 1981, p62.

53   Luce Irigaray, 'When our lips speak together', transl by Carolyn Burke, *Signs* 6 (1) (Autumn 1980) pp 69-79.

54   Julia Kristeva, *Desire in Language*, trans. Leon Roudiez, Blackwell, Oxford 1980; *The Kristeva Reader*, Toril Moi (ed), Blackwell, Oxford 1987.

55   Julia Kristeva, 'About Chinese Women', in Moi, *op cit*, p150.

56   Estella V. Welldon, *Mother, Madonna, Whore*, Free Association Books, London 1988, p26.

57   Parveen Adams, 'On Female Bondage', in *Between Feminism and Psychoanalysis*, Teresa Brennan (ed), Routledge, London 1989, pp247–265.

58   *Ibid*, p256.

59   *Ibid*, p258.

60 *Ibid*, p263

61 Elizabeth Grosz, 'Lesbian fetishism', *differences*, 3/2, 1991, pp39–54; and Apter, *Feminizing the Fetish*, pp104–5, where she summarises Grosz's forthcoming essay 'Lesbian Fetishism' in *Fetishism as Cultural Discourse*, Apter and Pietz (eds).

62 Indeed, we might even argue that where Lacanian analysis situates fetishism on the castration complex's rupture of the dyadic union – rather than the focus on anxieties around the loss of the phallus – we would be in broad agreement. Mary Ann Doane questions the precise relation between sexual difference and linguistic difference in Lacanian theory, arguing that it is never properly specified. However, she continues, 'if linguistic difference and sexual difference are merged in a way that allows them no relative autonomy, the theory indeed becomes totalising, leaving no room for feminist strategy'. This is a useful call for specificity and for a separating out of the meanings of the 'phallus' in order to identify those which are accessible to feminism. Doane, *op cit*, p46.

63 Jacqueline Rose, *op cit*.

64 S.M. Payne, 'Some Observations on the Ego Development of the Fetishist', *International Journal of Psychoanalysis*, 20, 1939, p167.

65 W.H. Gillespie, 'A Contribution to the Study of Fetishism', *International Journal of Psycho-Analysis*, 21, 1940, p411. Bak too, in 1953, stresses the Kleinian equating of the breast with the penis in one of his male fetishists.

66 *Ibid*, p414.

67 *Ibid*, p415.

68 Bak, 'Fetishism', *Journal of American Psychoanalytic Association*, 1 (1953), p291.

69 *Ibid*, p286.

70 D.W. Winnicott, *Through Paediatrics to Psycho-Analysis*, Hogarth Press, London 1975.

71 Melitta Sperling, 'Fetishism in Children', *International Journal of Psychoanalysis*, 32 (1963).

72 Melitta Sperling develops this case study in 'Trichotillomania, Trichophagy and Cyclic vomiting', *International Journal of Psycho-Analysis* ,(1968), Vol 49.

73 Phyllis Greenacre, 'Perversions: General Considerations regarding their Genetic and Dynamic Background',*Psychoanalytic Study of the Child*, 23 (1968).

74 *Ibid*, p50.

75 Masud Khan, *Alienation in Perversion* Hogarth Press, London 1979, p121.

76 Linda Williams almost does this in her discussion of Parveen Adams' 'Of Female Bondage', in 'Pornographies on/scene', *Sex Exposed: Sexuality and the Pornography Debate*, L. Segal and M. McIntosh (eds), Virago, London 1992, pp233–265. The discussion of lesbian sado-masochists' use of a dildo, coming immediately after the discussion of lesbian fetishism, appears to equate the dildo with a fetish. But in this case, as Williams explains, the dildo does not disavow the sexual object so much as playfully subvert phallocentrism.

77 *Ibid*, p164.

78 *Ibid*, p167.

79 Elaine Showalter, *The Female Malady*, Virago, London 1987.

4

Bulimia: the Fourth Fetishism?

No one who has seen a baby sinking back satiated from the breast and falling asleep with flushed cheeks and a blissful smile can escape the reflection that this picture persists as the prototype of the expression of sexual satisfaction in later life. *Sigmund Freud* [1]

I think at some point I decided ... between food and sex. And food won. It was actually a conscious decision. *Shelley Winters* [2]

The epidemic proportions of compulsive eating, anorexia and bulimia in women in the West indicate that something must have gone wrong in Western culture relating to female sexual identity. There are many psychoanalytic and cultural arguments offered to explain why women find themselves caught up in food obsessions, but none of them connect eating disorders with sexual fetishism.

We feel that there are similarities between explanations of sexual fetishism and those offered by the analysts of eating disorders. On the popular level some feminists, like Kim Chernin, have almost made the connection between food fetishism and eating disorder. When discussing contemporary female identity problems and eating obsessions, Chernin argues that they have all the elements of a 'rites of passage', gone wrong:

> a rite of passage accomplishes two things, the transformation of identity and the entry into culture ... Much of the obsessive quality of an eating disorder arises precisely from the fact that food is being asked to serve a transformative function it cannot carry by itself.[3]

Like sexual fetishism, eating disorder often involves a transitional mechanism for coping with underlying unconscious conflicts – Chernin is astute in her observation of this.

Anorexia is perhaps the most extreme form of eating disorder, since so many young women have actually died from the effects of it, including singer Karen Carpenter. Anorexia, like its obverse, obesity, has been explained as 'a flight from femininity' which unconsciously denies female sexuality and may involve a flight from 'the male gaze'. This denial takes the form of obsessions surrounding food which create body shapes that are often seen to be 'sexless' by men and women alike. (Even the *Sun* could not continue to eroticise Mandy Smith's body – ex-wife of rock star Bill Wyman – when in 1991 she became emaciated and anorexic-looking as a consequence of what was alleged to be a food 'allergy'.) The figures of both the anorexic and the obese, in Western culture at least, draw attention to themselves as 'deviations' from dominant feminine stereotypes.

The view of obesity and anorexia as a 'flight from femininity' has been substantiated by the research of Susie Orbach, of the Women's Therapy Centre, one of the most respected feminist writers on eating disorder. She has gone on to argue that anorexia, in particular, is a form of 'hunger strike' and part of a feminine 'protest'.[4] Other critics, such as Kaplan, have suggested that anorexia represents enactment of 'a perverse strategy', which she says differs from other psychological strategies in that it demands a performance.[5]

A Fourth Fetishism?

We would take Kaplan's rather general argument further and argue that the 'perverse' strategy of bulimia, the binging and vomiting of food in particular, could be seen as *fetishistic*. This is because the processes of 'doing' and 'undoing' (bingeing and purging) that comprise bulimic behaviour are comparable with orthodox descriptions of sexual fetishism.

Bulimia could be argued to constitute a fourth fetishism, comparable with sexual fetishism, though different enough to warrant its own category. Firstly, one needs to accept that fetishism:

1. is available to women.
2. is as much about the disavowal of individuation as of sexual difference.
3. carries a strong oral component.
4. allows direct sensual gratification.

Then it becomes appropriate to look also at women's relationship to food as the object of a fetishism. For the bulimic shares all these characteristics, as well as exhibiting the oscillating disavowal, characterised as doing-and-undoing, that allows the gratification of the pleasure principle in the 'real' world.

In our discussion of bulimia we draw attention to the comparable mechanism of disavowal. We also draw out the psychoanalytic links to individuation and to a gratification very similar to sexual release. We would also suggest that, just as sexual fetishism redirects the sexual urge, the element of bingeing in bulimia is in fact a pleasurable re-direction ('perversion') of the drive for nourishment. And just as sexual fetishism makes a fetish of an object in the external world, so bulimia fetishes food which is only subsequently injested. Actual consumption (bingeing) goes on, analogous to the actual genital orgasm of the fetishist. For this reason, we feel it comes under the category of a perversion, rather than a neurosis. It is notable that bingers tend not to devour the whole range of foodstuffs, eschewing the healthier fruit and vegetables to choose fattening, high-calorific foods. We would suggest that this specialisation, analogous to the fetishist's compulsive 'choice' of shoes, string or white stockings is largely culturally (rather than chemically) based: these are exactly the foods portrayed as dangerous and alluring to women trying to live up to the ideal of femininity.

Most discussion of bulimia concentrates upon the destructive and debilitating aspects of the compulsion. Of course we acknowledge these, fully, but they are not the whole picture.What we believe is missing from the account is the way food is being used as a creative, constructed compromise to disavow harsher anxieties. The first stage of bulimia (bingeing) grants the experience of direct, sensual pleasure. The second stage allows a denial of the 'threat' of consuming food (whatever that stands for in the subject's unconscious). This parallels the process whereby the fetish object allows the fetishist to experience direct genital gratification, while unconsciously denying the 'threat of castration'. Any account which does not acknowledge the self-granting of pleasure cannot fully grasp the structure of bulimia.

Bulimia – What is It?

Bulimia has really only been diagnosed since 1979 and all the literature agrees that it is a relatively new syndrome.[6] The debate as to whether it is a separate eating disorder from anorexia, or a further symptom of it, still rages. Discussion is often complicated by the fact that many anorexics have bouts of being bulimic during their anorexia, while many erstwhile anorexics later become bulimics. 'Bulimia nervosa' has thus variously being categorised as part of the: 'fear of being fat syndrome'; 'dietary chaos syndrome'; or as 'bulimarexia', the binge-purge syndrome.

The third revised edition of the *Diagnostic and Statistical Manual of the American Psychiatric Association* diagnoses as a criterion for bulimia:

1. Recurrent episodes of binge-eating.
2. A feeling of lack of control over eating behaviours during the eating binges.
3. The person regularly engages in either self-induced vomiting, use of laxatives or diuretics, strict dieting or fasting, or vigorous exercise in order to prevent weight gain.
4. A minimum average of two binge-eating episodes a week for at least 3 months.
5. Persistent overconcern with body shape and weight.[7]

We would concur with this description of bulimia but feel that any definition should recognise varying levels of the syndrome, not only in terms of duration (point 4 above) but also in terms of 'intensity'. Just as Gebhard proposes that fetishistic behaviour consists of different degrees of intensity we would argue that bulimic behaviour also could be analysed along a continuum. Many women may practise some of the symptoms without entering the 'pathological' status.

But not all the behaviour that involves bingeing is bulimic. Indeed, we would point out that bingeing is common to the three main eating disorders: 50 per cent of the obese binge; 50 per cent of anorexics also binge then purge; 100 per cent of bulimics binge and purge.[8] What distinguishes bulimic bingeing, it has been argued, is:

> the persistent, intrusive, and overdetermined concern with body weight and shape, and the intractable nature of eating binges, all of which hint strongly at underlying vulnerabilities in self-esteem, interpersonal adjustment, and identity formation.[9]

'Bingeing is not the same as eating. To binge is not to nourish oneself. On the contrary it is to make a mockery of the whole process of self-nourishment,' as Strober and Yager emphasise.[10] As such we can argue that it is a perversion, a deflection, of the oral drive for nourishment. Compulsive eating, we believe, is the active use of an outside object – food – and hence a 'perversion', rather than a passive 'hysterical' reaction on the body of the subject.

But the bulimic doesn't just binge, she also vomits. It is hard to imagine that some women might find vomiting pleasurable, but the American psychiatrist Stoller has found they do and has written about 'evidence of erotic vomiting' in women.[11] However, he rules out the relationship of erotic vomiting to the eating disorders of anorexia and bulimia.[12] His observation of three case studies brings forth the comment that 'even behaviour as rare or bizarre as erotic vomiting can have its reasons ... though not yet explicable.' We believe the explanation needs to make reference to the theory of sexual fetishism, and to the pleasures of disavowing threatening unconscious conflicts.

In order to justify our argument that bulimia should be seen as a fourth fetishism, which parallels sexual fetishism, we will show:

1. how the literature on bulimia illustrates the syndrome as a coping strategy (against anxiety or dysphoria).
2. how it is identified with the problems of individuation (separation).
3. how its oral gratification can also be linked to aspects of sexuality.

Just as Juliet Mitchell argued that the sexual fetishist could 'have his cake and eat it', through his disavowal, so Dana and Lawrence use the same metaphor for the bulimic:

> Bulimia initially looks like the perfect solution; she really can have her cake and eat it. She can have her fill - vast amounts of food; she can succumb to her overwhelming needs, shut them up with a binge and yet not have to carry the consequences with the fat showing on her body.[13]

Bulimia as a Coping Strategy: the Psychoanalytic Links with Sexual Fetishism

Many critics have posited bulimia as a 'coping strategy'. One of the earliest writers on the subject of female psychology and food was Hilde Bruch. In her groundbreaking book *Eating Disorders: Obesity, Anorexia Nervosa and the Person Within*,[14] published before bulimia was recognised, Bruch argues that eating disorder patients,

> perceive, or misperceive, their bodily sensations so that the nutritional function can be misused in the service of complex emotional and interpersonal problems.[15]

One explanation of eating disorder offered by Bruch stems from her observations of breast feeding. She ascribes eating disorder to the consequences of inappropriate responses by mothers who attend to all the baby's various cries (for comfort, cold, tiredness, etc, as well as food) with milk or feeding. The baby thus becomes unable to distinguish the urge to eat from other analogous bodily discomforts that have no relation to a need for food. Neither, at this oral stage, can it learn to distinguish hunger from psychological conflicts and tensions. So Bruch theorises that some adults have learned to confuse psychological or even sexual needs with hunger signals. For, she argued, the experience of hunger is culturally constructed, rather than innate.

In later life, these adults use eating disorders as a mask or coping strategy for dealing with deeper, psychological problems:

> Preoccupied as these patients are with eating and not-eating, and in their use of the eating function as a pseudo-solution of personality problems, they have in common the inability to identify hunger correctly or to distinguish it from the other states of bodily need or emotional arousal.[16]

Contrary to the usual medical theory that one should reduce weight to improve physical and emotional health, Bruch was therefore one of the first to argue that obese sufferers may run the risk of succumbing to depression if they are removed from their compensatory mechanism. 'It is my impression that the overeager propaganda of reducing diets ... overlooks a basic human problem, the need for satisfaction of vital needs.'[17]

People who eat in response to stress, it has been found, eat in response to external cues (the sight of food, nearness to a 'meal-time'), rather than from the internal cues (hunger).[18] The behaviourist, Joyce Slochower, similarly argues that obese people who eat in response to emotional states do so particularly when the anxiety is 'diffuse' rather than in response to a specific event. She argues, 'much internal conflict is believed to be (in part) unconscious, the individual may not be aware of the source of the anxiety.'[19]

It needs to be said that as a coping strategy, bulimia is extremely painful and inadequate. Nevertheless it is experienced as a coping mechanism as can be observed from the comments of bulimics:

> I'd get the urge to fill up the emptiness and sadness I felt inside. Usually I'd turn to food ...[20]

> I think about food nearly all the time. It's frightening to be so obsessed with it, but at least it stops me worrying about anything else.[21]

Several researchers have investigated the perverse 'coping' mechanism of bulimia. Troy Cooper, for example, says that 'bulimia is useful and necessary to the lives of so many women' because it is 'a position taken in order *not* to have to say something.'[22] She explains:

Because of Western socio-religious history, bulimia has been seen as a loss of control. However I shall argue that it is in fact the method used by the bulimic for keeping control over elements of her life which she considers would be destructive, disruptive and frightening if expressed.[23]

The question of what is being disavowed, what bulimia is coping with, depends on which theorist is describing it. There are various interpretations made by the different therapists and psychologists who have studied it. Those giving a cultural (as opposed to psychiatric) answer point to the conflicting expectations placed upon women since the feminist revolution of the 1960s. R. A. Gordon argues that bulimia is a social epidemic embodying the inner conflict women feel. He suggests that bulimic women are caught between conflicting cultural demands which require integration of contradictory values 'of achievement and mastery with an underlying self-concept that is defined in terms of nurturance, physical attractiveness …'[24] C. L. Johnson, D. L. Tobin and S. L. Steinberg agree that bulimia is due to the destabilisation of gender role norms.[25] Troy Cooper has argued that bulimia is a defence against the inability to live up to the 'Superwoman' image. In Chernin's model too, bulimia is a consequence of contradictory cultural messages about female identity. Some women find it difficult to make the transition from 'girl' to 'woman', or from 'woman of the past' to 'woman of the future' because there is so much confusion as to the contradictory roles of 'the new woman'.

Marlene Boskind-Lodahl's influential writing also sees the syndrome as a reaction to female role models. But she argues that whereas anorexia is a rejection of 'feminity', bulimics embrace it. The anorexic rejects the rounded feminine shape synonymous in Western culture with being accommodating, receptive and passive. Bulimics embrace the traditional assumptions that 'wifehood, motherhood, and intimacy with men are the fundamental components of femininity.'[26]

Boskind-Lodahl's analysis may well appear to make sense, in the way that the different syndromes are symbolically represented on the body. The anorexic's painful emaciation could be seen to be refusing to inject the feminine role. The bulimic, a more secret syndrome hidden behind the facade of a successful, coping woman of acceptable size, could be seen as accommodating the societal role.

But we would argue that the reality belies this symbolic reading adopted by many feminist critics, some of whom, to our dismay, have seemed to admire the anorexics's restraint and denial.[27] In 'Sex Role Ideology among woman with Anorexia Nervosa and Bulimia', S. Srikameswaran, P. Leichner and D. Harper found evidence that pointed in the opposite direction from these arguments that bulimic women adhere to traditional codes of femininity. Instead they assert that 'women in the bulimic group were significantly more feminist in their views than were those in the anorexic groups'. [28] They go on to argue:

> we have also observed that many of these bulimic patients are quite career-orientated and involved professionally. On the other hand, we have also found anorexic patients to be clinically more traditional in their goals as women.[29]

With consideration, we believe the anorexic's debilitation, and refusal to abandon the 'child' role, could as easily be read as a bid for dependency. [30] Conversely, the bulimic can be seen to strive to succeed and so to challenge passive feminine role-models. Her less debilitating compromise, or disavowal mechanism, allows many to have successful, high-flying careers both as professionals and as feminist activists. Many bulimic feminists are well aware of the significance of slender images in contributing to some women having problems with food, and this points to a view that eating disorders arise from irrational unconscious anxieties.

Individuation and Bulimia: the Key
to Female Fetishism

The cultural analyses of bulimia may diverge, but the various object-relations psychoanalysts tend to have more of a consensus that eating disorders have a strong relationship to unconscious problems with separation. Although discussion around eating disorder has never focussed on fetishism, they have nevertheless many similar connections in the psychoanalytic models used.

Hilde Bruch was the first to identify a familial pattern for eating-disorder sufferers, where the father was weak and unaggressive or absent (ie, subordinate role) while the mother was domineering. The mother's over-involvement was seen as a consequence of her using the child as a compensatory object for her own lack of fulfilment in marriage or life. A similar familial pattern is often argued for fetishists, especially by Melitta Sperling.

The 'vital need' which Bruch believed that obesity fulfils, is the individual's desire to be big and powerful enough to live up to the mother's expectations, whilst still remaining dependent upon her. This orthodoxy of the familial pattern was also agreed in relation to bulimia by Sights and Richards who write that 'it is believed that parents of bulimic daughters refuse to allow them to individuate normally from the family. Mothers especially seem to intrude unduly into the lives of their offspring at times when it would be more natural to encourage separation.'[31]

Incidentally, the orthodoxy of the above ideas generated a rather off-the-wall experiment whereby obese women were put into a deep sleep and then played a tape repeating the 'soothing' words, 'Mommy and I are one, mommy and I are one'.[32] It was hoped that the message would be taken up subconsciously by the women as a reassuring subliminal communication to deny that individuation had taken place. Although some success was reported with this technique, we must admit to some scepticism.

The practitioners of the Women's Therapy Centres in London and New York adopted more traditional methods of counselling and therapy to treat women with eating disorders. They too view the mother-daughter relationship as central to eating disorder but mobilise a differently focussed theory of individuation in order to develop treatment techniques. Dana and Lawrence assert:

> The shame and agony involved in vomiting up the nourishment is a compensation, a suitable punishment, for having greedily swallowed it in the first place. It is not just that too much food has been consumed and the fear of becoming fat makes vomiting inevitable ... It is that needs have been perceived which are so terrifying that they must simultaneously be denied ... It is about having a clean, neat good, un-needy appearance which conceals behind it a messy, needy, bad part, which must be hidden away.[33]

The model utilised by the Women's Therapy Centre explains bingeing and purging in Kleinian terms. The split in the female ego that activates eating disorder is seen as being related to to the baby's early relation to the breast: its desire to swallow the breast (to incorporate it, to be sure of it) simultaneous with its fear that this destructive neediness might damage the source of love.[34] Susie Orbach reinforces this analysis in both *Hunger Strike,* and *Outside In ... Inside Out,*[35] co-edited with Louise Eichenbaum.

These descriptions of bingeing and purgeing, as being related to the defensive ego mechanisms developed by the baby's relationship to the breast, have strong parallels to both Payne's and Gillespie's reading of the mackintosh fetishist. In chapter three we outlined how the mackintosh was seen by analysts as a similar mechanism for saving the love object (mother's breast/parent imago) from sadistic attack.

The Psychosomatic Study Group of the Psychoanalytic Association of New York, while concentrating predominantly on anorexia in their book of essays, *Fear of Being Fat,* make some similar links. They argue that in bulimics, 'the gorging of food and laxatives reflects a loss of impulse control and is related to unsatisfied infantile yearnings for food, closeness and security, as well as agressive discharge'.[36] Again, there are clearly links to be made with the Kleinian explanation of bulimia in women as put forward by the Women's Therapy Centre, as well as with Payne's and Gillespie's reading of the male mackintosh fetishist. All locate inability to individuate (the 'me/not me' split) as a causal mechanism of bulimia and fetishism.

'Popular' feminists working on eating disorder, as well as the treatises written by the psychiatric profession, locate identity conflicts and issues about separation as central to eating disorder. Kim Chernin, for example, as mentioned earlier suggests that eating obsessions have all the elements of a rite of passage gone wrong. She says that women fail to move from one stage in the life cycle to the next and get caught up with food, hooked on their relationship to it.[37]

Most of the work that has been done on anorexics and bulimics in recent years has focussed upon the college student, since that is often where the syndrome is first seen to manifest itself. College, unlike school, expects individuals to take responsiblity for themselves and is perhaps the first big 'separation' for many women from parental-style authority. It is at this point, in adolescence, that the regression to the earlier phase of orality seems to be activated - often in quite epidemic proportions. This work on college students is important because it surveys some of the cultural characteristics of the widespread proportions of bulimia, rather than locating all its arguments on the evidence of 'exceptional' cases. The adolescent student, of course, moving away from home possibly for the first time, is undergoing exactly the 'rites de passage' Chernin describes. Melanie Katzman describes a bulimic student, Rebecca, as using the bulimic ritual as a way of avoiding the autonomy her new life demanded from her:

> The bulimia, as it slowly insinuated itself into Rebecca's life, provided a welcome relief from this tenuous, dizzying position. In an inflexible daily schedule of eating and exercise she discovered a retreat from the burdensome chore of self-directed living. The bulimic ritual offered a safe structure wherein she might 'go on automatic', relinquish her responsibilities, and create a self-controlled world, a temporary respite. The loss of the stabilising family system was compensated for by the substitution of a mind-numbing panacea rooted in rigid regimentation ... Rebecca main-

tained her dependency by transferring it from the family to a self-deluding reliance on the mythical power of caloric computations and a rigorous exercise regimen. All meaning and control derived from the strict adherence to this guiding bulimic mythology. It was her existential security blanket.[38]

Katzman also explains bulimia as involving problems with identity and individuation. Her reading of Chernin's *The Hungry Self* and Orbach's earlier *Fat is a Feminist Issue* is central to her explanation. Bulimia is connected to the daughter's oscillating feelings of panic and guilt. Guilt is experienced at the choice of surpassing the mother, showing her up by doing better, and thereby leaving her behind. Panic ensues from the fear of remaining with her, and thus also becoming frustrated and unfulfilled.

Object relation models focus on surpassing the mother as the cause of the symptoms, because they describe individuation as separation from the mother (the mother's breast). We prefer to describe individuation as the me/not me split rather than the separation from the mother, since it points more to the consequent threat of exposure of the infant self (and hence to its fear of a narcissistic wound). This shift also moves away from seeming to constantly blame the mother. However, we would agree that the sucking becomes a safe activity, which is regressed to if and when the psychic trauma occurs.

The two strands of explanation which we have been discussing, in fact, are connected and link into each other. The psychoanalytic explanations need to also embrace the cultural change in female norms and to acknowledge the changing social roles of women as well as the expansion of the codes of femininity. More is available to the young female students of the 1980s than may have been to the students of the 1950s and 1960s, but more is also being demanded of them. [39]

As we began by saying, most psychoanalytic readings of bulimia see it as in some way due to a faulty transaction of the individuation-separation process: anorexics may be denying the separation process; bulimics, by disavowing it, are allowed a significantly more comfortable social compromise. Bulimia is, we would argue, not a conflict[40] as with anorexia, but a compromise, a creative coping mechanism. And, we would also argue that it follows a very similar path to sexual fetishism in the pattern of its disavowal.

Sperling noted the similarity between bulimia and fetishism although in 1968 she wished to make a distinction 'between childhood fetishism and sexual fetishism'.[41] Considering psychosomatic disorders, within which she includes 'vomiting anorexics'(this is before bulimia was diagnosed as a separate disorder), Sperling argued that the sufferers regress to a need to control their transitional objects as if they were fetishes. The case study she cites is of a girl who ate hair and subsequently, with the onset of her menses, began cyclic vomiting, subsequently developing into a 'vomiting anorexic'. Sperling analyses this behaviour within a Freudian framework: she argues that the vomiting was due to the trauma of the little girl's passage through the castration complex and that the hair eaten symbolised the pubic hair 'hiding' the mother's phallus. Although we would want to question why the little girl was going through such a classic male castration reaction, we find it fascinating that Sperling's case study reveals a vomiting eating disorder that also incorporates a fetish. [42]

We have, in passing, noted that some other of the fetishists also had eating disorders : the female fetishist with white socks, of the Lacanian study group of Paraguay, was a bulimic; one of Gillespie's male fetishists would at times rush off and compulsively gorge on cream cakes.[43] Since no one has ever tried to connect bulimia and sexual fetishism, the significance of this has never been picked up on before.

Bulimia has been diagnosed, predominantly by various Kleinian-related theorists (who have done the bulk of the work on eating disorders), as stemming from a faulty individuation transaction. This flaw becomes activated when the child's narcissistic self-image is challenged (often with contradictory messages to go out and succeed *and* remain passive and 'feminine'). Unable to deal with the demands placed upon it in adolescence, the person regresses and, displacing the oral drive for nutrition, uses food as a form of transitional object. Such a coping mechanism, though irrational and compulsive, nevertheless allows a compromise that prevents the bulimic from having to face more threatening unconscious anxieties.

Bulimia and Sensuality

Our earlier discussion of sexual fetishism, while incorporating all the elements that we have been discussing above, also explains how sexual orgasm is achieved from an object which becomes the sole focus of the sexual aim. We now want to argue that an important further parallel between bulimia and sexual fetishism is that they both allow the experience of direct, unmediated and unsublimated sensual pleasure by their doing-and-undoing processes. The gratification is oral, in the case of the food fetishist, and genital in the case of the sexual fetishist, but some research has in fact argued for an interesting cross-over of the two drives in its analysis of bulimia.

Alan Goodsitt has taken up the question of whether bulimics *are* using food strictly as a transitional object. He argues instead that there is a strong auto-erotic element in the bingeing,

> using the term auto-erotic in a loose sense to refer to an internal state of stimulation characterized by a pressurised, driven demand for discharge and satisfied by the individual. [44]

Goodsitt argues that auto-erotic elements in bingeing are accomplished by the *extreme* sensations of hunger and fullness experienced by both anorexics and bulimics.[45] He suggests that binge-eating to distract or subdue rising tensions has strong parallels to the baby's sucking of its thumb (an auto-erotic stimulation) and not to its clutching at a piece of blanket (transitional object). Goodsitt ends by citing the case study of Dr Gedo whose bulimic patient shifted from using bingeing to pacify anxiety, to orgasmic pleasure:

> His patient suffered from severe deficits in the capacity for self-organization and self-regulation of her internal states. She was thus subject to experiences of over-stimulation and ate as an emergency measure to pacify her mounting tensions. Later in therapy, the function and nature of the bulimia changed. It shifted from an obligatory emergency measure used to combat tensions to an aspect of sexuality, a perversion accompanied by orgasm. The unconscious fantasy concomitant with the distention of her abdomen became that of identification with her idealised pregnant mother. This functioned to restore her self-esteem ... Dr Gedo (1982: personal communication) believed he was no longer treating an eating disorder as before, but rather an aspect of sexuality.[46]

Eating disorders have usually been seen as something to combat sexuality, to help deny or pacify it. Whereas anorexics and the obese may 'deny' sexuality, it has been noted that bulimics are often sexually active. What we want to argue is that some bulimics use food as a redirection of the pleasure principle, in exactly the same way as fetishists use sex, and that bingeing also carries with it an important element of sensual gratification.

Oral gratification, we would argue, is a re-direction of the pleasure principle experienced in sexual gratification. Unlike sublimation, where the urge is denied and moved onto a metaphorical plane, in bingeing the pleasure is experienced in the plane of the real. Even though some analysts seem to have missed this point, bulimics themselves have been aware of the connections between food and sex for years:

She also connected her eating impulses with the need for sex. She would gorge herself, often on ice-cream, 'like a baby', with a feeling of oral greediness and desire which she compared to masturbation.[47]

Often I used to go out and eat for my sensual, sexual experience of the day. I actually would be turned on by it.[48]

Reviewing the Connection Between Sexual and Hunger Drives

The parallels between the sexual and hunger drives, the contiguity of the two, has been identified by most psychiatric analyses of infantile development. Freud famously wrote:

The satisfaction of the erotogenic zone is associated, in the first instance, with the satisfaction of the need for nourishment. To begin with, sexual activity attaches itself to functions serving the purpose of self-preservation and does not become independent of them until later. No one who has seen a baby sinking back satiated from the breast and falling asleep with flushed cheeks and a blissful smile can escape the reflection that this picture persists as the prototype of the expression of sexual satisfaction in later life ... There are thus good reasons why a child sucking at his mother's breast has become the prototype of every relation of love. The finding of an object is in fact a refinding of it.[49]

In the earliest stage then, psychoanalysis argues, the baby exists in the *oral phase*, where its libidinal pleasure and its experience of satisfaction, comes from sucking. Between the ages of two and four, the libido develops into the *anal phase* and focusses on the expulsion or retention of faeces. Only in the third, the *genital phase*, does the libido locate itself on the genitals.

The link between oral and sexual gratification, at least in the first years, is thus an orthodoxy within all the schools of psychoanalysis. It therefore becomes a legitimate target for regression. Havelock Ellis came tantalisingly near to making the connection between a boy's sexual fantasies and a girl's eating disorder in 1910. He linked a young man's erotic symbolism with discussion of a young woman's anorexia, connecting the two with the sentence: 'It is worthy of remark that the instinct for nutrition, when restrained, may exhibit something of an analogous symbolism, though in a minor degree to that of sex.' Nonetheless, the paragraph on the young woman, Nadia, concludes with the unsubstantiated assertion : 'the deviations of the instinct of nutrition are, however, confined within the narrow limits, and, in the nature of things, hunger, unlike sexual desire, can not easily accept a fetish'.[50]

We, of course, argue differently from Havelock Ellis, and suggest that the hunger drive can accept a fetish. Overall we argue that food can be the object of fetishism, and that some cases of bulimia (thought not all) do in fact constitute something comparable to sexual fetishism in the fourth degree.

Given that we are dealing with an actual object, food, we have been questioned as to why we do not just term it an addiction. The reason we analyse it as fetishism, instead of addiction, is that addiction has a clear chemical explanation for the fixation. Alcohol itself, for example, is provenly addictive. Alcoholics drink not for the experience of drinking, *per se*, but for the chemical effects of being drunk. Bulimics eat for the experience of bingeing (since the food is almost immediately purged). And there are no 'chemical' explanations of why they should choose biscuits, cakes, and milk products for example. Bulimics often say they use soft food such as icecream and puddings entirely, or at the end, to enable them to vomit the food more easily. Alongside the pragmatic functions of the food it may also accommodate the fantasy element of returning to the breast (ie, not having to make the me/not me distinction) and hence a preference for such soft, milky foods.

Whatever dysfunctional psychoanalytic reasons move the addict to take up the addiction, psychoanalysis is not puzzled by the processes of ingesting alcohol or heroin. The effects given are easily explained. The effects gained by eating enormous amounts of non-addictive food are less easily explained and so the perverse strategies of the bulimic point to the unconscious's distortion of oral needs. Some work has been done on the possibility that sugar and chocolate can be 'addictive' to many women, but this can not explain the bulimic's behaviour, since she would purge the substances before they were adequately ingested. Imagine an alcoholic who drank a bottle of whisky, and then made himself throw it up again before he felt the effects of getting drunk. This illustration demonstrates both the perverseness of the bulimic's strategy and the inadequacy of the notion of addiction to explain the behaviour. Addicts 'do'; bulimics 'do-and-undo'.

Most women recognise that food is alluring and dangerous and has sexual connotations. This central understanding is played around with by many of our cultural discourses that connect food and copulation, from jokes told by female comics to adverts which link food and sex to sell products. As we write, the Häagan Dasz ice-cream adverts (see Illustration 8) are causing controversy for their sexually explicit couple and the literally orgasmic effects of the icecream. Many newspapers are running diet sheets that connect food and sex. The *Daily Express* has run 'The Good Sex Diet'[51] and during the same week, the *Sunday Mirror* ran 'The Lovesexy Diet'. It has even been argued that some advertisements acknowledge that 'for women, chocolate is superior to male company in every way'.[52]

We wanted to do our own research as to whether or not women typically have such cravings around food, indulging in 'binges' (that only becomes pathological in certain extremes) and so we organised a brief survey.[53]

Women, Sex and Food: Our Survey Findings

Our thesis was that this bingeing behaviour was practised by a wide proportion of women, not only those with eating disorders, and was in fact a common experience within our culture. Food is a vehicle for women to pleasure themselves ('indulging themselves') and carries messages of being both alluring and forbidden, without being actually taboo. Our survey women certainly found it much easier to talk about food than about sex, even within the anonymity of a questionnaire. In this brief, introductory survey, every returned questionnaire answered the section on food cravings, usually with a high degree of specificity (Marks and Spencer's products did exceptionally well). However, 29 per cent left the section on sex unanswered. Of the 71 per cent who filled in the section on sex, 60 per cent never revealed their cravings or fantasies to either their partners or their friends. Only 21 per cent of all the answers in the food section kept their cravings and binges a secret.

Chocolate headed the list of 'guilty pleasures,'. 73 per cent named it as a source of pleasure.[54] Only potato chips, nuts, cream, and salad dressing came anywhere near a significant number (15 per cent each); otherwise the choices were specific to the individual: mince pies, smoked salmon, fudge, babyfood, etc. In a minority of cases, the expensiveness of the items played a part in their feelings of guilt and self-indulgence, but overall it was the calorie content - the fattening properties - that they identified as being the thing that made them feel 'guilty' and often led to them consuming the items in secret. The survey findings reflect the power of Western culture's reification of slenderness, an evaluation which the bingers felt they were transgressing.

We were curious to see how women internalised the cultural evaluations of consuming food, so we asked them how they described their binges to themselves. The answers covered the whole range of responses to being transgressive, from the celebratory to the ashamed. There were positive explanations such as 'hedonism' and 'treating myself'; through to 'an endearing failing - I'm only human' (a favourite ending, this one, that came up time and again); to the much more negative 'pig-out' and 'shameful, guilty, weak!'

In order to satisfy the desire when it came upon them, some might go to the lengths of walking three-quarters of a mile to buy it; others get up in the early hours of the morning, dress, and drive to an all-night garage shop; another woman retrieves discarded jars from the dustbin, in order to scrape out the last remaining traces; others starve all day to justify to themselves being able to indulge in the desired food. It was clear that many 'ordinary' women in our survey felt disturbingly 'out of control' around food.

Everyone cited similar circumstances for bingeing – while feeling depressed or bored, during pre-menstrual tension, or while experiencing themselves as unwanted, unloved, undervalued. Bingeing filled up 'that empty feeling'. A few answers also described having the craving in the opposite circumstances – when they were busy, hyperactive and wanted to 'reward' themselves. 71 per cent would *not* prefer to be doing anything else, when they are having a binge. Of the others, having sex and buying clothes cropped up as answers.

Those who answered on the sex section included 29 per cent who said they would prefer to be doing something else, usually something to do with status, indulging in conspicuous wealth, power, or even revenge. One specific example (which probably had a lot to do with the survey being done in London during June) would specifically have preferred to be 'winning Wimbledon' rather than having sex. The favourite sexual fantasies were bondage ones. 30 per cent of those answering expressed a fantasy of being tied up. 20 per cent fantasised about having sex in exotic places, like Brazil, and 15 per cent about having sex with a complete stranger. For the most part, these were secret fantasies since, as we have already mentioned, 60 per cent never told their sexual fantasies to their partners.

Curious to know if there were any parts of their lovers' bodies that the women favoured, in a more traditionally fetishistic sense, we asked what parts of their partner they fantasized about. Just under a third of those answering the sex section, said they did have fantasies about parts of their partners' bodies. The penis was a recurrent and dominant fantasy object of 50 per cent of the survey, while 20 per cent also said muscular arms and another 20 per cent, the face. Bottom, back, neck, and chest also were mentioned, in that order of prefer-ence. We noticed a lack of specificity of detail, a lack of warmth or excitement, in the answers on sex in contrast to the answers on food. Except, that is, for the answers which managed to combine both food and sex: one woman's fantasy was of having maple syrup poured over her body and having her partner massage it in then lick it off. Another woman's fantasy included fucking the whole England soccer team after getting them to lick chocolate off her body at Wembley to a packed crowd cheering her through it. On the whole, however, the discussion of sexual cravings were soft-focused or generalised, when they were not being denied altogether, exhibiting little of the devoted specificity found in the section on food (eg, Marks and Spencer's whole brazil nuts, rather than just any old brazil nuts). There was also little of the disturbance and sense of 'danger' in the descriptions about sex, perhaps because on the whole they remained safely within fantasy.

Food was clearly viewed as the more 'speakable' outlet for women, though one often surrounded by guilt, for pleasuring themselves. While we are wary of claiming too much based on our survey, this response indicated to us that many ordinary women do use food as coping mechanism. The practice only appears as a pathologised 'eating disorder' when the compulsion becomes extreme and debilitating.[55] The redirection of oral stimulation from nutrition to pleasure is thus a common cultural experience that forms a whole continuum of degrees, from giving oneself a chocolate as a reward to the compulsive bingeing of the entire contents of a supermarket trolley.

The question of why women form the majority in eating disorders whereas men form the majority in sexual fetishism, is clearly one that needs to be addressed. In the following chapter we look at the cultural issues surrounding women's relationship to food and why it may impinge on their notions of identity. In this chapter we have argued for bulimia as a food fetishism, a fourth fetishism to add to the earlier three (anthropological, commodity, sexual), and one in which women predominate as practitioners. On the grounds that it functions in ways analogous to those identified in the models of sexual fetishism, we argue that some women 'pervert' the oral drive for sustenance to assuage narcissistic feelings of inadequacy in relation to their self-identity. In chapter five we begin to tease out how food relates to the cultural codes of femininity, in order to understand why coping with this individual faulty 'ego transaction', through bingeing and purging, has developed from almost nothing to relatively epidemic proportions since the 1960s. We look, in other words, at how culture impinges on identity, on how identity is inscribed through the cultural codes available.

If bulimia is a food fetishism, and this food fetishism has only recently developed and become an epidemic, then a psychoanalytic model is not sufficient, in itself, to fully discuss the phenomenon, because it is unable to incorporate change (the epidemic). On the other hand, a sociological model which can account for change is not sufficient because it is unable to grasp the irrational displacements of the unconscious (the fetishism). What is needed is a model that is able to structure the two discourses and include both in its analysis. Just as saying that women fetishise sexually ends up in a challenge to the phallocentrism of the traditional psychoanalytic models, saying that bulimia is a food fetishism points to the need for a psychoanalytic model that can incorporate cultural change.

Emily Apter points out that in the nineteenth century, a common object choice of shoe fetishists was the 'sabot', the heavy working-shoe worn by servants (to whose charge the children would often be relegated). Times change. The prevalence of employing servants ended with the first world war, and after the second world war fashion focused on 'feminizing' women (to leave the factory work for the de-mobbed men). The icon of shoe fetishism from the 1950s and 1960s, has been high heels. The type of the object fetishised thus varies from culture to culture. Gosselin and Wilson lamented the loss of variety in the objects chosen between the nineteenth and twentieth centuries. The nineteenth century saw an enormous variety of fetish objects – hair, fur, feathers, silk, handkerchieves – whereas the fetish groups they canvassed in 1980 fell into only two categories, leather and/or rubber.[56] If there can be shifts in the types of objects chosen as fetishes, can there not also be shifts in the objects themselves, a shift onto food? We answer in the affirmative, that food can be fetishised, and that the shift is largely culturally constructed.

Notes

1 Sigmund Freud, 'Three Essays on Sexuality', *Standard Edition*, Vol 7, Hogarth, London 1953, p182.

2 Shelley Winters, interviewed by Christina Appleyard, *Daily Mirror*, 2.10.89.

3 Kim Chernin, *The Hungry Self*, Virago, London 1987, p166–7.

4 Susie Orbach, *Hunger Strike: The Anorectic Struggle as a Metaphor of our Age*, Faber, London 1986.

5 L. Kaplan, *Female Perversions*, Pandora, London 1991, p10.

6 Eating disorder was being observed in the eighteenth and nineteenth century: and there has been discussion about 'Holy Anorexics', women who were so religiously devout that they did not eat.

7 Initially it was diagnosed as;

a. Recurrent episodes of binge-eating (rapid consumption of a large amount of food in a discrete period of time, usually less than two hours).

b. At least three of the following:

i. Consumption of high-calorific, easily ingested food during a binge.

ii. Inconspicuous eating during a binge.

iii. Termination of such eating episodes for abdominal pain, sleep, social interruption, or self-induced vomiting.

iv. Repeated attempts to lose weight by severely restrictive diets, self-induced vomiting, or use of cathartics or diuretics.

v. Frequent weight fluctuations greater than 10 pounds due to alternate binges and fasts.

c. Awareness that the eating pattern is abnormal and fear of not being able to stop eating voluntarily.

d. Depressed mood and self-deprecating thoughts following eating binges.

e. The bulimic episodes are not due to anorexia nervosa or any known physical disorder.

However, this was felt to leave out the concern for body-shape and the handicapping nature of the syndrome so it was revised to incorporate these elements.

The above list appeared in Strober and Yager, 'Some Perspectives on the Diagnosis of Bulimia Nervosa', in *The Bulimic College Student: Evaluation, Treatment and Prevention*, L. C. Whitaker and W. N. Davis (eds), Haworth, New York 1989, p10.

8 W. Stewart Agras, *Eating Disorders: Management of Obesity, Bulimia and Anorexia Nervosa*, Pergamon, London 1987, p6.

9 Mira Dana and Marilyn Lawrence, *Women's Secret Disorder: A New Understanding of Bulimia*, Grafton, London 1988, p41.

10 Strober and Yager, *op cit*, p10.

11 R. Stoller, in *The Erotic Imagination, op cit.*

12 *Ibid*, p158.

13 Dana and Lawrence, *op cit*, pp115–6.

14 Hilde Bruch, *Eating Disorders: Obesity, Anorexia Nervosa, and the Person Within*, Routledge, London 1974.

15 *Ibid*, p50.

16 *Ibid*, p45.

17 *Ibid*, p208.

18 See for example: Sara Gilbert, *Pathology of Eating: Psychology and Treatment*, Routledge, London 1986; Glucksman, 'Psychiatric Observations of Obesity', *Advances in Psychosomatic Medicine*, 7, 1972, pp194–216; Joyce Slochower, *Excessive Eating: the role of emotions and the environment*, Human Sciences Press, New York 1983.

19 Slochower, *op cit*, p29.

20 B. French, *Coping with Bulimia*, Thorsons, Wellingborough 1984, p29.

21 *Ibid*, p59.

22 Troy Cooper, 'Anorexia and Bulimia: The Political and the Personal', in Marilyn Lawrence (ed), *Fed Up and Hungry*, Women's Press, London 1987, p176.

23 *Ibid*, p175.

24 R.A. Gordon, 'Bulimia: A Sociocultural Interpretation', in *The Bulimic*

College Student, pp41–55; the theory is developed in further detail in his *Anorexia and Bulimia: Anatomy of a Social Epidemic*, Blackwells, London 1990.

25 C.L. Johnson, D.H. Tobin, and S.L. Steinberg, 'Etiological, Developmental and Treatment Considerations for Bulimia', *Bulimic College Student*, pp57–73.

26 M Boskind-Lodahl, 'Cinderella's Stepsisters: A Feminist Perspective on Anorexia Nervosa and Bulimia', *Signs*, 2 ,Winter 1976, p346. This argument is continued in *Bulimarexia: The Binge/Purge Cycle*, Marlene Boskind-White and William C White Jr, Norton, New York 1983.

27 Troy Cooper is good at analysing how bulimia is seen as more of a 'failing', a self-indulgence that could be prevented, than anorexia which is often half-admired for its self-denial.

28 *International Journal of Eating Disorders* 3 (3), Spring 1984, p42.

29 *Ibid*, p43.

30 The obese woman, on the other hand, may be symbolically trying, by becoming 'outsize', to deny the fact that she has less power than men as a consequence of patriarchal relations in the West.

31 'Parents of Bulimic Women', *International Journal of Eating Disorders*, 3 (4), Summer 1984, p5.

32 Silverman *et al*, 'Effect of Subliminal Stimulation of Symbiotic Fantasies on Behaviour Modification Treatment of Obesity', *Journal of Consulting and Clinical Psychology*, 46 (1978), pp432–41.

33 Dana and Lawrence, *op cit*, p42.

34 *Ibid*, p81–82.

35 Susie Orbach, *Hunger Strike*, and Orbach and Eichenbaum, *Outside In … Inside Out: Women's Psychology, a Feminist Psychoanalytic Approach*, Penguin, Harmondsworth 1982.

36 Ira L. Mintz, 'Psychoanalytic Description: The Clinical Picture of Anorexia Nervosa and Bulimia', in *Fear of Being Fat: The Treatment of Anorexia Nervosa and Bulimia*, C. P. Wilson, C. Hogan and I. Mintz (eds), Aronson, New York 1985–88, p87.

37 K. Chernin, *op cit.*

38 Melanie Katzman, 'Is it true eating makes you feel better?: A Naturalistic Assessment of Food Consumption and its Effect on Stress', in Leighton Whitaker (ed), *Bulimic College Student*, Haworth Press 1989, pp208–9.

39 Though it should be added that this is true of most young women in the West and that bulimia is not just a college student phenomenon. Bulimia usually manifests itself at a later age in the sufferer than anorexia. It is agreed that bulimia, as it has emerged in the West, has no specific race or socio-class connections (as anorexia supposedly has). Bulimics appear to come from all classes, races, generations and walks of life. Dana and Lawrence argue that they work with women 'from a variety of class and cultural backgrounds', p16.

40 Dana and Lawrence specify a conflict: 'Given that bulimia seems so clearly to be a symptom symbolising conflict … ', p27.

41 'Trichotillomania, Trichopagy and Cyclic Vomiting', *International Journal of Psycho-Analysis* 49 (1968), pp682–90.

42 In 'Transference Neurosis in patients with psychosomatic disorders', Sperling argues that both perversions and vomiting anorexia are psychosomatic disorders and so part of a similar problem. *Psychoanalytic Quarterly* 36 (1967), pp342–55.

43 See Gillespie, 'A contribution to the study of fetishism'.

44   *International Journal of Eating Disorders* 2, Spring 1983, p51.

45   'To accomplish this, the [anorexic] resorts to primitive pathological defenses of denial, splitting and disavowal. The body's basic need for nourishment to remain healthy is disavowed. Delusions of fatness are justified. The patient actually treats her own bodily needs cruelly, or at best indifferently. She splits off her body as part of herself. One may be justified in characterising this relationship to the body as sado-masochism.' *Ibid*, p56. This is an argument with which we would strongly concur, apart from the term 'disavowal'. We would see the rejection as a denial, a complete repression, rather than as a compromise with reality that allows the delusion to stay in place.

46   *Ibid*, pp58–9.

47   Dana and Lawrence, *op cit*, p269, describing a vomiting anorexic.

48   S. Abraham and D. Llwellyn-Jones, Oxford University Press, Oxford 1987, p28. Sex therapist A.V. Offit also made the connection between food and sexual 'hunger'. She did not present a very rigorous psychoanalytic model of eating disorder, and almost seems to conceptualise the bulimic as cross-eyed as a consequence of brain circuit overload. Nevertheless Offit does manage to recognise the redirection of the sexual pleasure principle in terms of the relationship to oral gratification:

> The most prevalent disorder, the act of excessive eating, of continually placing food in one's mouth, tasting, chewing, and swallowing, so resembles intercourse that the most successful sex manual of the last decade took its title from a cookbook. A sexually troubled woman may easily make the transition from being afraid to fill her vagina to cramming her mouth with alternative delights ... Both men and women may use the act of eating to distract from sexual urges; sexual hunger may become permanently confused with a call to the larder. As odd as these mix-ups may sound to the layman, they do not surprise psychiatrists. We human beings possess so many brain circuits that it is a wonder more of them don't get crossed.

49   Freud, 'Three Essays on Sexuality', p182.

50   Havelock Ellis, *Studies in the Psychology of Sex*, Vol 3, p7.

51   See for example, *Daily Express*, 3.9.91 and 4.9.91.

52   Lucy Ellman, 'Love and the Coffee Mates', *New Statesman and Society*, 14.2.1992.

53   'Naughty but nice' survey conducted through Middlesex University, in 1991. We advertised for participants in the Middlesex University newspaper *North Circular*, and among our friends. The questionnaires were distributed to both heterosexual and known lesbian circles, to ensure that we canvassed a range of sexualities in relation to food. We sent out hundreds of questionnaires but received only 35 per cent completed. Although we would not claim our survey constitutes any form of scientific proof, given the narrow range of the sample, we do feel it helps to illustrate the way some women relate to food in our culture. We have noted that many much larger and more rigorous surveys come to similar findings.

54   Chocolate contains phenylethylamine, a chemical which the body produces when the person 'falls in love', and so has clear sensual connotations: 'research from the New York State Psychiatric Institute reveals that chocolate produces the same chemical effects as love', G. Roth, *Feeding the Hungry Heart*, Grafton Books, London 1986, p22. Also argued in *40 Minutes: Chocolate*, BBC2 Television, 18.12.90.

55   '50% of women binge, 25% of women vomit - it is a very normal behaviour (for women) that has been labelled abnormal'. Bulimia expert on *Diana the End of*

a Fairytale? made by ITN for ITV, 6.9.92. Although we might query the figures here, we would concur with the comment.

56   Gosselin and Wilson, *Sexual Variations: Fetishism, Sado-Masochism and Transvestism*, Faber, London 1980. The lack of variety may well have been because they canvassed groups self-selected by their prediliction for leather and rubber, e.g. the Mackintosh Society. The psychoanalytic case studies do suggest a slightly wider object choice.

5

Food Fetishism:
The Cultural Arguments

Women have long since made the choice between men and chocolate and have chosen chocolate. You don't need a condom, in fact, part of the pleasure is in taking the wrapper off. You control the frequency and the quality of the experience, and the calories make it dangerous. Ads acknowledge that for most women, chocolate is superior to male company in every way. *Lucy Ellman* [1]

To displace the pleasure of sex into the pleasure of food is peculiarly appropriate. It still focusses on the hungry clamour of the body. *Margaret Reynolds* [2]

If we are attempting to map a cultural framework onto the psychoanalytic model, in order to fully understand why bulimia may have developed in the later twentieth century, one of the first things we need to investigate is what food means to us. We need, in other words, to comprehend how food is encoded within our society. Once we have some idea of how food impinges on the codes of femininity, we can begin to understand why some women may have developed food fetishism as a coping mechanism to disavow certain anxieties about identity. Further, we can go on to question how to adequately incorporate cultural change into the psychoanalytic model.

Talk Dirty to Me: Food Metaphors

Women are well aware of the connections between food and sex. A recent collection of women's erotica edited by Margaret Reynolds, as well as including fiction from a great variety of authors, from Sappho and George Sand to Christina Rossetti and Angela Carter, also included recipes by the cookery writer Elizabeth David. [3] We were not surprised by this. For many women, reading about food, we would argue, is almost comparable with reading about sex. In many cultures nouns about eating food are frequently used to explain sexual practice.

Similar words for consuming food are used to describe copulation and recur across a variety of different cultures. Few English-speaking lovers ask for the Latinate 'cunnilingus' or 'fellatio' but instead use their own phrases, from words like 'eat me' to 'suck my lollipop', to direct their partners to their sexual needs. Jeremy MacClancy, who has looked at the behaviour of many different nationalities who perceive eating and love-making in the same linguistic terms, observes:

> We say we have lusty appetites, we hunger for love, feast our eyes, eat out our hearts, and suffer devouring passions. Vulgar Frenchmen do not seduce their womenfolk, they fry them *(faire frire)* or put in the pot *(passer a la casserole)* ... The Ancient Greek term *parothides* can mean either 'hors-d'oeuvre'or 'foreplay' ... Among the Yoruba to 'eat' and to 'marry' are covered by the same verb ... The Yanomami of the Amazon use one word to mean 'eat like a pig' and 'copulate excessively' ... The Ilahita Arapesh of Papua New Guinea make the link between food and sex in a rather different way, for they have the saying 'Cooked meat goes in the mouth and *down* the body: raw meat goes in the vulva and *up* the body.'[4]

Anthropologist Levi Strauss further illustrates this point. Writing in the 1960s, before MacClancy, he shows how food and sex are linguistically connected by some of the Indian tribes in South America:

> The Tupari express coitus by locutions whose literal meaning is 'to eat the vagina' *(kuma ka)*, 'to eat the penis' *(ang ka)*. It is the same in Mundurucu. The Caingang dialects of Southern Brazil have a verb that means both to 'copulate' and 'eat'; in certain contexts it may be necessary to specify 'with the penis', in order to avoid ambiguity. A Cashibo myth relates how a man had no sooner been created than he asked for food; and the sun taught him how to sow or plant maize, the banana tree, and other edible plants. Then the man asked his penis, 'and what would you like to eat?' The penis replied, 'The female organ.'
>
> However, it is worthy to note that in the myths just discussed the sexual code should be apparent only in its masculine references...When the references are feminine, the sexual code becomes latent and is concealed beneath the alimentary code.[5]

What is especially interesting, in such cross-cultural data, is the way that sex and the food are gendered. Food is seen as the women's realm and sex as the men's. In the West, statistics reveal a similar gendering: whereas the majority of sexual fetishists are male, the majority of food fetishists are female.[6]

Cultural connotations associated with food associations are taken for granted and entrenched in the 'bricks and mortar of daily life'[7] so that even courtship is connected to food rituals. Just as food and sex are connected and inform 'commonsense'[8], food is metonymically connected to 'courting'. In the West couples that are sexually attracted to each other, heterosexual, homosexual, lesbian, etc, often meet for a meal on the first date and thus feed before fornication.[9] MacClancy observes that in some non-Western groups, individuals are more up front about the connections between food and copulation, and it is intended that eating 'a meal together ... should to lead to intercourse'.[10]

The gendering of food in our 'culture of plenty' however, is more than just a 'natural' association of sex and food. Food associations are a site where gender distinctions can be enacted. MacClancy further cites a group of women surveyed in the North of England who, despite changing attitudes to sexual equality, admit they feel it is 'natural' to serve 'their husband and sons larger helpings of food and choicer cuts of meat'.[11] Indeed the relationship between meat and the meaning of masculinity has been something that has fascinated feminists for years. Nicole Ward Jouve, for instance, when writing about the 'Yorkshire Ripper' has observed that 'real' men in the North of England partake enthusiastically of offal and tripe, because it is expected of them and learned by one generation from the other. She quotes John Sutcliffe (father of serial sex murderer Peter Sutcliffe) boasting that, 'it has stood me in good stead to this day that I can eat *anything* out of a butchers, be it trotters, or be it cow-heel or be it tripe or chicklins – anything at all in the offal line. I *love* it ... man's food'.[12] His son Peter didn't like offal and his father 'saw this lack of appreciation of man's food as one of the many signs of his weakness'.[13]

This gendering is reinforced by the way food is advertised, as we will go on to explore, for in post-industrial Western society food is big business. It is regulated by the profit motive, despite the fact that the consequences of this form of organisation include food shortages in many parts of the world, resulting in millions of people starving to death. In most countries the conglomerates in the food industries influence political decisions about food production as well as about national diet. In Britain, for example, four big retail outlets control the supermarkets.[14] Overall in the West we consume far too much food altogether.

This culture of 'plenty'[15] has paradoxically produced many diet-related illnesses from obesity to heart disease. It might seem ironic to some that the most expensive health farms in the world offer a third world diet (lots of grains and pulses as well as walking) in order to promote good health, but it has long been recognised by the medical profession that the rich Western diet is very bad for health. While half the world starves the other half tries to lose weight. The parallel is ignored by the diet industry which continues to make millions that could be better spent. Jeremy MacClancy, for instance, estimates that 'more money is spent each year in the West on slimming aids than is needed to feed all the world's hungry'.[16]

In 1990 in Britain alone sales of saccharine, calorie counted meals, excercise aids, slimming club fees and best-selling diet books reached an all time high. The diet industry was estimated at £850 million and growing by an average of ten per cent per annum.[17] This sort of turnover, we would argue, is comparable with the pornography industry in terms both of the economic investment, and the proliferation of related gendered fantasies.

Most Western women experience food as a site of struggle. They have easy access to food to accommodate the means of survival, as well as pleasure from eating. But they also know from cultural messages about what it means to be a woman, that they must exercise restraint around food. For many women, then, food appears to provoke more compelling fantasies and conversations than sex and is perceived as just as alluring and dangerous.[18]

Food Fetishism and the Culture of Slenderness

One explanation for female eroticization of food, therefore, could relate to the culture of slenderness itself. Tabloid newspapers as well as women's magazines from *Elle* to *Women's Realm* intersperse lavish images of food and pages of messages to swallow alongside those which explain how a new diet or exercise programme can help find the 'real you'. Ros Coward has pointed out that gourmet representations in magazines aimed at women constitute a sort of 'food pornography'.[19] Lavish recipes and images of food are packaged alongside pages which explain how diet or keeping fit can discover your new 'self'. This produces the sort of logic whereby individuals go to bed with recipe books whilst trying to keep on a strict diet and indulge in food, rather than sexual, fantasies.

Ros Coward points out that food imagery in women's magazines consists of lush food photographs that are touched up to deny imperfections. Cropped close-ups of perfect pastry flakes upon which plump sugar soaked strawberries lie oozing with fresh cream, just waiting to be eaten, are designed to tempt our tastebuds through the visual 'prompt' to our hungry eyes. If it is not the abundance of flesh and juice hanging off the fat golden honey-roasted chicken breast that gets the reader going, then her eyes are seduced and infatuated by the perfect texture of the oh so dark chocolate mousse presented in glossy 'four colour' as a potential pudding. Of course four colours are vital. How else to illustrate all the different layers of chocolate on offer, and to emphasis the 'delicious wickedness', that the dessert may contain in terms of calories? This representation, and the effect of food imagery, is similar in many ways, to the way in which representations of women are given the soft focus treatment in pornography; perhaps the ways in which both deal in idealized forms of imagery to work upon the imagination are also similar. Dean Hollowood's 'bondage food photographs' (see Illustration 9) disturb the women's magazine genre because they do not present the usual codes associated with soft focus 'food porn'. Instead the illustrated vegetables in 'leather poses' overtly sexualise food in a far more disruptive manner than those familar food images that Ros Coward describes. Consequently, Hollowood's photographs drew many humorous, but nevertheless knowing, comments from women when they were exhibited at the ICA.[20]

Ros Coward suggests that the luscious food images, often found in women's magazines in between diet sheets (and thus representing the 'forbidden') are pleasurable because 'pictures of food provide a photographic genre geared towards sex. Like sexual pornography it is a regime of pleasure that is incomprehensible to the opposite sex'.[21] She goes on to point out that whereas sexual pornography offers the male reader/viewer a display of images which confirms men's sense of having power over women, food pornography has the opposite effect on females as readers and viewers. According to Coward, food pornography, 'indulges a pleasure that is linked to servitude and therefore confirms the subordinate position of women. Food porn cannot be used without guilt'.[22]

While we agree that images of food are often associated by women with erotic messages, the word 'pornography' – whose meaning is constantly being challenged and renegotiated by feminists – is perhaps inappropriate to describe the phenomenon or the pleasure. Further, the association of women, eroticism, and food needs to be examined more closely because there are a range of 'non-use' messages coming from the advertisers and producers of food. The ways

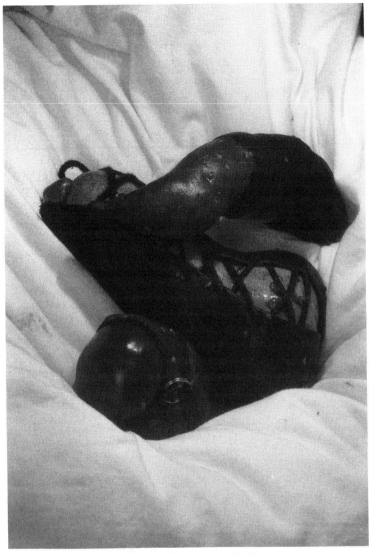

Bondage vegetables by Dean Hollowood

in which advertisements utilise and develop messages about the pleasures of food and sex are diverse.

Confectionary adverts, for example, frequently indicate that the pleasure of eating sweets is in itself a sexual experience. The notorious Cadbury's flake TV adverts of a woman's mouth consuming the phallicly-shaped chocolate, are only the most overt. But in this case the woman is also being sexualised; *she* is the consumable. As Ros Coward points out, the image of woman and food becomes blurred into an image of tempting sensuality, in a way that is customary in the commodification of women. Women consuming gourmet four-colour representations are a different phenomenon. There, the food is the desirable and consumable object, its full frontal pose promises a 'taste sensation' far beyond anything that the commodity itself possesses. The first uses women to sell chocolate (consumer fetishism of the erotic) the second uses the erotic pleasures around food (food fetishism), to sell to women. The recent Terry's chocolate TV advert of a woman attempting to sneak away to consume her chocolate bar mimics the way clandestine places are often sought out to conduct illicit love affairs. The advert carries the clear message that eating Terry's chocolate is as guilty and as pleasurable as casual sex. The underlying message of this ad, however, is more subversive: when the chocolate wrapper is flippantly discarded in the stationery cupboard after the female office worker's brief 'fling' with the chocolate, it implies that women can be as cavalier in their attitude towards chocolate as men often are in their sexual attitudes towards women.

But consumer fetishism of food also incorporates many other cultural messages about women's role as part of the sales pitch. The 'Naughty but Nice' cream cake campaign proved phenomenally successful by playing upon the dual elements of the sinful associated with women consuming calorific sweets. It managed to play upon both the world of secret desires and the anxieties about body shape normally utilised by the diet industry.

Advertisements for diet products play on female guilt and anxieties about body shape. As well as those adverts that promise 'you can enjoy the food you crave and watch your weight' (Lean Cuisine) other adverts for products like diet lemonade, mayonnaise or yogurt adopt a more subtle approach to subject/object identifications.

The diet product is often photographed as having 'female' curves itself, or the item is associated with idealised female figures. In some adverts, for example the Horlicks hot chocolate drink advert (see Illustration 10), women are not only connected with the product but

Consuming curves: Conflicting messages from the food industry

once again represented as the product. But here it is slenderness, rather than sexual pleasure, that is the desirable attribute used to sell the food commodity. Through the mode of address, potential customers are being persuaded to identify slenderness with 'consuming' the product. These messages, like the one accompanying St. Ivel Gold (see Illustration 10), communicate to cumstomers, at the level of the sign, that they too may have slender curves if only they consume the right products (rather than abstaining altogether). The language of consumerism is able to overcome the contradictions between 'eating' and 'slimming', transforming them into the same purpose. Critics from Raymond Williams to Judith Williamson have described this process as part of the 'magic' of advertising. [23]

The use of gender in the marketing of food commodities, through advertising, is widespread in Western culture and bears some relation to changing ideas about diet and healthcare. Indeed, discourses about healthcare are now harnessed by advertising as part of the sales pitch, in order to sell food products. Whilst diets have been central to medical regimes since the seventeenth century, it is only in the twentieth century that it appears to have become central to all debates about healthy lifestyle, particularly those aimed at women. [24] However, in the nineteenth century the first low carbohydrate diets, invented by physicians like Charles Bunting, were addressed towards men;[25] it is only in the twentieth century that the concentration of diet information has so bound up with the regulation of codes about 'femininity' and female sexuality. This emphasis on women as consumers of special diet foods has, as we have already mentioned, been encoded into the marketing of food products.

The 'health awareness' messages of adverts stress the succulency of food 'with half the fat' and then try to persuade us to consume double the amount and not ask too many questions about how it is produced. Women are mainly targetted by these conflicting messages which play on further contradictions about women's role. Women are implored to think about, prepare and buy lots of special diet food whilst refraining from eating too much in order to remain slender.

This 'displacement' of the direct pleasures of eating onto the pleasure of economic consumption creates conflicting messages about female identity. Our cultural obsession with slenderness is implicitly encoded in all food advertisements aimed at women (in these, like all other adverts, there are rarely images of fat women). Indeed, it could be argued that diet food representations say as much about 'cultivating female obedience to rigid codes of femininity' as they do about cultural perceptions of the meaning of flesh. These representations often deny unself-conscious eating, which becomes a dangerous and guilty vice for women, a cultural taboo. Even in the popular arena it is rare to find popular representations of women eating food. TV soap and film locates much of the dramatic action around the preparation and consumption of food: yet it rarely shows women actually swallowing any of it.[26]

Slenderness and Eroticism

The thin erotic aesthetic is so central to the Western beauty ethos that for women, eating has become associated with sinning. As Shelley Bovey has pointed, out to many people 'being fat IS a sin'.[27] Recent medical surveys provide confirmation of female fears about fat and the oppressive nature of female psychological conditioning through compulsive weight control. They reveal that on any day 25 per cent of all American women are on diets. Although 40 per cent of men, compared to 32 per cent of women are overweight, almost 60 per cent of UK and US women in the sample group, compared to 10 per cent of men, had been on slimming diets in the twelve months previous to the date of survey.[28]

Obsessions with weight control contain so many other anxieties that it is common for women to fantasize that all their problems might be resolved if only they could lose a few more pounds[29] Even very young girls are identified as showing signs of being obsessed with dieting. Hilde Bruch in the 1970s found that 'concern with weight and feelings of fatness have been seen to be increasingly prominent among younger children, even as early as the age of 7'.[30] It seems that messages about slenderness are inscribed onto the female psyche at a young age - at the same time as the messages about how to be 'feminine'.

While contemporary discourses about femininity have forged a direct association between sexual attractiveness and the 'thin' aesthetic, the development of the thin woman as cultural icon has a short history. Despite the nineteenth century penchant in Western Europe (and the USA) for small waists and tightly laced corsets, it was not until the beginning of the twentieth century that thinness became culturally emphasised in the West as an ideal for women.[31]

At the end of the nineteenth century historians like Veblen were noticing the slender wives of the wealthy.[32] By 1908, the Paris fashion correspondent for *Vogue* magazine was proclaiming that 'the fashionable figure is growing straighter and straighter, less bust, less hips more waist and a wonderfuly, long slender suppleness about the limbs, ... how slim, how graceful, how elegant women look. '[33]

It is fascinating to consider that the shape of the western female body appears to have significantly altered around the periods 1912-1919 and 1967–1974, periods which, as Juliet Mitchell has pointed out, were both characterised by mass movements of women as well as political and cultural rebellion.[34] Indeed, the boyish gamine first made her entrance in the 1920s with the arrival of the flapper who tightly bound her bosoms and created sexual ambiguity about the female form. The flapper's 'boyish androgynous body' was clearly a forerunner to the anti-maternal emaciated look that emerged in the 1960s.[35]

Models like Shrimpton (the 'Shrimp') and Twiggy took the fashion world by storm in 1965 when they arrived alongside of the pill and sexual liberation a little ahead of the second wave women's movement (but without any theoretical framework to explain the significance of this new female body ideal). [36] In retrospect, it is clear that the rounded icons of the 1950s post-war period – Monroe, Hayworth and Mansfield – went out of fashion at the same time as the emphasis on domesticity started to lose its allure. Into the spotlight came women with skinny 'hard' bodies, who looked more like adolescent boys than the softly curved female icons of the previous decade, and who were ready to take their place in a man's world.

It seems ironic that today, when western women have been undergoing such a vast change and expansion in their social roles, they should be represented as being 'less', that is, physically smaller. Elizabeth Wilson argues that technological inventions may have as much to do with the culture of slenderness as with patriarchal relations. She cites the influence of photography on fashion images as 'influencing and changing the actual appearance of the women in the street'.[37] She points out that photography accentuates width, and therefore makes the fashion industry over-conscious about fatness. She argues that because photography has come to dominate fashion journalism, 'it has contributed to the fashion for extreme thinness and length of leg'.[38] Although Wilson notes that photographic *illusion* may have come to change the appearance of real women, she is wary of oversimplifying:

> Foucault ... puts the body back into the social sciences. As anyone who has tried to diet knows, it is rather difficult to radically alter the shape of one's body. Yet dress and adornment in all cultures has been used to do

precisely this: from tattooing and neck rings, to the dyeing and curling of hair and the use of high heels, both women and men have worked hard to produce a 'different' body.[39]

Recent research by Silversteen *et al* would agree with Wilson about the difficulties of changing body shape, but nevertheless draws our attention to the contradictory effect of social change upon female identity. They argue that periods of female leanness correlate with periods where women's economic and social position improved.[40] After analysing photography of women from the nineteenth century to the present day, they argue that at the historical point when women start to achieve 'male status' they desire and start to look like men.

There is no denying that since the 1960s thinness in women has been celebrated. We can't simply 'blame' representations for 'causing' eating disorder but we note that even the average weight of the Playboy Playmate centrefold, has dropped.[41] Janine Cataldo has pointed out that 'in the last 20 years the current female body ideal has shown a decrease in weight, bust and hips and an increase in waist size'.[42] Less than 5 per cent of Western women are estimated to be born with the genetic predisposition to meet the modern ideal. [43] The thin 'ideal' remains despite the real conditions of female existence: at the same time, 'the weight of the average [American] woman has become steadily heavier than that of 20 years ago'.[44]

This recent Western phenomenon of eroticising images of underweight women has been the subject of many studies. Feminists like Shelley Bovey, Kim Chernin, Elizabeth Wilson and Naomi Wolf point out that thinness is a new fad even in the West. Previously, in portraits of women for example, 'various distributions of sexual fat were emphasised – big ripe bellies from the fifteenth to seventeenth centuries, plump faces and shoulders in the early nineteenth century … generous dimpled buttocks and thighs until the twentieth century'.[45]

Cross-cultural data is also employed by critics in order to make similar points. Plump women seem to have stopped being aesthetic 'ideals' in the West after the rise of mass communications technology. But in cultures where technology is not as 'developed' as in the West and famine is not a too distant memory, plumpness is viewed as a visible sign of prosperity and fertility. Gordon identifies that fatness is still valued over thinness by the Gurage of Ethiopia 'who were troubled by collective anxieties of scarcity'. He also notes the existence of 'fattening houses' in some parts of Nigeria where young girls are sent in order to transform them into alluringly fat women. [46]

During their lifetimes many modern Western women experience a variety of body sizes, and become accustomed to imagining themselves in the sort of transitions reflected in 'before' and 'after' diet pictures. This experience relates not only to pregnancy and ageing, but also to the long-term effects of dieting. Janine Cataldo has pointed out that such unrealistic female body perceptions result in many women feeling that they never attain their 'true' body size, but are always 'en route'.

Western black women may experience an even more complex relationship to body size. Marion A. Bilich suggests that the argument that eating disorders are a middle-class white phenomenon may largely be due to the fact that the questionnaires and experiments are drawn from the college campuses where most of the participants will be middle-class, and that it also focuses on the predominantly white colleges, rather than the black or minority-strong ones.[47] Dana and Lawrence state that at the London Women's Therapy Centre they work with women 'from a variety of class and cultural backgrounds'.[48] Gordon, in contrast, claims bulimia is 'less prevalent among black women and subjects from minority groups', arguing that this is because they are less caught up in middle-class values and Western ideals of female achievement.[49] Yasmin Alibhai-Brown, in a *Guardian* article, 'Having it and Flaunting it', appears to agree with Gordon. She argues that it is only recently, as black women are being included in the targetting of beauty products and the consequent consumer idealisations, that a concern for body size has arisen and incidences of bulimia are beginning to appear. However, there has been little research which attempts to map the difference of 'race' onto the complexities of gender and body shape, and Alibhai-Brown's position is largely unsubstantiated.[50]

Her view fits in with our arguments that cultural codes of femininity are implicated in the incidence of eating disorders – but the theory that Western black women, because they have been excluded from the dominant beauty myth, have therefore had no relationship to those codes of femininity, is clearly a simplistic one. It ignores the experience of many black women who live in the West and internalise Western beauty myths (which of course have negative implications for black women which extend far beyond the question of body shape). Susan Bordo argues for a more sophisticated reading of how black women have been affected by the 'normalizing discipline' of the coercive ideals of beauty. And she points to the racial standards functioning beneath the idealisation. Black women's experience can

be effaced if the 'hegemonic power of normalizing imagery' is not
adequately acknowledged. Bordo cites the experience of a black high-
school student, locked into the battle of bingeing and dieting, who
sought help:

> only to be told that she didn't have to worry about managing her weight
> because 'black women can go beyond the stereotype of woman as sex
> object' and 'fat is more acceptable in the black community'. Saddled with
> the white woman's projection onto her of the stereotype of the asexual,
> material Mammy, the young woman was left to struggle with an eating
> disorder that she wasn't 'supposed' to have.[51]

Alibhai-Brown's *Guardian* article seems to reinforce this stereotyping
in its argument that being excluded from the dominant Anglo-Saxon
beauty image leaves black women free to be totally self-directed. We
would argue that this is an idealisation that refuses to acknowledge
the hegemonizing power of the culture of white slenderness, and of
how such 'normalizing', dominant meanings articulate black wom-
en's marginality, and hence 'inferiority'. Why would a creative and
talented black celebrity such as Oprah Winfrey consider that losing
70lbs was one of her greatest achievements, if not for internalisation
of the dominant slender ideal.

Bordo's discussion illustrates how the Afro-American fashion
magazine, *Essence*, consciously strives to promote beauty features that
challenge Anglo-Saxon standards and promote black self-acceptance.
This positive ideological input into the magazine, however, she argues, is constantly undermined by advertising images which reinforce
insecurity, 'by insisting hair must be straightened (and eyes lightened)
in order to be beautiful'.[52]

Caught up in the paradoxical messages about feminine beauty,
and ideals of slenderness, black women are no more 'free to be themselves' than white women. Indeed their relationship to such idealisations
perhaps takes an even more complicated toll, which is just beginning
to be explored, and clearly warrants further research.

Dieting is promoted as a strategy of self-improvement for women.
The bookshops bear testimony to the epidemic of 'self help' books
now available in the marketplace. Aerobics and body-building may
also be seen as 'self help' strategies which need to be viewed scep-
tically. While many women clearly enjoy exercise, critics like Jean
Mitchell have called into question whether exercise for women is always
simply 'positive' and promoting of strength.[53] Mitchell argues that
some women (and men) who pump iron obsessively have much in
common with anorexics. Anorexics and some (but obviously not all)

body-builders use an almost sadistic control over their bodies as a substitute for controlling the real issues in their life (over which they often have very little power). Body-building, aerobics and anorexia all reappropriate notions about the weakness of the flesh and the spiritual goodness of 'transcending' the body. The transformation of such ideologies into practices like body-building, it has been suggested by Mitchell, produces feelings of moral superiority. The individual feels superior, but is actually trapped within an oppressive rigidity of what is acceptable or not acceptable in terms of body shape. Elizabeth Wilson has called these regimes 'invisible corsets'[54] and contrasts them with the wearing of visible corsets to regulate femininity in the nineteenth century. This idea that dieting is like an invisible corset is illustrated by Kelly Harrison's sculpture (see Illustration 11) which features a corset made of fattening sweeties (Smarties) and plays with the paradoxical notions of indulgence and restraint which cluster around the issue of female body shape.

Certainly it is clear that many women, and not just those who take strenuous and regular exercise, are often alienated from their bodies, and frequently have unrealistic expectations about body shape. Evidence of this is not only found in the literature on eating disorder but is further corroborated by many psychological surveys. One undertaken by the University of Pennsylvania revealed that female students, compared to male students, tended to overestimate their body weight and choose much larger images to identify themselves with.[55]

Culture and the Female Unconscious

Some women *do* fetishise non food objects sexually, some men *are* bulimics and fetishise food. However, statistics claim that: 95 per cent of all fetishists are presumed to be male[56] and similarly 90 per cent of all bulimics are thought to be female.[57] Traditionally, our culture constructed masculinity as he who fucks, femininity as she who cooks (the nurturing role is even more vital than that of bearing children).

Women still take on far more of the household tasks than men, but, as we have already mentioned, women are expected to maintain rigid self regulation of their own consumption of food. Often mum doesn't eat the same food as the rest of her family. If she does partake of the family meal she is advised by slimming magazines to take smaller portions and to weigh them to make sure she is not consuming too many calories. Thus an inequality of food consumption, where women

Smarties corset by Kelly Harrison

do more of the preparation but are expected to eat less, is reflected in the accommodation of domestic labour. [58]

Unequal gender constructions still dominate despite changes in the female role; and we believe that this socially constructed inequality has permeated the unconscious psyches of both sexes. This would explain why 'aberrant' sexual behaviour by men and women appears to reproduce gender stereotypes. This leads us to question how the psyche might be informed by cultural norms. And, as we mentioned earlier, the relatively recent emergence of bulimia leads us to question how the psychoanalytic models could be adapted to incorporate historical change. We therefore turn to a critical examination of some attempts to accomodate cultural shifts within psychoanalysis.

Initially Lacan seemed to be extremely useful to feminists. His redefining of the importance of the language element within the construction of the self and his specific idea that the unconscious functions like a language, seemed for the first time to pay concrete attention to material definitions of reality within the psyche. However, many feminists have begun to realise that although this model helped to explain the existence of patriarchal relations, it did not challenge the universal, transhistoric nature of the psychoanalytic model. In fact the Lacanian model reinforced phallocentricism, by implying the inescapable psychic hold of the significance of the phallus. The feminist philosopher, Judith Butler, considering the concept of identity argues:

> By instituting the Symbolic as invariably phantasmatic, the 'invariably' wanders into an 'inevitably', generating a description of sexuality in terms that promote cultural stasis as its result ... This structure ... effectively undermines any strategy of cultural politics to configure an alternative imaginary for the play of desires.[59]

Similarly, discussing subjectivity and identity, Helen Crowley and Susan Himmelweit come to the conclusion that for Lacanian theory,

> *historical* difference is of no consequence to the way we conceive the subject, whose meaning, along with that of sexual difference, is fixed within the unconscious. Although his account proposes a synthesis of social and psychic meaning, in the final analysis this synthesis is weighted towards the unconscious. Lacan marginalises questions of social process and historical change. Unconscious desire, however, is socially mediated and this means that its significance is historical and not just psychostructural.[60]

Rather than try to adapt the Lacanian model to incorporate cultural changes, feminists have tended to drop psychoanalysis and to adopt

Foucault's model of the discourses of power, and discussing the reasons for the subject's position within them.

Kleinian Models of Food Fetishism: Susie Orbach

Kleinian theory has been able to incorporate some element of social change. Perhaps that is one reason why Kleinians have predominated in the analyses of eating disorders. In her essay, 'Sexuality as the Mainstay of Identity', Ethel Spector Person argues for object relations theory being able to incorporate change in a way that Freud, dependent on a fixed biological model of drives, could not. [61] Object relations theory, she argues has a model which is able to formulate the internalisation of the historical moment, 'not just in the organisation of perception and affective relationships but in the very creation of subjectivity.'[62] The emphasis on early object relations, such as the process of individuation, and the infant's development of its body image, allows subjectivity to be influenced by the experiential, the experience of the external world. Person points up the need for such an incorporation of culture into the psychoanalytic model, with her insistence that 'the fantasies attached to desires reflect interiorisation from the culture'.[63]

However, one of the problems in the way object relations writers such as Kim Chernin and Susie Orbach connect eating disorder and cultural definitions of femininity stems from the model of the 'Self' they mobilise. In her groundbreaking book *Fat Is A Feminist Issue*, analysing why women overeat, Susie Orbach utilizes diagrams of a 'fat' self and 'thin' self. [64] Her overall thesis is that 'unconsciously' many women want to be fat and fear thinness because of the difficulties they experience in coping with the conflicting demands society places on them. Many women therefore cover up the 'real' thin self with layers of fat to obscure their fears . Orbach's book goes on to suggest that dieting doesn't help women to get over their fears or obsessions and that the need to 'release' and recognise the meaning of the 'thin self' in their life is absolutely crucial in helping them get/ remain slim. The book (which we abbreviate in further references to FIFI) proposes that a new form of 'consciousness raising' group is needed to help women deal with their fears about sexuality. The Women's Therapy Centre, which Orbach helped to set up, took these ideas into the therapeutic practice. Of course, the Women's Therapy Centre uses more than one psychoanalytic framework and don't confine all their therapeutic strategies to those outlined in FIFI.

The claims made in FIFI stirred up considerable controversy, not only among dieticians who felt the anti-diet strategy was misguided, but also among feminists who felt that Orbach was aligning herself with cultural stereotypes in promoting thinness as invariably the desired goal. Nicki Diamond in 'Thin is a Feminist Issue'[65] argues that FIFI's stance is actually 'anti-feminist', while Cath Jackson in 'Fast Food Feminism' argues for Orbach's political naivety: 'I suspect Orbach is nothing more sinister than superficial. Her heart is in the right place, but she fails to see beyond the immediate problem.'[66]

Our own problems with the analysis lie in the concept of a fat-and-thin, divided self. Such arguments about these 'fat' and 'thin' selves suggest that women can be made whole (ie, can let the 'authentic' thin self emerge) when contradictions about female identity are understood and redefined by the individual. This humanist model is often associated with R. D. Laing whose ideas about schizophrenia and the 'divided self' have been influential in the past. Lacanian psychoanalysis, however, brings a challenge to the notions about the self as used by Laing and Orbach, and presents a radical critique of the humanist notion of any simple 'split' in the ego that can be healed.

The Lacanian model of subjectivity rejects ideas about the 'true self' and instead introduces the concept of the 'fragmented subject'. This model of the subject arises as a consequence of Lacan's formulations of the Mirror Phase which suggests that our notions of identity are always a *misrecognition* of our apparent external unity. The infant 'I' that looks into the Mirror (the subject) sees itself as the 'I' of the mirror reflection (the object). When we learn to recognise ourselves in the mirror, and to speak about this recognition, our subjectivity is guaranteed, but it is unfortunately constructed on the misconception that we are a unitary whole.

Lacan's concept of the 'fragmented subject' is a useful one. It reveals as a fantasy Orbach's argument for an authentic 'thin self' lurking inside the 'fat' self which can be freed if women only work on what their fat symbolically means. The Lacanians would suggest that the split in the subject can never be healed. They challenge the concept of an increasing mastery of this 'authentic' self, since for them the 'authentic self' is itself a misrecognition. The Lacanian model would therefore suggest that the sort of 'consciousness raising' proposed by Orbach as a treatment for eating disorder, however self-affirming, could never go far enough to reach the unconscious. The changes that arise from 'consciousness raising' come about in the realms of our *conscious* awareness of ourselves whereas effective remedy lies in affecting the *unconscious*.

As we mentioned in chapter three, see page 113) Jacqueline Rose indicates how the object relations school, though able to include change, has lost the full implications of the concept of the unconscious. They have become more sociological. Nancy Chodorow's analysis of mothering,[67] which Chernin in particular mobilizes in *The Hungry Self*, is effectively challenged by Rose. She shows how Chodorow has sidestepped the issues of the unconscious and of the baby's initial bisexuality. Instead of accepting a problematic process of acquiring self and sexual identity, she has made use of Stoller's concept of *gender imprinting* – 'the establishment of an unambiguous and unquestioned gender identity'. As Rose argues, Chodorow's theory thereby becomes simplistic and unquestioning in the sociological stance it takes:

> the problem needing to be addressed – the acquisition of sexual identity and its difficulty – is sidestepped in the account ... [She sets herself] to question sexual *roles*, but only within the limits of an assumed sexual *identity*.[68]

Feminist attempts to challenge the 'universal' model of psychoanalysis by incorporating a concept of cultural change, therefore, have on the whole tended to either shift outside the psychoanalytic model or to go for a unproblematic model of the self or a simplified sociological assumption of what sexual identity constitutes.

Challenges to Psychoanalysis's Universal Model

In an attempt to hold onto a notion of the dynamics of the Unconscious, while still incorporating generational change, we had to look elsewhere for a theoretical model. Neither the Lacanian nor the Kleinian models in themselves were adequate to explain all the phenomena that we had uncovered in our examination of bulimia and the change in desire, fetishism, and hence the dynamics of the female unconscious.

Psychoanalysis has been criticised over and over again for being transhistorical: from Deleuze and Guattari's *Anti-Oedipus* which argues that desire is not structured by each individual's reaction to the incest taboo, but is generated 'machinically' by a society as a whole [69:] through to Frantz Fanon's *Black Skin, White Masks* which argues that psychoanalysis needs to take on board issues of race, in its analysis of the contradictions constructed within black subjectivities, when living in a colonized country. [70] Most critics have focussed on the shortcomings of assuming the Oedipal triangle as universal, but a few anthropological psychologists have attempted to be more positive. They have sought to use examples of non-Western cultural practices as a way of adapting the model to incorporate cultural differences. The Lidzs in particular have sought to question the 'universal model' in their *Oedipus in the Stone Age*, and 'Masculinization in Papua New Guinea'. In the latter they argue that a different resolution of the Oedipal conflict exists in certain cultures : 'The studies of the cultures of Papua New Guinea are important to us because they ... make it apparent that ways that challenge basic psychoanalytic theories of development can work, indeed have worked for thousands of years and therefore require our attention.'[71]

Amongst the Sambian culture, for example, men and women are rigidly segregated and children remain with the women. Boys therefore form a strong (feminine) identification and erotic attachment to their mothers up until the ages of eight to twelve when they undergo the 'masculinization' initiation rites. Removed from their mothers and isolated in the ritual dwelling, they are made to bleed and vomit to cleanse them of the feminine contaminations of menstruation and umbilical feeding. Isolated and shocked by the cleansing rituals, the boys experience loss and emptiness which the Lidzs define as individuation. Instead of the breast, they are then given a penis to suck and the boys perform fellatio on the 'bachelors' of the group. The Lidzs claim that the Sambians believe that they thereby becoming masculinized through ingesting the semen necessary to make them men. Whether such a 'belief' is literal or symbolic is not explored. While they are swallowing sufficient amounts of semen, the boys are also being instructed on the dangers of contamination in women. Once they have made the transition, they become 'bachelors' in their turn until they are given a wife.

Care needs to be taken with the Lidzs's explanations, and with their 'recognition' of 'essential' (ie, transhistorical) needs similar to Western needs. The humanist model they adopt and some of their implicit assumptions about 'universal needs' are elements we would want to distance ourselves from. Nevertheless, their attempt to argue for a form of sexual identity developing in a pattern different from the classic Oedipal rivalry, of son against father for the mother's affections, is worth noting. The Lidzs argue that this Oedipal rivalry is avoided in Sambian culture, by the eroticised homosexual period. Many of the cultures they studied, they felt, had similar periods of passive and active homosexuality as a way of gaining a masculine subjectivity. Awareness of different cultural practices is one possible way of challenging the essentialist claims of the Western psychoanalytic model. The Lidzs claim that such differing models of the formation of subjectivity are not only possible but have been 'workable over thousands of years.'

Towards a Tentative Conclusion

Certainly the Lidzs seem to offer the scope to incorporate cultural change into a model of human subjectivity and the development of the individual psyche. And cultural change, especially change across the generations, needs to be fully conceptualized within psychoanalysis. We would hope that the institutions that regulate psychoanalysis would at last acknowledge the influence of cultural change upon the individual psyche, without jettisoning the unconscious. Unfortunately, none of the psychoanalytic models we considered have done this adequately. On the whole they are unable, when they contemplate the dynamics of desire and the feminine unconscious, to also bear in mind generational contradictions, such as those of women's liberation in context of the oppressive culture of slenderness. Without such a model, the unconscious relationship of women to food, to desire, and to the mechanics of disavowal, which, we believe, has produced bulimic epidemics of food fetishism, will never be adequately conceptualised.

We would point out that within the Lacanian model, our subjectivity takes place in relation to the gaze of the [m]other. And that gaze (the mirror) is always located within a cultural space. Whereas the pre-Oedipal baby may not yet know of an outside world, the mother clearly does experience herself in relation to it, and this is surely reflected in her gaze. The baby is constructing its subjectivity in relation to a culturally informed 'mirror'.

It is interesting that the Lacanian concept of 'misrecognition' bears such a strong similarity to most Western women's experience of not being able to recognise their actual body shape (even when they are looking at themselves in the mirror). We have begun to map a theoretical model onto the empirical data of food obsessions. Perhaps in turning their attention to the incidences of bulimia Lacanians will inescapably encounter History. Unconscious desire, however it is generated, is always socially mediated. Whatever the internal mechanisms of the anxieties around the me/not me splitting, the vocabulary with which the individual expresses this must be a cultural one. There is nothing else. There is nothing outside of language. The unconscious, in dreams, uses the objects of the every-day world to express itself, as we will try to explain, metaphorically. It is only the strangeness (the 'uncanny') that is unique to it.

When you dream of falling off the Eiffel Tower at the height of the rush-hour, the Tower and the rush-hour are clearly part of our cultural language. It is simply the fact that the Tower is made of cheese that signals the presence of the unconscious which is expressing itself in relation to the possible meanings of 'cheese'. The cheese itself and its meanings are also part of the vocabulary, but it is the way in which it is being used that forms the uncanny.

The sexual fetishist chooses a leather shoe, the food fetishist chooses chocolate cream cakes – and the shoe and the cake are cultural objects with a definite relationship to the cultural norms of masculinity and femininity. In both instances, the objects are found 'wanting' by the norms, which form part of that culture. A man having a sexual relationship with a shoe is seen as deficient in his masculinity, a woman having an excessive relationship to a cream cake is seen as deficient in her femininity. The various pathologisings of the fetishisms all agree on that.

What the various fetish practitioners agree on is that in some way and for some moments, fetishistic practices allow psychic anxieties to be disavowed in a burst of experiential pleasure. And pleasure is always preferable to pain and denial. The fetishist has found a compromise with society's construction of the gendered self, and that is in itself a celebratory victory. We would certainly argue that the denials and repressions practised by other people towards fetishists tends to be a lot more damaging to them than the actual fetishism.

Notes

1 Lucy Ellman, 'Love and the Coffee Mates', *New Statesman and Society*, 14.2.92.

2 Margaret Reynolds (ed), *Erotica: An Anthology of Women's Writing*, Pandora, London 1990, p250.

3 *Ibid.*

4 Jeremy MacClancy, *Consuming Culture*, Chapman, London 1992, pp70–1.

5 Claude Levi Strauss, *The Raw and the Cooked*, Translated by J. and D. Weightman, Cape, London 1970, p269.

6 R.A. Gordon, in '*Anorexia and Bulimia*', Blackwells, London 1990, claims that 90 per cent of all bulimics are found to be female. (p8). Kaplan argues that 20 men to every 1 woman are perverts.

7 P. Willis in 'Shop Floor Culture: Masculinity and the Wage Form' defines

culture as 'not artifice and manners, the preserve of Sunday best, rainy afternoons and concert halls. It is the very material of our daily lives, the bricks and mortar of our most commonplace understandings, feelings and responses'. In C. Critcher *et al* (eds), *Working Class Culture*, Hutchinson, London,1977.

8 Antonio Gramsci, *op cit.*

9 Jeremy MacClancy, *Consuming Culture*, Chapman, London 1992.

10 *Ibid*, p2.

11 *Ibid*, p138.

12 Nicole Ward Jouve, *The Street Cleaner: The Yorkshire Ripper Case on Trial*, Marion Boyars, London 1986, p84.

13 *Ibid*, p85

14 MacClancy, *op cit*, p214.

15 By the 'culture of plenty' we mean the way advertising represents the myriad available consumables, as part of the cultural identity. Many people cannot afford to share in this 'plenty' and we are not arguing that eveyone within a 'culture of plenty' can. In Los Angeles, for example, armed guards outside the hospitals prevent women in labour from entering if they lack adequate health insurance. Yet the image of America, both to foreigners and Americans themeselves, remains a culture of choice and plenty.

16 MacClancy, *op cit*, p142.

17 Figures quoted in Penny Chorlton, 'Where Do The Pounds Go?', *Observer*, 20.1.91, pp24–36.

18 Elizabeth Gleick, 'Food on the Brain', in *Cosmopolitan*, August 1990, pp98–9; includes interviews with women who prefer to talk about food rather than sex. Our survey findings bore this out.

19 R. Coward, *Female Desire: Women's Sexuality Today*, Paladin, London 1984, p101.

20 Exhibited during the '*Preaching to the Perverted*' Conference, ICA, 12 July, 1992. Subsequently some of the pictures were commissioned to illustrate *Skin Two*, the fetish magazine.

21 Coward, *op cit*, p102.

22 *Ibid*, p103.

23 Raymond Williams, 'Advertising the Magic System', *Problems in Materialism and Culture*, Verso, London 1980; Judith Williamson, *Decoding Advertising: Ideology and Meaning in Advertising*, Marion Boyars, London 1978.

24 Elizabeth Wilson, *Adorned in Dreams*, Virago, London 1985, p114.

25 *Ibid*, p115.

26 Suzanne Moore, *The Guardian*.

27 Shelley Bovey, *Being Fat is not a Sin*, Pandora, London 1989.

28 Naomi Wolf, *The Beauty Myth*, Chatto & Windus, London 1990, p151.

29 R.A. Gordon, *op cit*, p48.

30 Richard A. Gordon *Anorexia and Bulimia: Anatomy of a Social Epidemic*, Blackwell, London 1990, p71.

31 *Ibid*, p77.

32 T. Veblen, *The Theory of the Leisure Class*, Macmillan, London 1899, pp148–9.

33 V. Steele, *Fashion and Eroticism*, Oxford University Press, Oxford 1985, p227.

34 Juliet Mitchell, 'Feminist Theory and Feminist Movements: The Past Before us', in *What is Feminism?*, Juliet Mitchell and Ann Oakley (eds), Blackwell, London 1986, p58.

35 William Bonnet and Joel Gurin, *The Dieter's Dilemma*, Harper Row, New York 1982, chapter 7.

36 Twiggy was initially received with a certain amount of amusement by the popular press, as the deliberately ironic name suggests. We are indebted to Ian Birchall for reminding us of the popular joke of the time, 'Forget Oxfam: feed Twiggy'.

37 Wilson, *op cit*, p116.

38 *Ibid*, p116.

39 Julie Ash and Elizabeth Wilson, *Chic Thrills: A Fashion Reader*, Pandora, London 1992, p10.

40 Cited in R.A. Gordon, *Anorexia and Bulimia*, *op cit*, p7.

41 Researchers found the body size of the *Playboy* centre fold decreased from 11 per cent below the national average in 1970 to 17 per cent eight years later. Gardener *et al*, 'Cultural Expectations of Thinness in Women', *Psychological Reports*, 47 (1980), pp483–9.

42 Janine Cataldo, 'Obesity: A New Perspective on An Old Problem', *Health Education Journal*, Vol 44 (1985), p213.

43 K. Chernin, *Womansize: The Tyranny of Slenderness*, Women's Press, London 1981.

44 R.A.Gordon, *Anorexia and Bulimia*, *op cit*, p69.

45 Naomi Wolf, *The Beauty Myth*, Chatto & Windus, London 1990, p150

46 R.A. Gordon, *Anorexia and Bulimia*, *op cit*, p76.

47 Marion A. Bilich, 'Demographic Factors Associated with Bulimia in College Students: Clinical and Research Implications', *Bulimic College Student*, pp13–25.

48 Dana and Lawrence, *op cit*, p16.

49 R.A. Gordon, 'Bulimia: A Sociocultural Interpretation', *op cit*, p43.

50 Yasmin Alibhai-Brown, 'Having it and Flaunting It', *Guardian*, 27.8.92, p35.

51 Susan Bordo, 'Material Girl: The Effacements of Postmodern Culture', in *The Madonna Connection: Representational Politics, Subcultural Identities, and Cultural Theory*, C Schichtenberg (ed), Westview, Boulder, Colorado 1992, pp265–90 (pp.279-280).

52 *Ibid*, p281.

53 Marilyn Lawrence (ed), *Fed Up and Hungry*, Women's Press, London 1987.

54 Ash and Wilson, *op cit*, p10.

55 R. Fallon and P. Rogin, 'Sex Differences in Perception of Desirable Body Shape', *Journal of Abnormal Psychology*, 94, (1985), pp102–5.

56 Kaplan, *op cit*, 1991, argues 20 men to every 1 woman are perverts, p8.

57 R.A. Gordon, 'Bulimia: A Sociocultural Interpretation',*op cit*, p43.

58 A 1991 survey by MORI, for instance, revealed that 74 per cent of British men said 'they would not take responsibility for domestic chores'. G. Nedell, 'Still Cleaning After All These Years', *Guardian*, 16.8.92.

59 Judith Butler, *Gender Trouble: Feminism and the Subversion of Identity*, Routledge, London 1990, pp55–6.

60 Helen Crowley and Susan Himmelweit, *Knowing Women: Feminism and Knowledge*, Polity/Open University, Cambridge 1992, pp235–36.

61 Ethel Spector Person, 'Sexuality as the Mainstay of Identity: Psychoanalytic Perspectives', *Signs* 5 (1980).

62 *Ibid*, p615.

63   *Ibid*, p630.

64   Susie Orbach, *Fat is a Feminist Issue*, Paddington Press, London 1978. See also Kim Chernin's *Womansize*, Women's Press, London 1983, for similar analysis. *Fat is a Feminist Issue* (FIFI One) has been developed, into FIFI Two, and issued as a recording – the FIFI cassette stands testimony to its popular success.

65   Nicki Diamond, 'Thin is a Feminist Issue', *Feminist Review*, 19, Spring 1985, pp45–64.

66   Cath Jackson, 'Fast Food Feminism', *Trouble and Strife* 7, Winter 1985, p43.

67   Nancy Chodorow, *The Reproduction of Mothering: Psychoanalysis and the Sociology of Gender*, University of California Press, London 1979. Published in America in 1978.

68   Jacqueline Rose, 'Introduction II', *Feminine Sexuality*, *op cit*, p37.

69   Giles Deleuze and Felix Guattari, *Anti-Oedipus: Capitalism and Schizophrenia*, trans. Robert Hurley, Mark Seem and Helen R Lane, Viking, New York 1977. Originally published in 1972. Deleuze and Guattari, in their reformulation of the Unconscious and desire, set out to challenge the Oedipal model but continue on to deconstruct psychoanalysis altogether. Arguing that Lacan didn't go far enough in his re-formulation of Freud, they attack the notion that the Unconscious is located in the family triangle and concerned only with the incest taboo. Instead, they argue the Unconscious is not generated in the individual, but within society: out of a collective cultural experience. The Unconscious, 'is not essentially centred on human subjectivity. It partakes of the spread of signs from the most disparate social and material flows.' Deleuze and Guattari's radical attack on the Oedipal complex and its claim to universality (sharing much in common with Foucault) leads to a rejection of psychoanalysis as a repressive discourse. Despite linking the unconscious and the cultural, their focus on a free-flowing desire does not help to unpack the issues of subjectivity in relation to the social. Dogmatic assertions about 'desiring machines' do not lead us very far. And they are themselves also 'universal'.

70   Frantz Fanon, *Black Skin, White Masks*, trans. C. Markmann, Pluto, London 1986, Originally published in 1968.

71   T. Lidz and R. Lidz, 'Masculinization in Papua New Guinea', *Psychoanalytic Review* 73, Winter 1986, pp117–36 (p133).

Female Fetishism Conflated: Representations of 'Fetishism'

Now we have propounded our argument about women as active practitioners of fetishism, we want to return to earlier feminist work that has looked at women as *objects* of sexual fetishism and the objectifying male gaze. Griselda Pollock has summarised the position as follows:

> woman is fetishised, ie, parts of her body are taken out of context and made to function both as erotic thrills and threatening danger for the male viewer'.[1]

This school of research is based on a post-castration model of sexuality and the idea that female sexuality – and the fetishistic gaze itself – is regulated by Lack.[2] Consequently, it is unable to explain how women would be able to fetishise, nor it is able to adequately conceptualise female libido as active. (Freud claimed the only model for the libido was the masculine one.) Feminist work has persuasively mobilised psychoanalytic concepts associated with Sigmund Freud and Jacques Lacan in order to interpret the way women's oppression is encoded in many cultural forms.

By reviewing previous discussion of fetishism we hope to show how other feminist writers – as a group – have dealt with the subject and how their accounts differ from ours. The work we refer to includes some ground-breaking ideas that have changed and influenced feminist theory over the last twenty years. We approach discussion of these ideas about fetishism in four sections.

First, we look at theories of the gaze which posit women as objects of male fetishism, particularly ideas associated with the film critic Laura Mulvey.[3] We review all the work we could find on the gaze that relates to the concept of sexual fetishism, and suggest, for a variety of reasons, that Freud's model has been applied inappropriately by film critics to formulate the analysis of codes and conventions of the cinema.

Second, we look at theoretical ideas about the mother as prototype fetishist which artist Mary Kelly[4] developed and pioneered in the late 1970s with regard to her own art work. We consider whether her work constitutes an illustration of sexual or anthropological fetishism by women.

Third, we look at the work of a number of feminist literary critics, including Naomi Schor[5], Emily Apter[6] and Marjorie Garber[7], who have all used ideas about penis envy to explain fetishism by women in the literary texts they have engaged with. Here, we consider the limitations of trying to adapt ideas about penis envy in order to develop an adequate model of female sexuality.

Finally, we look at the implications of some of the confusions and conflations of meaning embedded not only in the work of the writers just mentioned, but also in more general discussion about fashion, popular fashion, culture and fetishism.[8]

We would clarify that our discussion of previous authors on the subject of fetishism is not included to argue that they have all been 'wrong'. We refer to previous research, and the stumbling blocks we associate with it, in order to point out the wider repercussions of our theoretical argument and to simply explain why we have approached our case studies from a different angle.

Woman As Object (of Fetishism): The Male Gaze Revisited

The best known article which refers to ideas about 'the male gaze' is without question Laura Mulvey's 'Visual Pleasure and Narrative Cinema'.[9] In order to understand the significance of this influential piece of criticism, which inspired so much further feminist writing, it should be noted that Mulvey provided a theoretical framework to substantiate what many other feminists had been asserting for some years. From Betty Friedan's *The Feminine Mystique* (1963)[10] to the anthology of writings from the early 1970s collected in Robyn Morgan's *Sisterhood is Global* (1984)[11], much second wave feminist writing about advertising and fashion had made connections between women's subordinate social role and the overdetermined emphasis on their appearance.

Many feminist critics had in some way made associations between women's objectification and their lack of power within patriarchal discourse. Mulvey's writing, however, gave the women's movement a theoretical basis to further understand the meaning of the fragmentation of the female form in Western culture. Mulvey looked at fetishism in the work of artists like Allen Jones and later raised the issue of fetishism of women in cinematic texts. In this work she related objectification of women's appearance to the unconscious fetishistic practices of men involved in artistic production.

Writer and critic John Berger made similar connections between women's objectification and their fragmentation in the visual arts and for that reason we start discussion of the gaze with a look at his writing. Even though Berger never actually used the word 'gaze' his discussion of the way women are 'surveyed' by men was one of the first to implicitly discuss it and to connect visual images to ideas about fetishism.

John Berger

John Berger's collaborative book and four tv programmes called *Ways of Seeing*, published in 1972, were very influential even before Laura Mulvey's seminal article on the gaze appeared in print in 1975. We would argue that Berger's work certainly fed into, and may even have prompted, much feminist analysis of the male gaze.[12]

In *Ways of Seeing* Berger discussed how and why oil paintings in the European tradition privileged unequal relations of looking:

> The convention of perspective, which is unique to European art established in the early Renaissance, centres everything on the eye of the beholder … The conventions called those appearances *reality*. Perspective makes the single eye the centre of the visible world … .

> According to the conventions of perspective there is no visual reciprocity.[13]

The argument that perspective denies reciprocity and at the same time gives the artist the ability to play god is made through comparison: 'There is no need for god to situate himself in relation to others: he is himself the situation … '[14] What Berger is referring to here is the fact that the spectator of European oil painting is positioned as omnipotent by the conventions of realism. Berger suggests that the codes and conventions which govern European oil painting as a historically specific form also govern what can and cannot be seen by the spectator.

When his focus on the codes and conventions of perspective is further developed Berger introduces the terms 'surveyor' and 'surveyed'.[15] Here he implicitly makes an argument about commodity fetishism:

> a way of seeing the world, which was ultimately determined by our new attitudes to property and exchange found its visual expression in the oil painting... Oil painting did to appearances what capital did to social relations. It reduced everything to the equality of object. Everything becomes exchangeable because everything was a commodity.[16]

Whereas Marx had argued that the commodity form produced fetishised relations between men and women, Berger extends his argument to explain how commodity fetishism has impacted upon relations of looking. He suggests that relations emanating from class divisions, colonial contexts and gender differences are also encoded in the image-making process. The separations of power involved in such relations, he argues, are comparable to those occuring during the exchange processes of commodity fetishism. (Edward Said has made similar observations about the impact of colonial relations on visual and other discourses about the Orient.[17])

Clearly Berger's Marxist analysis of perspective in European oil paintings is a controversial one which has been attacked by many critics for reducing appreciation of the aesthetic to economic questions[18]. Yet his arguments still seem relevant to us today when trying to understand 'fragmented' representations of women and other oppressed groups in advertising and other popular forms.[19] In 1972 Berger could argue: 'men look at women. Women watch themselves being looked at.' He went on to explain that in our culture the spectator is 'usually assumed to be male' because:

> A woman must continually watch herself; she is almost continually accompanied by her own image of herself. While she is walking across a room or whilst she is weeping at the death of her father she can scarcely avoid envisaging herself walking or weeping. From earliest childhood she has been taught and persuaded to survey herself continually.[20]

In the above quote Berger acknowledges that gender relations and relations of looking are constructed through and by consumer representations. But he goes on to point out that images of women in representation are designed to flatter 'the ideal specator who is always assumed to be male'. Here then Berger has expanded his rather simplistic Marxist model to explain how power inequalities deriving from patriarchal discourse impact upon the commodity form. His point is persuasive but unfortunately lacks precision. For example, in his discussion of nude women in paintings, he sees the depiction of woman as object as a 'reflection' of women's social subordination. He does not further analyse the relationship between ideology and representation, nor how images of women themselves impact on definitions of femininity and masculinity.

Berger does not really offer an adequate model of consciousness and ideology in his discussion in *Ways of Seeing*. Indeed, it must be said that his account of visual images and the way they impact on spectators is extremely limited (even though he has implicitly connected such relations to the Marxist model of consumer fetishism). Geoff Dyer has commented that one of the central 'weaknesses of the book is its lack of precision, detail and academic thoroughness'.[21] Nevertheless, *Ways of Seeing* opens up some very suggestive lines of enquiry.

Michel Foucault

John Berger's writing implicitly has a model of 'power' which is connected to ideas about consumer fetishism and the operations of capital. But it certainly does not address power relations in the specific way, for example, that Michel Foucault's writing has done. Yet when referring to the 'male spectator' Berger does seem to be implicitly addressing similar ideas about the discourses which regulate power/knowledge/observation. Discourses that Foucault has suggested produce:

> An inspecting gaze, a gaze which each individual under its weight will end by interiorising to the point that he (sic) is his own overseer; each individual thus exercising the surveillance over, and against, himself. A superb formula, power exercised continuously.[22]

The quotation above is from Foucault's discussion of the perfect prison, the panoptica, where prisoners learn to internalise their supervisors' inspecting gaze. This discussion about the way discourses of power culminate, in effect, to assure 'internalization' of specific values by individuals, relates to more than just prisoners. It perhaps explains the experience of those oppressed by 'others' who have the ability to define things. Fanon has made many persuasive observations about the way racism is internalized by its victims.[23]

Foucault's discussion of the way prisoners learn to internalise oppressive discourses, and are often 'appellated' by them, seems appropriate to describe the experiences of women. The processes that inform the subjectivity of women, who experience themselves as more visible (like the prisoner being watched), and learn to appraise themselves through male eyes, seem comparable to us. Women in Western

culture, despite feminism, continue to experience more social 'surveillance' and objectification than men. This point has been made by
Sandra Lee Bartky, who applied this Foucauldian model to the female
experience of being looked at. She argues that 'a panoptical male
connoisseur resides within the consciousness of most women'[24], a point
that has also been made by Catherine Hopwood.[25] Bartky aligns herself
with Foucault in arguing that this situation is not 'universal' or biological. Foucault suggests that individuals can resist the impact of the
gaze in certain circumstances, because:

> one doesn't have ... a power which is wholly in the hands of one person
> who can exercise it alone and totally over the others. It's a machine in
> which everyone is caught, those who exercise power, just as much as those
> over whom it is exercised ... Power is no longer substantially identified
> with an individual who possesses it by right of birth. It becomes a machine
> no one owns ... .[27]

A psychoanalytic perspective would probably look at power relations differently from Foucault, who argues that at the root of the gaze
are conscious power relations rather than unconscious primal repressions. And it is the psychoanalytic influence, as has already been
mentioned, which has been formative in much feminist writing,
particularly since Laura Mulvey applied the ideas of Jacques Lacan,
and introduced consideration of the gendered 'unconscious' to the
debate on the gaze.

When Mulvey raised questions about the scopophilic pleasure
individuals get from watching film, she moves Berger's arguments
about the fetishism of relations of looking in commodity production,
on to a consideration of castration anxiety and sexual fetishism associated with Freud's model of the unconscious.

Laura Mulvey

There is no doubt that Laura Mulvey's article on 'Visual Pleasure and
Narrative Cinema'. prompted engagement with psychoanalysis by
many feminists interested in the visual arts.[27] As Judith Mayne has
suggested:

> It is only a slight exaggeration to say that most feminist theory ... of the
> last decade has been as response, implicitly or explicitly, to the issues raised
> in Mulvey's article: the centrality of the look, cinema as spectacle and
> narrative, psychoanalysis as critical tool.[28]

Mulvey's article suggested that unequal gendered relations of looking
were a universal effect of the way men acquire sexual identities and

resolve castration anxiety. Though Mulvey's article didn't construct many women as archetypal 'peeping Tomina's' or make the case that female voyeurism constitutes fourth degree sexual fetishism (as outlined by Gebhard), it did recognise that some individuals (primarily men) get pleasure from erotic contemplation.

Published at a time when women's objectification by men was a crucial issue for many feminists, Mulvey's analysis of cinematic viewing to explain how sexual difference was culturally constructed broke with sociological accounts. Implicit in Mulvey's model of the male gaze are issues of gendered identity, as well as 'sexual looking'. It must be noted, however, that Mulvey's model was originally intended only to explain classic narrative cinema, not the many other forms of popular culture it has been used to decode by so many subsequent critics.

Such discussions of cinematic viewing and classic narrative cinema started with Christian Metz in his book *The Imaginary Signifier*.[29] Crucially he introduced the idea to film theory that the structures of signification in film could not be understood empirically and that the spectator 'made' meanings which needed to be conceptualised. Metz mobilized Lacanian theory in order to explain 'disavowal' in the cinema (a concept central to ideas about fetishism). He argued that by visually promoting the 'suspension of disbelief' film viewing engaged the spectators's subjectivity and ego, even though spectators know what they are seeing is not "real". For Metz the 'imaginary signifier' of the mirror image is reproduced wholesale in the cinema where strong images created by the camera offer 'ego ideals' to the audience who often identify with them and thus 'misrecognise' themselves.

So Metz is the originator of the model of spectatorship based on identification rather than economic or other power relations. He argues that the imaginary union provided by film images, which operate as imaginery signifiers, is a process comparable to the ways mirror images constitute us as subjects. Laura Mulvey takes the work of Metz as the starting point of her argument when she points out:

> important for this article is the fact that an image constitutes the matrix of the imaginary, of recognition/misrecognition and identification ...[30]

Like Metz, Mulvey suggests that the spectator's relationship to visual texts may accommodate 'narcissistic' relations of looking and identification with images on the screen. This occurs in the darkened arena of the cinema when images are bigger than ourselves and so idealised that they inspire us to identify with characters and even imagine that we are the characters we see before us, who are so much larger than life. But Mulvey also suggests that the relations of looking that articulate classic narrative cinema are voyeuristic, to the extent that the spectator's look stands in for the look of the camera. Mulvey discusses three types of looking in the cinema:

1. the look of the camera as it records the filmic event.
2. the look of the audience as it watches the final film product.
3. the look of the characters at each other in the visual images of the screen illusion.

She says that these looks are linked to the issue of gender (later explaining this in relation to castration anxiety and sexual fetishism) because all relations of looking in the cinema are informed and disrupted by erotic contemplation of the female form:

> In a world ordered by sexual imbalance, pleasure in looking has been split between active/male and passive/female. The determining male gaze projects its fantasy onto the female figure which is styled accordingly. In their traditional exhibitionist role women are simultaneously looked at and displayed with their appearance coded for strong visual and erotic impact they can be said to connote to-be-looked-at-ness. Woman displayed as sexual object is the leitmotif of erotic spectacle ... The presence of woman is an indispensable element of spectacle in normal narrative film, yet her visual presence tends to work against the development of story line, to freeze the flow of action in moments of erotic contemplation.[31]

Mulvey starts by identifying that certain 'erotic' scenes in film – like the famous one in *The Seven Year Itch* where Marilyn Monroe steps over an air vent and her dress rises up to reveal her legs – are not necessary to move the actual plot along. Instead, they give the male viewer scopophilic pleasure (visual images of woman connote 'to-be-looked-at-ness'). Mulvey develops her analysis of this phenomenon of woman as erotic spectacle in psychoanalytic terms when she argues:

> the female figure poses a deeper problem. She also connotes something that the look continually circles around but disavows; her lack of a penis, implying a threat of castration and hence unpleasure.[32]

Thus Mulvey suggests that the reason why women in film always looks so perfect, so glamorous – through the way their clothes, makeup and hair is stylised, and the way the camera lingers upon them - is linked to male castration anxiety and its resolution. Mulvey suggests that the way men deal with castration anxiety is to turn the woman, or the figure of woman, into a fetish object, because the body of woman is too frightening for men. So she argues :

woman in representation can signify castration and activate voyeuristic or fetishistic mechanisms to circumvent the threat.[33]

Many critics have voiced doubt about the relevance of this model to explain visual *pleasure*. Patricia Mellencamp, for instance, has observed:

> The dominant model of psychoanalysis developed for cinema is based on the unconscious, desire and the male subject. It relies on voyeurism and scopophilia, desirous seeing from a distance ... This is a model of anxiety rather than pleasure.[34]

Mulvey's model of visual pleasure also throws up other problems that are central to our inquiry into fetishism. In particular, since she concludes that the object choice (image of woman) is how the male spectator achieves disavowal of castration anxiety and hence 'pleasure', she universalises and centralises masculine experience. And her model of the male unconscious is far more 'logical' and 'rational' than Freud's writing would suggest. It requires further scrutiny, not least because it cannot encompass the idea of the differing degrees of intensity of visual pleasure (scopophilia) that can be gained from viewing, particularly from different types of viewer.

Furthermore, it seems to us that Mulvey tends to conflate the terms voyeurism and scopophilia with fetishism, and that these terms, at times, appear to be used interchangeably. Mulvey suggests that 'scopophilic' pleasure arises principally from using another person as an object of sexual stimulation through sight. Voyeurism and scopophilia for most cinematic viewers rarely replace other forms of sexual stimulation, nor are they preferred to sex itself. Thus these forms of pleasure cannot be encompassed within our definition of fetishism.

She argues that the images of women enjoyed by ordinary viewers and voyeurs are objects. By this route she is able to argue that the erotic contemplation of the image is a form of sexual fetishism. But voyeurism is the obsessive desire to look (at the other's genitals, etc), about which there is intense anxiety, and often no sexual orgasm. Fetishism on the other hand disavows anxiety via the object, to allow sexual orgasm. The difference between holding/experiencing an object oneself, and viewing someone else holding the object of desire, needs to be carefuly assessed. We do not believe that the path by which Mulvey shifts voyeurism into a visual kind of fetishism is adequate or has addressed these distinctions. It is true that Freud suggests that we are all fetishists to some extent and focus on some aspect of our lover's body that we like above others. But orthodox sexual fetishists rarely react to sight alone. Smell, feel and even taste are central to the orgasmic experience. Indeed, it is the physicality of the object that is important to the orthodox fetishist, an aspect of the experience which makes it quite distinct from voyeurism.

Mulvey's model is unable to conceptualise the notion of voyeurism in adequate terms. In particular, it is unable to make a distinction between ordinary (Gebhard 1–3) and orthodox (Gebhard 4) voyeurs nor, as mentioned above, is it able to conceptualise the differing degrees of their experience of voyeurism in the cinema. We think she conflates many differences between spectators in the cinema – and she conflates the degrees of fetishism in play (we think she really means objectification) – within the ubiquitious male gaze of classic narrative cinema.

Carol J. Clover has argued that the concept of the male gaze is not even adequate to explain the experiences of men, let alone women. She argues that 'assaultive gazing' at women is not the only position available to men in the cinema and 'is by and far the minority position' in horror films. She goes on to suggest that even heterosexual men may narcissistically identify with the victim of horror genres (often women) as well as with male characters, or the voyeuristic camera. She points out that most of the pleasure from horror movies comes from the 'introjective' spectator position, and mobilises Kaja Silverman's analysis of masochism (in relation to the male gaze and the way men view images) in order to further substantiate her point.[35] This argument challenges the idea that the way men watch images of women is always about projective viewing (associated with Mulvey's use of the term fetishism).

Overall, we would question whether Freud's ideas about sexual fetishism are appropriate to discussing forms of visual pleasure deriving from the cinema. Mulvey argues that all classic narrative cinema texts that feature women are involved in some level of phallic replacement. What she means by this is that women wearing top hats, high heels, wielding canes or other phallic attire are perceived as 'masculinised' and hence phallicised. In Mulvey's terms these images constitute men putting the phallus back on the 'mother' to stop the anxiety her castrated body originally provoked. By this strategy Mulvey shifts the analysis of scopophilic pleasure to one of 'visual fetishism' and argues that such powerful female images serve to allay male castration fears.

This argument that 'fetishised' women constitute a phallic replacement has been taken on board by many feminist film critics. Some visual texts that feature women, from Marlene Dietrich to Madonna, certainly do seem to be overdetermined by phallic symbols. We wouldn't disregard Mulvey's analysis of this phenomenon, nor the important work of feminist critics, from Annette Kuhn to Mandy Merck, who have offered many insights about the subject of women and representation. Unfortunately, Mulvey's model has been applied wholesale to analyses of women in film by some less careful critics, so that at times it has seemed to us that every representation of a 'strong' woman is analysed in relationship to the phallus, rather than on its own merits. Clearly it is reductive to argue that all images of powerful women consitute phallic replacement. The omnipotent mother surely needs a space in her own right, within film theory, and can perhaps be looked at through female eyes.

What happens to Mulvey's account of 'fetishism' if the idea that women too fetishise is taken on board? Obviously, the way women look at women wouldn't be about the resolution of castration anxiety. But Mulvey's model is unable to address this. (Not that it necessarily follows that women can create different sorts of images in their own cinematic practice. The evidence from feminist film practice does not by and large corroborate this sort of essentialist thinking, although we do accept that feminism has brought some changes in representations of women in the cinema.) Perhaps the question that should be raised is what is at stake for women when viewing images of men.

Many images of men do look overdetermined by phallic references, but these are usually mainstream Hollywood films. One might be able to argue that this relates to an address to the female gaze, as well as to the sociological evidence that suggests that only one in seven men feel their penis is big enough.[36] Indeed, images of men associated with people like Arnold Schwarzenegger or Sylvester Stallone do seem to imbued with an inordinate amount of references to what we would call phallic replacement. So over the top are the number of phallic props male screen idols often wear, or are photographed wearing or posing alongside, that we feel they are begging to be decoded in terms of ideas about masquerade.

Mulvey's model of the male gaze doesn't say very much about men on the screen, or how images of masculinity may involve fetishism. Indeed, Mulvey bases her arguments about the male gaze on the assumption that 'the male figure cannot bear the burden of sexual objectification'.[37] This argument in particular has been refuted by feminist critics, including Suzanne Moore, who has drawn attention to shifts in the last ten years in representations of men and masculinity, which visually position men as objects of the objectifying erotic gaze.[38]

There are many other problems with Mulvey's arguments about spectatorship, as have been identified by a great number of feminist critics. Many have argued in various ways that Mulvey's framework 'cannot explain how other dynamics of identity – such as race, class, and generation – may influence identifications' of the audience.[41] In light of all these criticisms we would argue that Mulvey's use of psychoanalytic concepts, while ground-breaking at the time, does not accurately explain the way many of today's images of men and women work on the audience.

To acknowledge the male body as a site of erotic spectacle is absolutely necessary. This is not only because of the existence of gay porn[42] which rarely features women, but because social shifts in the last ten years have meant that the naked male model body has taken centre stage in many contemporary representations. In a social context in which sexual roles are changing, and where images have been influenced by ideas emanating from women's, gay, and lesbian as well as black liberation movements, it would be surprising if any one model could explain everything we see on our screens. Further, Mulvey's gaze model focusses on psychoanalysis and thereby ignores questions about historical change. It brings explanations of representations and spectatorship back to questions about a supposedly trans-historical phenomenon: resolution of castration anxiety. Such a model is unable to adequately accommodate post-modern aesthetic strategies such as kitsch, camp, pastiche and parody which have permeated many representations we see on our screen. Nor is it able to explain the way gay, lesbian, bisexual as well as heterosexual women (rather than men) get pleasure from erotic spectacle in their own right, without recourse to what Mulvey describes as 'psychic transvestism'.[43]

Consumer Fetishism of the Erotic in Visual Images

We would argue that the introduction of the concept of consumer fetishism of the erotic would be helpful in dispelling some of the confusion, and the conflation of voyeurism, fetishism and scopophilia. In other words, 'fetishised' images of women and men are not simply a product of both male and female phantasy. They are also an aspect of commmodity fetishism, even though representations of sex and sexual fantasies are involved.

In the 1990s 'fetishised' images of women and men are informed by the economic logic of post-modern culture. We suggest that the concept of consumer fetishism of erotic codes may begin to provide a model that can account for historical changes in modes of representation

The fetishism of the erotic often occurs through processes of consumerism designed to make products appear 'sexy'. This model often seems far more appropriate to us to explain visual images of men and women than mobilising Freud's ideas about sexual fetishism. Certainly, ideas associated with Marx about commodity fetishism could be applied to explain the commmodification of the codes and conventions of, for example, gay pornography, and to analyse how these codes have impacted on representations of 'new men' in the mainstream.

By 'returning to Marx' we are not saying that psychoanalysis is not useful in understanding viewing experience. Rather, as we have already argued, the model of castration anxiety and sexual fetishism mobilised by Mulvey carries all sorts of theoretical problems. It does not adequately explain women's experience. It needs to be more comprehensive and interdisciplinary in its analysis of the way the gaze works across popular representations. We would suggest that the blindspots of gaze theory become most evident when trying to conceptualise the meaning of images in a consumer society where spectacle informs all points of sale of the market economy.[44]

Despite the theoretical impasse we have discussed, many feminist writers have gone on to try to modify the male gaze framework to include the female gaze, and to make a case for female agency during spectatorship.[45] Many of these critics, as well as the fifty feminists who contributed to the journal *Camera Obscura* on female spectatorship in 1989, have attempted to negotiate ideas about fetishism and to suggest that women enjoy erotic spectacle without engaging in 'psychic transvestism'. Most of these writers, nevertheless, still remain 'loyal' to gaze theory and the psychoanalytic reading that female sexuality is regulated by 'Lack'.

The Fetishising Female Gaze: Della Grace, Madonna and the Queer Aesthetic

We have included discussion of Della Grace's work in this section, not only because Della Grace describes herself as a 'fetish photographer', but because we think her work challenges ideas about the ubiquitous male gaze. It is true that some critics have argued that her photographs are indistinguishable from a male photographers photographing fetishism. We would argue there are differences. Della Grace's photos often document lesbian subcultural experience and many critics have argued that gay and lesbian representations, and desire, pose a challenge to the Mulveyan framework. Teresa de Lauretis, Richard Dyer, Jackie Stacey and many of the contributors who wrote in *Stolen Glances*[46], have argued that the Mulveyan framework, which conceptualises all non-heterosexual male spectatorship in terms of 'psychic transvestism', is not adequate to explain all gay and lesbian experiences of viewing.

Looking at the photographs found in Della Grace's book *Love Bites* it was pretty clear from the number of images that promoted same sex choice (lesbianism) that men were not a significant ingredient to the photographic scenarios or meanings. We are not arguing that male spectators wouldn't enjoy them but we felt that the way the women looked at each other as well as back at the camera, and the S&M scenarios and subcultural fashion codes included in the pictures, made it impossible to pin the photographs down to any single reading. There is no controlling, female gaze in Della Grace's photos but a range of possibilities offered to the spectator. We suggest that this is because these images invite a multiplicity of spectator positions, including lesbian spectatorship. Certainly they do not appear to us to equate with Mulvey's notions about the male gaze or any simple 'inversion' of it. As Reina Lewis has summarised in her forthcoming discussion of Della Grace's work:

> There is an element of being looked at in this collection that does not simply relate to the stereotypical gaze of the (male) voyeur ... [it] forces us to theorize a lesbian gaze and prioritize an analysis of female fetishism ...[47]

There are two main points we would make in response to the above quotation and to Della Grace's work. First, we feel that the photographs in *Love Bites* document female S&M practices rather than fetishism per se (as we have explained in chapter two). In this context we feel that Reina Lewis has not defined what type of fetishism she is referring to in her article. Second, and more importantly, the photographs throughout *Love Bites* do not simply employ or invert codes and conventions associated with what Mulvey describes as the 'male gaze', but, to the educated eye, reveal 'resistance' to it, in the Foucauldian sense of acts of power engendering resistance.

The 'resistance' to the male gaze in Della Grace's work can be

observed not only from the way the female models appear self-consciously happy with their lesbian subjectivity: these models stare back
at the camera as well as erotically at each other; and the fashions they
are wearing, and other sub-cultural codes contained within the *mise
en scène* of the images, indicate a relationship to lesbian experience.[48]
Men and women who 'know' this history, or these codes, will be aware
that these visual cues are intended to address some female viewers
who will 'recognise' them.

Such codes can act to interpellate 'lesbian spectators' as well as
other knowing viewers (be they heterosexual, bisexual, lesbian or homosexual in their 'real' lives) and so address the spectator through
her relationship to knowledge about specific objects and products.
These objects, as a consequence of activities and histories associated
with contemporary sexual subcultures, carry heavy symbolic meanings and connotations. Not least because they have been used by gay
men and lesbian women to carve out more fluid gender identities for
themselves. Therefore, such codes are recognised by some knowl-
edgeable viewers who may sexually react to them. Thus we would
argue that the subcultural codes implicit in Della Grace's photos can
be central to processes of interpellation, identification and erotic
voyeurism.

Clearly all spectators can bring various 'cultural competences'
to the texts they peruse or enjoy. This point has been made in great
detail by Pierre Bourdieu when writing about the meaning of 'taste'
in western culture. We would argue that gaze theory has not paid
enough attention to the significance of interpretative communities
that frame experience. We would certainly wish to challenge the
idea that there is any one way of reading photos or cinematic texts.
We therefore take issue with Mulvey's central contention, at the
heart of her *Visual Pleasure and Narrative Cinema* article, that watching film in the cinema will automatically determine the identificatory
or erotic experience of the viewer. The cultural knowledge and
understandings the viewer brings to the cinema with him or her
may significantly affect the identificatory or voyeuristic experience.
Recent media effects research, for instance, shows that black women
have watched films like *The Accused* in quite different ways from
white women.[49]

The point we are making is that there are many visual clues which
generate interpellation, identification and voyeurism in the cinema.
These visual signs need more analysis and investigation. Gay and
lesbian erotic aesthetic codes, produced as a consequence of sub-

cultural activity, may not be recognised by all viewers, but this is not always the case. As Judith Butler points out, many representations cause 'gender trouble'. That is they mobilise 'subversive confusion and proliferation of those constitutive categories that seek to keep gender in its place'.[50]

We would go further and argue that careful attention to sub-cultural codes within gay and lesbian representations has enabled many artists to create images that address a variety of female and male erotic pleasures from scopophilia. We would suggest that a psychoanalytic model would not be able to interpret this phenomenan, nor the significance of how these erotic codes work upon viewers who may sexually react to them. This is because psychoanalysis cannot address the way in which codes associated with the sexual erotic change with history.

The march of time will make certain visual codes associated with gay or lesbian experience more or less familiar to the general population depending on the political context. Some critics, for instance, are arguing that the mainstream is now more 'Queer' than ever before. Madonna, it has been argued, by mobilising gay and lesbian sub-cultural codes as well as those associated with sexual fetishism, in her videos and many other visual performances, has opened up the popular arena to Queer viewing: ' ... for many young gay people in the United States, Madonna came closer than any other contemporary celebrity to being an aboveground queer icon.'[51]

Madonna is known for playing with sexual identity as well as the gender identifications of the audience. For this reason, it has been argued by some critics that:

> Madonna has increasingly subverted dominant gender categories ... She forces the spectator to question the boundaries of gender constructs and the cultural constraints on sexual themes and sexual fantasies.[52]

Madonna's contribution to the Queer aesthetic, though less informed than Della Grace's work, is perhaps more significant because of her international popularity. In chapter two we outlined Baudrillard's expansion of commodity fetishism. We would argue that Baudrillard's concept of fetishism is more relevant to analysing the phenomenon of Madonna than Freud is. Madonna is not what she is pretending to be: there is little reference to 'utility' function in terms of the way Madonna uses products to carve out identities for herself. The image of Madonna has as much to do with actual women as aeroplane food has to with the food we buy in the market; they are both simulacra.

Queer representations, like those mentioned in relation to Madonna, are prevalent in the 1990s more than ever before. They are subsequently thought by some critics to cause gender confusion in the minds of spectators and have been celebrated for precisely that reason. To explain such representations, the post-Oedipal model of sexuality, based on ideas about castration anxiety and lack, which is integral to gaze theory, is inadequate. It cannot fully comprehend all the positively perverse pleasure deriving from the gaze as 'gender fuck': nor can it encompass the way that the queer visual aesthetic plays around with sexual as well as gender signs.

Fetish Artists

Women in fetish outfits have become more familiar in the 1990s, even though these representations have been with us in popular culture as well as High Art for at least the last fifty years. But feminist discussions of fetishism on the art circuit have not taken the debate much further than Mulvey's ideas about women as fetishised 'object' of the male gaze. Only Mary Kelly has really looked at women as fetishists in the active sense. She was really the first to put the issue of female fetishism on the feminist agenda by arguing that the mother was the prototype fetishist, and we return to her work later.

While some women fetish photographers, like Della Grace and Grace Lau, or artists such as Many Harris the leather sculptor, or Penny Slinger, who creates fetish photo-montage objects, have gained the attention of some feminist art critics, they are not well known or discussed. Conversely, male artists such as Robert Mapplethorpe, Allen Jones, or Jeff Koons have achieved the sort of fame rarely bestowed upon their female contemporaries.

The work of women fetish artists seems to remain further on the fringes than the work of male fetish artists. Why? Is it simply that women artists are still being 'hidden from history' and/or are not valued by male critics (even though feminist art historians have attempted to reclaim them)? There could be several explanations for the lack of critical acclaim of women fetish artists. The 'hidden from history' argument has been made about most of women's creativity as has been outlined in many books including *Old Mistresses*[53] as well as *The Subversive Stitch*.[54] But perhaps this lack of discussion of women fetish artists is also an effect of theory's inability to positively explain why women artists also create fetishised images of women.

'Fetish' Art is often associated with 'deviant' female sexuality – lesbianism in particular. Clearly, lesbianism is marginalised much more than male homosexuality in terms of mainstream discussion and representation (as the editors and contributors to *Stolen Glances* have pointed out before us).[55] Even when lesbianism is not the cause of marginalisation there are other reasons why the voices and work of women practitioners of fetish art are rarely seen or heard. Recent issues of *Skin Two* magazine suggest there is more artistic work on the subject of fetishism being produced in London and other art colleges by women than ever before. Yet there appears to be little evidence that fetish art is seen as straightforward or legitimate work for women.

Christine Berry, who created S&M leather sculptures while at Chelsea School of Art in the late 1980s, reports that she had a hard time being taken seriously and was not given support by staff or students, who she felt were undermining in many ways.[56] On the other hand, when we interviewed a rubber textile designer, Amanda Ross, from the MA in Textile Design at Central St. Martin's School of Art and Design, she didn't view the situation in the 1990s as being quite so oppressive:

> I mean I get jokes about rubber all the time, with people sort of saying, aha, she's a pervert ... into funny sexual practices using rubber. There is a definite connotation but ... I think it depends on your make up and how much you let things affect you. People jibe and joke all the time, I do that myself. But the fact is that I can stand up and talk seriously about my work and make people understand why I want to do it, which changes the atmosphere.'[57]

The lack of critical attention to the subject of women and fetishism may be changing. Some of the resistance to taking work seriously may be because even feminist art historians have had trouble believing that women could be practitioners (rather than objects) of fetishism. Indeed art historian Lisa Tickner wrote in 1978:

> Voyeurism and even fetishism, which have provided the impetus for large quantities of erotic art and literature are both rare among women'[58]

Since that time, while there have been many shifts in feminist thinking, which would construct female sexual desire as 'active'[59], little has been said about women and fetishism. This may be because ideas associated with Laura Mulvey's work have been extremely powerful. The person who put the subject of female fetishism on the map more than any one else, as we have mentioned, is Mary Kelly. Her artistic practice influenced feminists into taking on board the idea that fetishism could be seen as a practice involving female agency. We discuss this work below in detail but question whether even Mary Kelly addresses women specifically as *sexual* fetishists.

Mary Kelly – Sexual or Anthropological Fetishism?

Mary Kelly's London exhibition *Post-Partum Document* was subsequently written up as a book. In it she displayed objects associated with her baby, charting his first move away from the breast, at weaning, to the move away from home to go to school. The work as a whole details the mother's experience and her sense of loss: 'It is an effort to articulate the mother's fantasies, her desires, her stake in that project called motherhood' (Mary Kelly).[60] The objects on the walls of the exhibition, Kelly argued, were the fetish objects that enabled her to disavow the separation. As such, the exhibition located itself as part of a 'real' process of dealing with an active female fetishism, corresponding to male sexual fetishism.

Kelly's view of the mother's memorabilia as 'female fetishism' fits in with orthodox Freudian thinking about the female passage through the Oedipus complex. The girl, envying the father's penis, desires to have a child by him, as her 'penis substitute'. For women, therefore, the threat of castration does not focus on genitalia but instead takes the form of fear about losing children.

Our main problem with Kelly's argument about 'sexual' fetishism is that the mother's memorabilia seems to us to be less about an individual history of sexual repression and more about that which is socially expected and determined. The fetishism of the child's memorabilia by women seems to us to be anthropological, standing in for the absent person (as mentioned in chapter one). Such rituals of motherhood legitimate social cohension (ie, the woman in the home as mother). There are however further theoretical ramifications of Kelly's work for any psychoanalytic understanding of female fetishism, which we should also address here.

The first half of *Post-Partum Document* was initially exhibited in 1976 when the press, alerted by the outraged reactions, dubbed it the "Dirty Nappies" show.[61] Located within a Lacanian framework, the six sections chart the development of the separation of the mother-child relationship. A series of used nappy liners, inscribed with details of the food consumed, forms the first section of the exhibition. The meticulousness of the detailed documentation conveys the mother's anxiety over the baby's progressive weaning from the breast and onto solid foods. The next section details the child's first pre-Oedipal utterances, ('da', 'diddy', etc). Section three continues the representation of the child's weaning from the dyadic union of mother and baby, in detailing the mother's anxieties over his attending nursery.

Section four locates itself at the Oedipal moment and presents a series of 'transitional objects' used by the child (his 'blankie') and by the mother (casts of his fist) to assuage their separation anxieties (see Illustration 12). The final two sections chart the child's entry into the symbolic codes, of firstly, sexual differentiation and secondly, language (both signified by the phallus in Lacan). Sexual differentiation is documented by the child's distinguishing between what is appropriate for men, and what is appropriate for women. Language is represented by the child's attempts at the alphabet, alongside the mother's difficulties in securing a school for him (see Illustration 13). The exhibition ends with the boy, almost four and a half, writing his name and entering into the symbolic, external world.

Post Partum Document thus charts a mother's reactions from her baby's first move away from the breast at six months, through to his access to written language and school. It locates the maternal experience within a materialist and a psychoanalytic discourse. The artwork rejects any literal figuration of the mother, refusing to make her the object of the viewer's gaze, and instead presents us with her subjectivity, her presence through her articulated desires and anxieties.

Within the work itself, and outside in her 'Preface' , Mary Kelly argues that *Post Partum Document* both is, and traces, a form of female fetishism:-

> In having the child, in a sense she has the phallus. So the loss of the child is the loss of the symbolic plenitude – more exactly the ability to represent lack … in one way, I have attempted to displace the potential fetishisation of the child on to the work of art; but I have also tried to make it explicit in a way which would question the fetishistic nature of the representation itself.[62]

Post-Partum Document is a multi-discursive, rich artwork that raises questions about the construction and subjecthood of the 'maternal project'. We would concur that it does challenge the objectification of art as commodity fetishism. This can be witnessed from the outcry over Kelly's practice in using actual stained nappy-liners, as opposed to the more usual and more kitsch painting of a mother changing a nappy, as Laura Mulvey has pointed out.[63]

The language of separation: Post-Partum Document, Mary Kelly

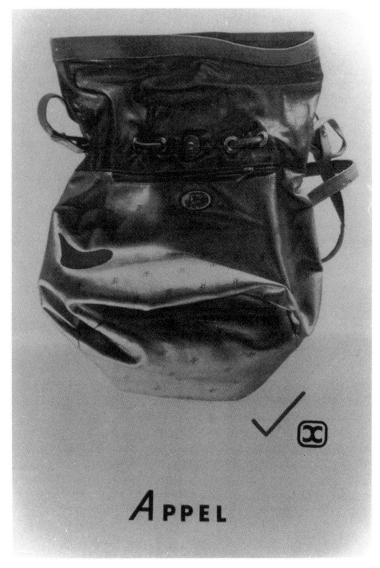

Interim Project 'Appel': Female desire in bondage
Mary Kelly

Post-Partum Document literally represents the process of the maternal fetishisation of the child. Visual accounts of the maternal 'hanging on to', are achieved by Kelly exhibiting her son's things: his nappies, hand-casts, gifts, drawings, writing, etc. However we would challenge the thesis that this fetishisation represents the psychological fetishisation of disavowing the separation and loss of the child-as-phallus. This is because we do not see this as a representation of sexual fetishism at all, since we argue that women have access to psychological fetishism in the same libidinal way as men. For us Kelly's transitional objects constitute anthropological fetishism seen from a peculiarly female point of view within the context of post-industrial Western culture.

The use of the hand-cast, the 'gifts' carefully saved, the drawings and transcripts of his baby conversations, are the mother's memorabilia of the baby at each moment of babyhood, captured and preserved, while the child grows away and grows up. We would go further and argue that these fetish objects Kelly uses in her work are directly comparable to the concert ticket and programme a fan uses to hold onto the experience of the concert once the actual moment has gone.

Unlike the masculine model of castration disavowal, there is no sexual arousal documented in relation to the objects. There is also precious little evidence of the unconscious at work in the dynamic of choosing them. The objects being fetishised lie within the conscious domain of disavowing the separation from the child. There is a logical connection between the choice of the child's drawings and nappy-liners to signify his presence, just as there is in a fan's choice of a concert ticket or the jacket worn by the star. These chosen objects are entirely different from the piece of string or the leather shoe chosen by the sexual fetishist, where the logical connection breaks down and the distortion by the unconscious becomes evident.

Just how much the concept of motherhood has silently subsumed female sexuality within the absorption of the child-as-phallus theory can be realised by thinking about a man in a similar scenario. Imagine a male artist documenting

1. the progress of his child
2. the movements of his dick over the same period.

Creating images to represent (1) and (2) would illuminate the differences between the social relationship of 'father' and the sexual identity of a 'male'. (The penis/phallus covers aspects of both cultural evaluation and libidinal desire, which the child-as-phallus does not.) We would not want to argue that either of the two constructs are simple or 'natural', but they are clearly different things. Were the same hypothetical male artist to develop his series to document

3. objects that signified the presence of his child
4. objects that aroused his dick to erection

the differences between the two processes would exemplify the difference between anthropological and sexual fetishism.

Kelly's acceptance of the psychoanalytic model of female castration, and in particular of penis envy, allows her to conflate these disparate elements in a way that actively denies woman as a sexual subject in her own right. But, as many of the art critics at the time of the exhibition argued – either overtly, like Jo-Ann Isaak[64], Margaret Iversen[65] and Laura Mulvey,[66] or covertly like Lucy Lippard[67] – the 'castration' reading is but one of many in this rich work. In its complex representation of female anthropological fetishism and in its radical documenting and problematising of the social and psychical roles of motherhood, *Post-Partum Document* remains an exciting work.

Kelly's later work, *Interim*,[68] explores the cultural and psychic experiences of being a middle-aged woman; a woman in between (interim) childbearing and old age, in a culture that only values women for their potential fertility. The psychoanalytic framework for this work is of the female hysteric,[69] but the work does encompass aspects of the commodification of women and of the lack of a symbolic, which we feel links to our arguments on fetishism.

The five sections of 'Corpus' each uses an article from a woman's wardrobe: a leather jacket, a handbag, boots, negligee, embroidered dress. These objects are represented in three similar ways: firstly, neatly folded and emblematic of a woman's groomed appearance; secondly in disarray, signifying the ageing body's disintegration from the youthful ideal; thirdly in bondage. The bound image (see Illustration 13) we would argue, is emblematic of female desire and fantasy, bondaged by our culture's lack of a language through which to express itself. Alongside each image runs a discontinuous narrative formed from conversations on middle age with over a hundred women. The narratives for the images of groomed appearance use the discourse of fashion; those for the disarray of the ageing body, use the medical language of objectification of women's bodies. The images of female fantasy and bondage are accompanied by narratives using the debased discourse of Romance and Disney fairytale.

The images focus on the commodity fetishism of consumer articles/signs associated with women (the ubiquitous black negligee, the 'apple-pie' embroidered white dress, etc). The absence of the woman in the frame, and the objects standing in for her, have been interestingly commented on by two critics, who also focus on the lack of a discourse for feminine pleasure within a phallocentric symbolic order.

Parveen Adams, in an article arguing that *Interim* works on the spectator in 'the discourse of the analyst', focuses on the absent signified, the woman, and questions whether this representation of absence points to a lack of 'a feminine order of signifiers ... Perhaps, indeed, what *Interim* does is to whet your appetite for a feminine ego ideal',[70] a feminine Imaginary. Laura Mulvey, commenting on the third, 'bondaged' image, also hones in on the absence of a feminine symbolic:

> its explicit sexual reference to a discourse of perversion opens up the question ... the problem of female sexual desire. Mary Kelly implies that desire cannot be expressed without an image that can represent itself. This third panel then speaks to ... the common need to redefine *women's* relation to their image, beyond the question of male appropriate image for masculine pleasure, to discover a feminine desire and understand female sexuality.[71]

Within the domains of fetishism, both anthropological (in *Post-Partum Document*) and commodity (in *Interim*), Mary Kelly has created artworks which challenge and document women's complex passage through a phallocentric culture.

Feminists on Literary Fetishism:
The Repercussions

Feminists have long explored literature, questioning the status of the canon and analysing the texts as sites of resistance to, and inscriptions of, patriarchal discourses. Lacan and the work of the French Feminists Kristeva, Cixous and Irigaray, have enabled even further insight into the analysis of these discourses. The field of psychoanalytic criticism is large, but that which relates specifically to the issue of fetishism is remarkably small. It appears to have been initiated mainly by the American scholar, Naomi Schor.

During the 1980s an interest in sexual fetishism began to emerge in feminist literary circles, particularly in America. Schor's influential essay on George Sand (written in 1986) seems to have been used by the other writers in the field as an inspiration on which to model the readings of their own authors: Emily Apter on Maupassant and other nineteenth century French writers; Marjorie Garber on Shakespeare. In 1987 the Modern Language Association Conference held annually in New York included a special session on fetishism, which both Schor and Apter attended. In 1988, the discussion of fetishism continued at the University of Pennsylvania's conference 'Eroticism and the Body Politic' organised by Lynn Hunt.[72] In what follows we try to chart the theoretical ramifications of feminist literary discussion of fetishism.

Naomi Schor

In the 1986 essay, 'Female Fetishism: The Case of George Sand,'[73] Naomi Schor argues that Sand's novels illustrate cases of fetishism and so, being written by a woman, problematise Freud's assertion that women do not fetishise. Her discussion of Freud's argument that, as Schor put it, 'female fetishism is, in the rhetoric of psychoanalysis, an oxymoron'[74] is extremely cogent, and she lists a range of examples of female fetishism that she has found in case studies, to challenge his view. Mobilising Kofman's argument that fetishism, a paradigm of undecideability, should be adopted by feminists, Schor argues that feminist criticism in the 1980s adopted a similar strategy, through its readings of 'bitextuality'.

Our main argument with Schor's essay, however, is that the examples she chooses from the work of George Sand are not in our eyes fetish practices at all, but sado-masochistic examples of the typical 'bruised lips' syndrome associated with representations in romance fiction. Schor cites a moment from Sand's novel *Valentine* (1869) where the heroine's foot is scalded before the consummation takes place. 'What,' asks Schor, 'is the significance of this unusual foreplay, this pre-coital wounding followed by the eroticisation of the injured limb?'[75] Were it any other limb, the answer might well have been the sadist's eroticization of his partner's pain, but since it is a foot, Schor makes the connection with Freud's discussion of Chinese footbinding in his essay 'Fetishism'. Turning to *Mauprat* (1837) she gives a second example of Sand's fetishism when the character Bernard eroticises his partner's scratched arm. She locates fetishism in the quotation 'I gently lifted the lace which fell over her elbow, and, emboldened by her drowsiness, pressed my lips to the darling wound'.

Schor, we feel, is conflating the two sexual practices she observes. She argues that wounds are not fetishised by men and that this therefore makes them a specifically female form. She further interprets the wounds as signifying 'a refusal to firmly anchor women ... on either side of the axis of castration'[76] but why and how the wounds serve this symbolic function is never fully explained.

In her discussion of the case studies of female fetishists, Schor seems to accept Bonnet's Lacanian theory that the female fetishist 'becomes', in her own body, the mother's (desired) phallus (and is thus a case of hystericisation rather than a perversion). She argues that Sand had 'a possessive mother who used her daughter as a phallic substitute'.[77] She thus accepts the view that women necessarily experience penis envy.

Schor goes further and states: 'there is more to female fetishism than the masculinity complex'[78], but she shifts the use of fetishism to a textual reading. What also happens here is a slippage in direction and in applying the theory to representation. Schor gives up on fetishism as a possibility for 'real' women and ends up teasing out the lack of fixity in the representations of gender. She concludes the essay by asking whether an attempt to appropriate fetishism is 'in fact only the latest and most subtle form of penis envy?'[79]

As we have stressed, this is an interesting and challenging discussion of the theory of fetishism. It is one that lists a range of cases of female fetishism and strives to assert a feminine practice even though it never really challenges the Freudian concept of penis envy. It inspired both Emily Apter and Marjorie Garber to develop readings of female fetishism within literature.

In the essay, 'Fetishism and Its Ironies', published two years later,[80] Schor links irony to fetishism, arguing that both have a similar trope: 'Just as the fetish enables the fetishist to simultaneously recognise and deny woman's castration, irony allows the ironist to both reject and reappropriate the discourse of reference, Romanticism in the case of Flaubert.' [81]

Looking back on her George Sand essay, she explains that what she was 'groping towards' was not fetishism as a strategy for feminism so much as irony. Fetishism as a concept now retains all of its perverse connotations of objectification and denigration of women. Schor seems quietly to have accepted that women do not fetishise sexually, that sexual fetishism is predominantly male. She is now focussing solely upon representation and the literary trope's potentially deconstructive 'uncertainties' .

In her definition of 'Fetishism', for Blackwell's *Feminism and Psychoanalysis*[82], Schor explains Freud's account of fetishism and states that female cases have been rare. In stressing its importance to feminism, she explains that fetishism is 'the linchpin' in privileging the phallus in Freud's theory and so 'underwrites the ideology of gender'. Fetishism, through its 'uncertainty', stands for the 'ultimate undecideability of female castration'.

Schor splits the feminist appropriations into three camps: those who use the paradigm of oscillation as a deconstructive political strategy for arguing for equal rights while retaining sexual difference; those who discuss the textual representations of fetishism by women writers (citing herself and Apter); and those who re-read Freud to allow female disavowal and splitting of the ego within lesbian practice (Grosz)[8].

The definition ends by locating Freud's theorisation of 'psychic' fetishism in the nineteenth century alongside a similar discursive practice of 'morcelisation' by capitalism. Schor argues for the need to find a different model for theorising sexual difference 'beyond late capitalism'.

Overall, Schor's work on female fetishism has been the major influence on feminist literary critics. She has opened up the debate to a level of theorisation and questioning that has been ground-breaking. However, her main interest has been in adapting psychoanaytic readings to literary tropes, rather than in challenging the psychoanalytic theories themselves, and for this reason we are not surprised that she still concurs that female fetishism is rare.

Emily Apter

Emily Apter's discussion of female fetishism, as evidenced in nineteenth century literature, takes a different tack to Schor. In the early version of the essay 'Splitting Hairs: Female Fetishism and Post Partum Sentimentality in the Fin de Siecle' (written in 1991) [84], and in the book, *Feminizing the Fetish: Psychoanalysis and Narrative Obsession in Turn-of-the-Century France* (written in 1991),[85] (where the later version of 'Splitting Hairs' becomes chapter five), Apter challenges the Freudian phallocentrism of fetishism.

She argues that, whereas nineteenth century psychopathology stops at the masculine examples of fetishism, the fiction goes on to illustrate female examples of fetishists. The works of Flaubert, the Goncourts, Mallarme, Maupassant, Mirbeau and Zola are used to demonstrate these literary 'case studies' of women by male authors.[86]

On the whole, as Apter acknowledges, the fiction tends to illustrate male fetishisation of women, rather than female practice, but she does extend the theory of female fetishism in two interesting ways. Firstly, in a chapter utilising, and critiquing, Riviere's theory of feminity in

'Unmasking the Masquerade', she argues for a feminine form of fetishism in fashion. She cites Freud's 1909 assertion that 'all women are clothes fetishists' in order to challenge Lacan's view that women masquerade as the phallus. Instead she argues for a 'sartorial super-ego' as a way of feminizing the fetish and challenging the assertion that the libido is essentially masculine.

Secondly, in her following chapter, 'Splitting Hairs'[87] she mobilises Mary Kelly's *Post-Partum Document* model of female fetishism, in her analysis of Maupassant's fiction. Maupassant's fictional accounts of women collecting melancholic memorabilia is well documented. However, the female characters collect 'relics' of their lovers in order to disavow the loss of the dead person, not for masturbatory purposes. We would therefore locate Maupassant's examples within anthropological fetishism, for the same reasons as we do Mary Kelly's *Post-Partum Document*.

In her final example from Maupassant, from *Bel-Ami* (1885), one woman winds her hair around the buttons of her lover's coat so that he will take something of her along with him. This reciprocal desire to be 'always with' the loved object does add another element to a woman's practice of anthropological fetishism, but it does not turn it into sexual fetishism simply because it is performed upon a lover.

Not all fetishism is erotic, as we have argued throughout this book. Both cases of Apter's discussion of female fetishism are fascinating and we would agree with her readings in all but one point – her examples of fetishism are not located in sexual desire. We would suggest they constitute firstly, commodity fetishism of clothes – which has, as she argues, been instrumental in the material construction of femininity – and secondly anthropological fetishism.

Apter's book[88] gives a detailed, sophisticated account of psycho-analytic theories of perversity and applies them to her reading and original interpretation of *fin-de-siecle* French literature. It doesn't really address sexual fetishism as a contemporary and active practice by today's women. Instead, it gives a useful history of psychopathology in its 'New History' contextualisation of the literature. While we would clearly endorse her attempts to de-phallicise fetishism, we feel that her discussion still lacks clarity in its descriptions of female sexual fetishism.

Marjorie Garber

Marjorie Garber's essay 'Fetish Envy'[89] begins with Schor's closing question from 'Female Fetishism', whether the attempt to appropriate fetishism is the latest form of penis envy. Garber argues that the answer is yes, because the question is tautological: 'phallus envy *is* fetish envy'. Garber therefore sees fetishism as pre-eminently about the protection of the phallus. Female fetishism is only passingly referred to, in relation to the Lacanian argument that since a woman fetishises her partner's penis, female fetishism goes unrecognised in our society because it fits within the model of normal heterosexuality.

Garber argues that any cultural signifier of the phallus is a fetish object. She links the cod-piece of Shakespearian theatre to Freud's patient who fetishised wearing an athletic support. Since a cod-piece can be removed, she argues, it therefore stands as a 'mark of undecideability'. We would question such a reading of the cod-piece because for us the cod-piece magnifies, and hence reifies, the phallus. It asserts the presence (and value) of the phallus, whereas Freud's patient's athletic belt concealed his genitals and so denied sexual difference.

On the whole, we think Garber has confused fetishism with exhibitionism. Her discussion of the significance of the cod-piece in Renaissance theatre conflates terms. She talks of a reification of the phallus to cover male anxieties of 'performance'. She links this to cross-dressing (and possibly vogueing in the final look at Madonna). Here, Garber has conflated fetishism's oscillatory disavowal with the fluidity available to theatrical representations of sexual identity. By misdirecting its thesis onto fetishism, her essay dilutes an interesting discussion of representations of sexual identities and their lack of fixity.

Despite our criticisms, it should be noted that literary discussions associated with Schor, Garber and Apter have opened up the debate about female fetishism in a number of ways. This discussion of fictional accounts of fetishism is not completely compatible with our project of trying to extend the theory, based on the experience of women, and so our analysis has emphasised the issue of conflation in critical definitions of fetishism. Nevertheless we hope that our response to these articles is seen as a constructive attempt to widen the definitions of fetishism circulating in the theoretical arena. Chiefly we believe that these feminist literary discussions have put on the agenda the question of female agency, even if they have not provided a model with which to argue for it. So we find ourselves challenging these as well as other feminist readings of fetishism, which

1. see fetishism as solely appertaining to the protection of the phallus and/or
2. equate female fetishism with forms of 'penis envy'.

Art, Fashion And Fetishism: The Problem of Conflation

As we have explained in detail, with a few notable exceptions most of the previous feminist work we have looked at on the subject of women and fetishism has not discriminated between anthropological, commodity and sexual fetishism. Conflation of the different types of fetishism was so widespread in feminist, as well as more general, discussions of fetishism that in one collection of essays on fetishism and popular culture we found discussion of advertising images, girlie mags, voodoo and even scholarship without any definition of the precise type of fetishism under scrutiny.[90] These essays, rather than 'interpreting present day fetishes in light of earlier and more regularised definitions' or 'updating concepts [of fetishism] to make them more use to the present day reader' – as was suggested by the editor Ray B. Browne in the introduction – in fact did the opposite.[91] Most of the essays tended to treat the word 'fetishism' as a blanket term that could contain all cultural fixations, accentuations, partialisms or personal obsessions. In our opinion this sort of writing often inapropriately interpreted consumer fetishism as sexual fetishism.

Even books that take fetishism as their main topic of discussion, such as David Kunzle's *Fashion and Fetishism*[92], have in our view been unable to make adequate distinctions between fetishism and *eroticism*. Descriptions of eroticism, inappropriately diagnosed as fetishism, are common to much of the literature we found under the subject index 'fetishism'. In what follows we consider Kunzle's book in detail because its problems are endemic to many other studies.

David Kunzle

The empirical methodology of David Kunzle's book *Fashion and Fetishism* attempts to identify female fetishism by quoting journals and correspondence which describes the feelings of Victorian ladies who enjoyed tight-lacing of corsets. Kunzle's position is that corset-wearing wasn't just 'fashion' for many Victorian women of all classes, but often constituted sexual gratification because:

> Tight-lacing, like all forms of fetishism certainly exists ... The capacity of modern woman for an active, rather than passive form of fetishism is confirmed by the practicing fetishist pairs personally known to me, amongst whom the female often assumes an active and sometimes leading role.[93]

Kunzle's argument is that a group of 'tight-lacers' – that is women who enjoyed the pleasures of constriction from wearing corsets as much the achievement of twelve inch waists– were sexually assertive women enjoying self-flagellation and thereby expressing female desire. (He uses the word 'fetishism' to categorise this behaviour but his descriptions are of S&M scenarios.)

Kunzle's book goes on to argue that those who saw the corset as simply 'oppressive', such as the dress reform movement or the physicians worried about women engaged in 'crushing' their ribs, were not always in an objective position to understand or judge the behaviour they condemned. Critics of the corset were either socially conservative and/or sexually puritanical because:

> the rebellion/restraints of tight-lacing is not merely a masochistic reflection of socio-sexual subjection of women by man, but a submissive/ aggresssive protest against that role.'[94]

Kunzle goes on to argue that his tight-lacers are women 'fetishists' and entirely different from fashion victims who endure discomfort to be fashionable.

Whatever we deduce about the activities of the 'tight-lacers' from the correspondence referred to by Kunzle, there is no denying there is much slippage in his terminology. Like other books on the subject of fetishism that try to read 'across' culture, Kunzle is unable to distinguish between the different types of fetishism he encounters in his case studies. Some cases of corset fixation may constitute sexual fetishism of clothing by women, but Kunzle's book makes so many generalisations, on subjects as diverse as starch linen fetishism, breast eroticism (which he inappropriately describes as 'breast fetishism'[95]) as well as 'Zoo fetishism'[96], that it is hard to be sure what he means at all. It is almost impossible to decide from Kunzle's accounts whether or not the men/women he describes choose the object to bring them to sexual orgasm in preference to any other sexual stimulation. If they did this would clearly constitute sexual fetishism in the fourth degree as outlined in chapter one when discussing Gebhard's model of the intensities of sexual fetishism. But Kunzle is not clear at all, either about the intensity of, or even the sexual nature of, the behaviour he is talking about.

His ideas about the sexual pleasure gained from 'constriction' or 'flagellation', for example, associated with women wearing corsets, more appropriately equate with bondage scenarios and the pscyhoanalytic concept of masochism than with fetishism. Yet Kunzle refutes the suggestion of masochism:

The dependency which tight lacing might induce is both psychological and physical. One young woman described her feelings when she wanted to be tighter than the corset could make her as 'really hurting' and 'being out of touch with my body' ... once the threshold of pain has been passed, it is experienced as pure pain, a condition the fetishist (as opposed to the masochist) does not seek.[97]

In the above quotation, fetishism is seen as pain that is not 'total', whereas masochism is associated with nothing but pain. Such an analysis ignores psychoanalytic theories of masochism and denies a notion of various intensities of gratification. This may be because Kunzle does not really address pscyhoanalytic concepts at all in his discussion of fetishism:

the reduction by psychoanalysis of human personality to intra-psychic traits, and its elimination of social factors, has rendered it useless, if not actually harmful, when dealing with fetishism.'[98]

Kunzle's dismisal of psychoanalysis is not as surprising as it might first appear, but is a political strategy. As Valerie Steele has pointed out:

Kunzle deliberately eschews any attempt to analyze the possible uncon-scious significance of fetishism, presumably because such an analysis might make tight-lacing appear to be a sexual perversion rather than an orthodox but legitimate and sexually liberated form of behaviour ... his work is a *defense* of fetishism.[99]

But by 'defending' fetishism Kunzle side-steps the issue of masochism and its pleasures and conflates ideas about eroticism and fetishism, a point we shall return to later.

How do we understand this apparent Victorian epidemic of fe-male masochism in terms of female desire rather than women's op-pression? Kunzle is of course right when he says it would be absurd to simply regard the corset as a metaphor of women's social restraints and subordination. As Elizabeth Wilson among other critics has pointed out, the corset has had so many different meanings in Vic-torian times as well as our own.

By focussing on corset 'fetishism' rather than on the issue of the 'masochism' of Victorian women, Kunzle implicitly refutes radical feminist arguments on corset-wearing: Mary Daly and Jane Caputi, among others, locate body modifications or uncomfortable fashions for women as further evidence of patriarchal oppression, and:

a primary means by which phallocratic fixers fix, tame, and train women for their own designs; the bad magic by which fakers attempt to destroy

female consciousness, embedding contagious anxieties and cravings, trying to trap women in houses of correction/ houses of mirrors ... [100]

Indeed, by implying that the meaning of the corset for women who
derive sexual pleasure from tight-lacing was, and is, connected to
ideas about social resistance, Kunzle is able to move away from a
negative reading of female agency. But it should be borne in mind
that only a simplistic understanding of 'masochism' would interpret
such pleasure from tight-lacing as unproblematically equating with
women's oppression; many feminists writing about cultural politics
certainly would not take this line.[101]

So while we sympathise with Kunzle's dilemma, and his reluctance
to accept the radical feminist argument that reads the corset as a
metaphor of women's oppression, we feel his methodology is inappropriate. By refusing to engage with psychoanalysis he prevents himself
from developing an informed analysis of the corset. A more sophisticated model of masochism and its pleasures would have served his
argument much more appropriately than the concept of fetishism. In
fact we found three main flaws to Kunzle's logic.

First, it must be noted that sexual pleasure derived from the tight-
lacing of corsets by a small group of specific women – even if this
interpretation could be proven – is unlikely to be representative of
the meaning of the corset in the lives of the majority of nineteenth
century women. (Kunzle's reading of Victorian journals and data, it
should be noted, are by no means conclusive in their findings.) Secondly,
the precise nature of the sexual pleasure Kunzle alludes to is not
specified. It seems unlikely from the accounts found in Victorian
journals that the corset, as an object in its own right, produced orgasm
in women. It is more likely that it was the element of bondage and
constriction that created sexual catharsis in women. Third, and finally,
the gender gap between sexual pleasure gained by an individual from
the process of achieving a tiny waist, and the widespread male erotic
interest in tiny waists (and the erotic charge from binding and
unbinding the waist and bosom) cannot be completely separated. Nor
can it be over-stressed. Kunzle's logic suggests a compatibility between socially learned gender roles concerning who is laced and who
isn't.

The tight-lacer may achieve pleasure from constriction (and release from it), associated with masochism; the viewer may achieve
erotic pleasure from visual images of tiny waists and heaving bosoms
and the fantasy of 'possessing' them, but Kunzle's gender equation
implies that it is always the women who enjoy being tied up and the

men who do the untying. This analysis, which to be fair may have only been meant to describe the tight-lacing pairs 'known' to Kunzle, nevertheless presents a restrictive and inaccurate analysis of S&M practice. Men as well as women are reported in great numbers to enjoy masochism. Despite the gender issues in the scenarios Kunzle describes, neither sex appears to be engaged in sexual fetishism, at the level that Gebhard described as the fourth degree.

This question of a *degree* of erotic charge seems to have escaped the curiosity of many fashion historians who connect fashion trends with fetishism. Laver, for example, suggested that 'fashion is the comparative of which fetishism is the superlative'. [102] He went on to talk about male appreciation of female fashion trends like 'frou frou fetishism' in a way that conflates terms. As Valerie Steele has pointed out 'fashion historians ... jump to the conclusion that the incidence of fetishism was significantly higher in the nineteenth century than in the earlier or later periods – an hypothesis that the available evidence does not necessarily support.'[103]

What is positive about Kunzle's work, however flawed the analysis, is that he does recognise and try to theorise female agency. Not many critics have in fact looked at women as practitioners of fetishism. We see this focus as 'radical' because much writing which does appear at first glance to be about female fetishism, doesn't look at women as *practitioners* of fetishism at all. Instead it looks at the construction and representation of 'women as fetish'.

With one or two exceptions, most of the research on female fetishism that we found (written in the 1970s and 1980s) focussed on women as objects of fetishism, rather than as agents of fetishism, in order to explore women's oppression as a consequence of the male gaze. This work was important for feminism and opened up debates about women and representation. Questions about women's objectification are obviously relevant to debates about images of women in popular culture. But we feel that in such a changing cultural context, where images are often ironic and may be read differently by different groups anyway, feminists have to be careful about applying theoretical models too monolithically.

The image of 'Emma Peel' from the TV series *The Avengers*, for instance, may have given many women and men pleasure because of the energetic sexual spectacle she made in leather clothing, but this sort of active image is rarely discussed by critics as pleasurable at all.[104] Yet frequently feminist criticism has not talked about the *active pleasures* on offer to women from obviously fetishised images. This may be partly due to the rather generalised definition of 'fetishism' that has emerged in some feminist debates, which virtually dismiss all images of strong women as enacting 'phallic replacement'. Here, if the critic is Andrea Dworkin, ideas about the male gaze can become a crude metaphor which correlates with radical feminist readings of 'patriarchy'.[105]

Summary

In conclusion we argue that by looking at the issue of conflation in the different types of fetishisms employed in feminist theoretical discussion, we have highlighted the discursive formation contributing to the widespread critical conclusion that fetishism is 'rare' in women. We have pointed to the fact that the subject area has been neglected to some extent because the theoretical focus on 'Lack' has become a discursive practice. The Lacanian model has led to a feminist reading of images of women in the cinema as always 'objects' and 'victims' of male fetishism, obscuring questions about female agency. It has also ignored questions about shifts in representations as a result of change in social roles, and more recently through the emergence of post-modern aesthetics.

Nevertheless, by spending so much time and effort explaining previous debates and important art work, this chapter has attempted to acknowledge that previous feminist cultural writing has created rich debate and thought-provoking arguments – even if such discussion has cumulatively led to a theoretical impasse, in terms of visualing both female agency and the female gaze at women's experience. Given the central role of psychoanalysis in contributing to this theoretical 'impasse' we would suggest that it is now necessary to take what is useful from Freud and Lacan (notions about subjectivity, ego identifications and the mirror phase, for example) and to be highly critical of the rest; to draw upon cultural as well as psychoanalytic concepts to explain aspects of female experience.

In fact, in order to develop a model of female sexuality that can adequately conceptualise female agency and female libido as active, perhaps it is necessary for feminist critics to behave like theoretical guerrillas[106]. This may mean engaging in theoretical promiscuity – taking on board what is helpful and positive from the all the different theoretical writings, critically assessing the prescriptions that cannot even see, let alone explain, female agency.

Notes

1 Griselda Pollock, 'Anonymous Notes Towards a Show on Self Image', 1982, reprinted in R. Parker and G. Pollock (eds), *Framing Feminism: Art and the Women's Movement 1970–85*, Pandora, London 1987, p242.

2 As a consequence of Freudian emphasis on castration anxiety, much previous feminist discussion of women as objects (and occasionally as practitioners) of sexual fetishism legitimates (or at least engages with) the idea that female sexuality is regulated by 'Lack'. This stems from the Lacanian reformulation, in particular, of Freud on Castration Anxiety and Lack, which theoretically under-pins much contemporary feminist writing. In this work the inflated importance granted to the father's unseen organ, as Juliet Flower McCannel points out, means that the focus on lack is 'problematic for feminism in three areas' because it inadequately conceptualises:

(i) feminine access to sexuality/psychical reality

(ii) women's epistemology, the question of lack in her knowledge and perception of sex

(iii) the political effects of penis envy in relation to notions about desire and jouissance described in the Lacanian system.

See E. Wright (ed), *Feminism and Psychoanalysis: A Critical Dictionary*, Basil Blackwell, Oxford, 1982, pp207–9.

3 Laura Mulvey, *Visual and Other Pleasures*, Macmillan, Basingstoke 1989.

4 See Mary Kelly, *Post-Partum Document*, Routledge, London 1984.

5 Naomi Schor, 'Female Fetishism: The Case of George Sand', in Suleiman and Rubin (eds), *The Female Body in Western Culture*.

6 Emily Apter, *Feminising the Fetish: Psychoanalysis and Narrative Obsession in Turn-of-the-Century France*, Cornell, Ithaca 1991.

7 Marjorie Garber, *Vested Interests: Cross-Dressing and Cultural Anxiety*, Routledge, London 1992, chapter 5.

8 R. B. Browne, *Objects of Special Devotion: Fetishes and Fetishism in Popular Culture*, Bowling Green University Popular Press, 1989.

9 Laura Mulvey, 'Visual Pleasure and Narrative Cinema', *Screen*, Vol 16, No 3, Autumn 1975.

10 Betty Friedan, *The Feminine Mystique*, Gollancz, London 1963.

11 Robyn Morgan, *Sisterhood is Global: the Women's Movement Anthology*, Harmondsworth, Penguin 1985.

12 '*Ways of Seeing*, despite its sometimes over-assertive simplifications, unlocked a whole spray of ideas to be argued over and refined by others ... I would point immediately to, among much else, important new work subsequently on the representation of women, and on the analysis and decoding of advertisements', Mike Dibbs, quoted in Peter Fuller, *Seeing Through Berger*, The Claridge Press, London and Lexington, 1988, p69.

13 John Berger, *Ways of Seeing*, BBC/Penguin, Harmondsworth 1972, p170.

14 *Ibid*, p16.

15 *Ibid*, p46.

16 *Ibid*, p87.

17 Edward Said, *Orientalism*, Penguin, Harmondsworth 1975.

18 Peter Fuller, *op cit*, for example, first a disciple of Berger's then his most persistent critic, takes this view, and virtually suggests that Berger can't distinguish

208 FEMALE FETISHISM

between photographs and paintings. He bitterly points out that Berger's book has been reprinted every year since it was first published in 1972 and is a key text in art colleges so its influence should not be under-estimated.

19 He is particularly lucid about the way photographic techniques such as 'cropping', can over-emphasise one element of a whole painting above others, and thus change its meanings, so that an allegorical figure from Botticelli's *Venus and Mars* can become simply 'a portrait of a girl'. The point Berger is making is that these reproductions that appear everywhere, on postcards, chocolate boxes, and other forms of publicity for consumer products, often become more 'real' to the average person than the original. Berger utilises some ideas of Walter Benjamin's influential essay 'The Work of Art in the Age of Mechanical Reproduction' in order to analyse the significance of the flood of unanchored reproduced images that have flooded Western culture. His point is that the codes and conventions of European oil paintings have permeated other visual forms, such as film and advertising, and indeed our very consciousness itself.

20 J. Berger, *op cit*, p46.

21 Geoff Dyer, *Ways of Telling: The Work of John Berger*, Pluto, London 1986, p97.

22 Colin Gordon, (ed), *Power/Knowledge: Selected Interviews and Other Writing 1972-77 by Michel Foucault*, Harvester, Brighton 1980.

23 See Frantz Fanon, *Black Skin, White Masks*, Pluto, London 1986.

24 Sandra Lee Bartky, 'Foucault, Femininity and the Modernization of Patriarchal Power', in Irene Diamond and Lee Quinby (eds), *Feminism and Foucault: Reflections on Resistance*, Northeastern University Press, Boston 1989.

25 Catherine Hopwood made this point in 'My Discourse, My-Self', a paper presented to the Canadian Sociology and Anthropology Association, Victoria, B.C., May,1990.

26 Gordon (ed), *op cit*, p156.

27 Mulvey, 1975, *op cit*.

28 Judith Mayne, 'Feminist Film Theory and Criticism', *Signs*, No 1, Autumn 1985, p83.

29 C. Metz, *The Imaginary Signifier: Psychoanalysis and the Cinema*, Indiana University Press, Bloomington 1975.

30 Mulvey, 1989, *op cit*, p18.

31 *Ibid*, p19.

32 *Ibid*, p21.

33 *Ibid*, p25.

34 Patricia Mellencamp, *High Anxiety: Catastrophe, Scandal, Age and Comedy*, Indiana University Press, Bloomington 1992.

35 Mulvey, 1989, *op cit*, p17.

36 See Carol J. Clover, *Men, Women and Chainsaws: Gender in the Modern Horror Film*, BFI, London 1992, p221.

37 Mulvey, 1989, *op cit*, p20.

38 Chrissy Illey report 'Men on men and women', *Options*, August 1993, pp16-21.

38 S. Moore, 'Here's Looking at You Kid', in L. Gamman and M. Marshment (eds), 1988,*op cit*.

41 L. Gamman, 'Watching the Detectives' in L. Gamman & M. Marshment (eds), *op cit*. See also forthcoming article Caroline Evans and Lorraine Gamman 'What a drag – (1) the Gaze and (2) Masquerade Revisited', in Paul Burston (ed), *Queer Cultures*, Routledge, London 1994.

42 Gay porn, for example, which does not often feature women at all, contains levels of fetishism. How do we explain this phenomenon? Clearly psychoanalytic concepts that relate to the gaze may be useful, but definitions of fetishism here relate not only to the sexual and the unconscious but also to the promiscuous economic logic of capitalism. Profit is the reason gay porn has won a space in the market in the first place. Even the most homophobic of pornographers is able to repress unconscious anxieties when focussing upon that most erotic spectacle of all, money, connected to the burgeoning pink pound.

43 As Paul Burston, in a forthcoming book from Routledge on 'Queer Cultures' identifies, Mulvey's model cannot explain homosexual and lesbian experiences of viewing.

44 Guy Debord, *Comments on Society of the Spectacle*, Translated by Malcolm Imrie, Verso, London, 1988.

45 There have been so many articles, by Mary Ann Doane and Teresa de Lauretis among others, that it is impossible to list them all here. However, we would draw attention to the bibliographies, as well as the essays contained in the following collections: E. D. Pribham (ed), *Female Spectators*, Verso, London 1988: L. Gamman and M. Marshment (eds), *The Female Gaze*, Women's Press, London, 1988; Tessa Boffin and Jean Fraser (eds), *Stolen Glances*, Pandora, London 1991.

46 Tessa Boffin and Jean Fraser, *op cit*, see Introduction, pp9–29.

47 Reina Lewis, 'Disgraceful Images', forthcoming, *Feminist Review*, 1993.

48 Della Grace's models look like they know what lesbian sex is about unlike some of the fake lesbian models found in male pornography.

49 In *Women Viewing Violence*, edited by Philip Schlesinger *et al*, BFI Publishing, 1992, London, researchers argue that 'ethnicity proved to be a strong differentiating factor between different groups of women. Evidently, many black women viewers felt alienated because of the 'perceived irrelevance of some of the images to them'.

50 Judith Butler, *Gender Trouble*, pp33–4.

51 Lisa Henderson 'Justify Our Love: Madonna and the Politics of Queer Sex', in Cathy Schwichtenberg (ed), *The Madonna Connection: Representational Politics, Subcultural Identities, and Cultural Theory*, Westview Press, Oxford, 1992, p108.

52 Ann E. Kaplan, 'Madonna Politics: Perversion, Repression or Subversion? Or Masks, and/as Master-y', in Cathy Schwichtenberg, *op cit*, p175.

53 Rozika Parker and Griselda Pollock, *Old Mistresses: Women, Art and Ideology*, Routledge Kegan and Paul, London 1981.

54 Rozika Parker, *The Subversive Stitch: Embroidery and the Making of the Feminine*, Women's Press, London 1984.

55 Tessa Boffin and Jean Fraser, *op cit*, pp9–29.

56 *Skin Two* Video 2, 1990.

57 In the summer term of 1992, many students at Central St. Martin's School of Art and Design, entered and took seriously a competition designed by us to try and create specifically female images of fetishism, some of which appear in this book.

58 Lisa Tickner in 'The Body Politic: Female Sexuality and Women Artists Since 1970', reprinted in Rosika Parker and Griselda Pollock (eds), *op cit*, p266.

59 The debates Ros Coward took up and applied to her analysis of female sexuality in popular culture in *Female Desire*, Paladin, London 1984.

60 *Post-Partum Document*, Mary Kelly's 'Preface', p xvi, Routledge, London 1984.

61　Sections four and five were added in 1977, and the final section in 1979. Also a book form of the exhibition was published in 1984, tying in with the interest of the literary critics in the 1980s.

62　*Ibid*, p xvi.

63　'Post Partum Review', *Spare Rib*, 40 (1976). Reprinted in the Appendix to *Post-Partum Document* ,p201.

64　'But this reading is only one of several inscriptions found in the text .... The Lacanian theory is displaced in the work through the reiteration of the primacy of the material and historical over the "natural".' 'Our Mother Tongue: Post Partum Document', *Vanguard* April 1982; Reprinted in the Appendix to *Post-Partum Document*, p204)

65　'I believe Kelly is simultaneously serious about Lacan's theory and perhaps gently parodying it – a self-conscious witness to women's alienated position in relation to the Symbolic Order'. 'The Bride Stripped Bare by Her Desire: Reading Mary Kelly's Post-Partum Document', *Discourse* 4 (1981); reprinted in the Appendix to *Post-Partum Document*, p207.

66　'Mary Kelly is limited by a theory biased – though not invalidated – by patriarchal assumptions. The influence of French psychoanalyst Jacques Lacan is heavily apparent in Post-Partum Document. But one important aspect of the exhibition prevails: it gives voice to the pain and pleasure women have lived as mothers, understood by each other, despised as domestic by dominant culture.', Appendix, *Post-Partum Document*, p202.

67　Lucy Lippard silently distances herself from Kelly's view of the work, through the use of parentheses. 'The result is a poignant attempt to understand the mother's personal sense of loss (loss of the phallus is her interpretation) when a child leaves the home...' 'Issue and Tabu', introduction to *Issue: Social Strategies by Women Artists,* ICA, London 1980.

68　We have only had access to 'Corpus', published as *Interim* (Fruitmarket Gallery, Kettle's Yard and Riverside Studios, 1986). During February-March 1990, four sections were on show at the New Museum in New York: 'Corpus', 'Pecunia', 'Historia' and 'Potestas'.

69　The artwork is structured around the five phases which Charcot (the nineteenth century French neurologist) designated as degrees of 'attitudes passionelles' in the hysteric. Feminism has both uncovered the ways in which nineteenth century psychoanalysis repressed women's sexuality, by pathologising resistence as hysteria, and the ways in which hysteria might be recuperated as a potential site of rebellion since the hysteric's symptoms find a voice outside of the phallocentric symbolic discourse. (Corpus makes reference to both Freud and 'Dora' in two of its third sections, and so to the feminist re-readings of 'Dora's Case'.)

70　'The art of Analysis: Mary Kelly's *Interim* and the Discourse of the Analyst', *October*, 58 (1991) 81-96 (92).

71　'Impending Time', in *Interim*, p7.

72　Published in 1990, L. Hunt (ed), *Eroticism and the Body Politic,* Johns Hopkins, Baltimore 1990, contains an earlier version of Apter's 'Splitting Hairs: Female Fetishism and Postpartum Sentimentality in Maupassant's Fiction'. The later version, see below, credits Naomi Schor and Carla Hesse with useful criticisms of her paper, during the conference discussion.

73　Susan R. Suleiman and Susan Rubin (eds), *The Female Body in Western*

Perspectives: Contemporary Perspectives, Cambridge, Mass., Harvard University Press, London 1986.

74 *Ibid*, p365.

75 *Ibid*, p364.

76 *Ibid*, p369.

77 *Ibid*, p362, footnote 2.

78 *Ibid*, p368.

79 *Ibid*, p371.

80 *Nineteenth Century French Studies*, 17 (1) Fall 1988, 87–97. Her book, *Reading in Detail: Aesthetics and the Feminine* (Methuen, London 1987), similarly is concerned with literary tropes, rather than psychoanalytic definitions of fetishism, though she does argue that nineteenth century realism, obsessed with detailing domestic things and objects, is itself a form of 'literary fetishism'.

81 *Ibid*, p94.

82 Elizabeth Wright (ed), *Feminism and Psychoanalysis: A Critical Dictionary*, Blackwell, Oxford 1992, pp113–17.

83 Elizabeth Grosz compiled the entry on 'fetishization' in the same dictionary, pp117–18.

84 *Body Politic*, Lynne Hunt (ed), *op cit*.

85 Emily Apter, *Feminizing the Fetish: Psychoanalysis and Narrative Obsession in Turn-of-the-Century France*, Cornell, Ithaca 1991.

86 Needless to say, there are problems with taking fiction as medical case studies, for all that many of the writers were fascinated by medical case studies and may have used them as the originals for their stories.

87 'Splitting Hairs: Female Fetishism and Postpartum Sentimentality in Maupassant's Fiction'.

88 We were unable to get Emily Apter and William Pietz (eds), *Fetishism as Cultural Discourse,* Cornell, Ithaca (forthcoming) before going to press.

89 *October* 54 (Fall 1990) pp 45-56

90 R. B. Browne, *Objects of Special Devotion: Fetishes and Fetishism in Popular Culture*, Bowling Green University Popular Press, 1989.

91 *Ibid*.

92 D. Kunzle, *Fashion and Fetishism: A Social History of the Corset, Tightlacing and Other Forms of Body Sculpture in the West*, New York: Ravan & Littlefield, 1982.

93 *Ibid*, p36.

94 *Ibid*, p250.

95 *Ibid*, p16.

96 *Ibid*, p9.

97 *Ibid*, p39.

98 *Ibid*, p14.

99 V. Steele, *Fashion and Eroticism: Ideals of Feminine Beauty From the Victorian Era to the Jazz Age*, Oxford University Press, Oxford 1985, p30.

100 Mary Daly (with Jane Caputo), *Websters' First New Intergalactic Wickedary of the English Language*, Beacon Press, Boston, 1987, p198.

101 `See definition of masochism by Ellie Rayland-Sullivan in *Feminism and Psychoanalysis*, discussed in E. Wright, *op cit*.

102 V. Steele, 1985, *op cit*, p30.

103 *Ibid*, p30.

104 L. Gamman and M. Marshment (eds), *op cit*, p10.

105 This argument about fetishised images of women has become so general that Andrea Dworkin, known for her biological essentialism and sweeping radical feminist statements, applies wholesale ideas about 'fetishised' images of women and argues: 'men look at women in an abstracting or fetishizing way; the voyeurism, the displaced excitement (displaced to the mind), puts the physical reality ... into a dimension of numbed abstraction', Andrea Dworkin, *Intercourse*, Martin & Secker, 1987, London, p33.

106 Lorraine Gamman was rather flattered to be accused by Beverly Alcock and Jocelyn Robson of being 'a theoretical guerilla' in *Feminist Review*, 35, p43, Summer 1990.

Fetishism – The Postmodern Condition?

For Baudrillard ... the power of femininity lies in this superficiality rather than in chasing after the falsehood of depth. Or to put it another way the postmodern condition has always been women's condition. *Suzanne Moore*[1]

We started writing this book based on the hunch that those who had previously argued that women do not fetishise had got it wrong. After extensive research into the subject we found not only that our initial intuitions about women as active practitioners of sexual fetishism were correct, but that women fetishised in more ways than had been dreamed of. But what sort of fetishism did women engage in? In order to answer this question, there was a need to clarify the often conflated discussions surrounding fetishism. Indeed, in order to attempt a radical look at women's relationship to the practice, we recognised that there was a need to find a new model of fetishism, one that could include women but move beyond artificial notions about femininity, and beyond pathologising individuals as perverts. A model that could address the wider cultural context of fetishism, without ignoring that complex and contradictory phenomenon, the human unconscious.

It didn't escape our notice that, as well as finding lots of women involved in various types of fetishism, we found that across western culture generally, consumer fetishism seemed to have reached a different level of intensity. The 'post-modern condition' describes the situation in some areas of Western culture in which 'hyper-reality'[3] is the order of the day: a cultural space where objects are no longer purchased for their use value but for what they signify to others; where images no longer reflect objects or subjects in the real world but have their own logic and meaning.

It occurred to us that, as hyper-real images of femininity and sexuality had clearly affected the experience of individual women,

perhaps such meanings had even mapped on to the female unconscious and had permeated individual psyches in complex and varied
ways. We looked at the way that women seemed to be increasingly
involved in fetishism, choosing objects like food to gain some form
of sexual satisfaction; and we wondered how this related, if at all, to
shifts in contemporary culture.

So we found that, having started off with arguing for the position
that women do fetishise, and engaging with psychoanalytic theory in
order to include women, we needed to move the analysis out of the
realms of individual pathology and into the realms of cultural context. As we described in earlier chapters, the central tenet that connects all the types of fetishism is the notion of separation, or more
specifically, 'disavowal'. The cultural space for women in contemporary culture seems to be full of fetishistic disavowals – or, more simply
put, half-truths that mask threatening information about women.

In the Freudian account of sexual fetishism, disavowal takes place
because the male fetishist appears to know, yet doesn't know, that
women do not have a penis. The substitution of the fetish object in
preference to the body of woman enables the fetishist to continue to
believe the lie (that women do have a penis) while rejecting the certain
truth that women are castrated (which is why her body is not found
erotic in the first place). Unlike displacement or sublimation, fetishism does not involve repression of the desire experienced. Instead,
through the mechanism of disavowal, that desire is granted a 'safe'
expression in the world, without having to take on board the 'threatening' knowledge involved. Similarly, in commodity fetishism, disavowal occurs not only because objects become separated from the
meaning of the labour power that created them (as Marx originally
explained), but also because the intensity of the separation between
the object and its meaning is exacerbated by marketing and advertising, which attributes qualities and auras that are not 'intrinsically'
part of the commodity.

So disavowal informs both commodity and sexual fetishism, and
relates to a process involving separations of meaning. Such processes
seem familiar to us. In everyday life, our exposure to advertising and
media hype involves us in doing two things at the same time : knowing
that superficial things won't really change our lives, and not knowing
this because we find ourselves wanting these things anyway.

Baudrillard has suggested that the over-production of images, the
saturation of mass communications, has intensified the experience of
fetishism within consumer culture. Images no longer mean what they

used to mean because their original significance has been lost or recreated. Baudrillard has severed his relationship to the Marxist account of commodity relations and argues that mass technology has meant that simulation, not production, is the structuring principle of social organisation:

> We are at the end of production ... Production is the dominant scheme of the industrial era ... Simulation is the dominant scheme of the present phase of history governed by the code.[4]

Baudrillard argues that we live in a situation in which there 'is ... generation of meaning by models of the real without origin or reality, a *hyper-real*'.[5] Such a reading of communications in the post-industrial age constructs disavowal of meaning as an inevitable condition of post-modern consumer culture. Baudrillard is using the logic of Marxist thinking in order to deconstruct it. He argues that consumer culture is all about simulation, and fetishism.[6]

Baudrillard argues that fetishistic disavowal is at the heart of our cultural life since signs in consumer society – which he attempts to theorise – have become unanchored. Suzanne Moore has summarised the position as follows:

> So signs are no longer tied to one-to-one relationships with their referents, but have become adulterous, producing illegitimate offspring wherever they go – pure simulacrum. Meanings are carried weightlessly around the circuit which is no longer involved in exchange with the real, instead, in this 'liquification of all referentials', signs only refer to each other and reality becomes redundant. The threat of illegitimacy has undermined the paternal fiction – for these bastard signs reproduce among themselves, not knowing or even caring who their father was.[7]

This post-modern reading of the meaning and influence of signs is an important part of analysing a subject like eating disorder. It suggests that it is not only individuals who are confused about their body image, but that society also is confused, and somewhat divorced from its definitions – and ultimately from meaning itself.

Jameson has made similar observations about society being confused (although unlike Baudrillard he does not completely disregard his original relationship to Marxism). Jameson acknowledges that post-modernism originated in connection with aesthetic developments in art and architecture, but he also argues that it is about more than just 'style'. He suggests that post-modernism is the cultural dominant of post-industrial society, which he links specifically to the economics of multinational capitalism. He argues that the consequence of this form of capitalist economics is a consumer society which promotes depthlessness and dislocation, and ultimately creates a breakdown in perceptions of temporal reality (periodization), as well as a break-down in the signifying chain. Jameson notes that as mass culture has come to dominate our lives, so unanchored images replace reality, and history loses meaning. The consequence of this breakdown in the signifying chain means that today's consumers become 'schizophrenic':

> When that relationship breaks down, when the links in the signifying chain snap, then we have schizophrenia ... If we are unable to unify the past, present and future of a sentence then we are similarly unable to unify the past, present and future of our own biographical experience of psychic life.[8]

Jameson is referring here to a multiple breakdown of temporal reality: the old boundaries between high art and mass culture, reality and spectacle, selfhood and otherness, have also become dislocated. Everything takes on a hallucinogenic and confused quality as a con-sequence of the way the media represents reality. Signs are not there for what they mean in historical terms, but simply because they are there and can be plundered and mobilised to sell us things.

Femininity and Post-Modern Culture

We are arguing that disavowal is central to fetishism and to post-industrial capitalism, and that subjectivity within post-modern cul-ture is characterised by oscillation between two subject positions (resulting in what Jameson has termed schizophrenia). We would point out that this process of oscillation is also absolutely central to the experience of gender in post-modern culture. We suggest, for that reason, that it is not in the least surprising that women have a re-lationship to fetishism.

Women are expected to construct themselves as objects, as well as to experience themselves as subjects, and to oscillate between the subject/object dichotomy in order to maintain a notion of successful femininity. But what is successful femininity? If it is culturally, rather than biologically, constructed then it is always about simulation, a simulacrum. To define 'simulacrum' Baudrillard quotes *Ecclesiastes* as follows:

> The simulacrum is never that which conceals the truth, it is the truth that conceals there is none. The simulacrum is true.[9]

In saying that femininity is a simulacrum, are we saying it doesn't really exist at all? We agree that femininity is not 'real' or 'natural', but are only too aware of the material reality of signs about it. Joan Riviere argued that femininity has no natural reality but is all about masquerade, and we would concur with this position, (and suggest that it also applies to men). We feel that the concept of masquerade is just as appropriate to discussing masculinity (the average man knows he does not possess the phallus either, only a penis). In post-modern terms this means that gender is the perfect simulacrum – the exact copy of something that never existed in the first place.

Often the female body, as Suzanne Moore has pointed out, has become the prime text of post-modernism. This is because critics like Baudrillard have argued that femininity is only ever about appearance. Rather than challenging superficial models of femininity in order to argue for a depth model, Baudrillard suggests that feminists should go to the opposite extreme and celebrate superficiality.[10] In reply to this sort of logic many post-modern feminist writers, including Christine Di Stefano, have argued that only men can afford to make this sort of case. Only men can afford the pleasures associated with the fluidity of identity, because they have access to power and can afford a decentred self; whereas for women to take on such a position 'is to weaken what is not yet strong'.[11]

Certainly, many feminists who have engaged with psychoanalysis have done so in order to explain how subjectivity is constructed by history and context. They have aligned themselves with the idea that femininity is not real but has been 'made' by culture. They have done this mainly in order to figure out how such oppressive and often sexist definitions for women can be 'unmade' through engagement with cultural politics.[12]

Clearly women's relationships to their own bodies is informed not simply by their instincts, Oedipal traumas and unconscious fantasies, but also by the specific cultural context they inhabit. But what actually is the female body? Too often in discourse it becomes a metaphor at the cultural level of the sign, far removed from its relationship to biological reality. These signs impact upon minds as well as bodies, and many people, especially women, find themselves caught up in an unrealistic system that promotes the desire to transform their bodies into 'better' (often unrealistic) slender feminine 'ideals'[13]. In such a context, where signs have lost their relationship to the signified, the female body is perhaps the final site of struggle over meaning. There is a limit to the extent to which women can change our biological bodies to accommodate the hyper-real meaning of signs about the feminine; beyond these limits our bodies become sick, or disintegrate altogether.

In post-modern culture, then, the behaviour of the female of the species has an intense relationship to simulation because femininity is not real in the first place. The bulimic who binges and purges, so as to really have her cake and eat it too, could be described as

1. illogical, in the individual sense, because she is unable to transform her unconscious perverse drives into creative/civilised activity (as psychoanalysis suggests humans do) and
2. logical, in the cultural sense, as a response to the overproduction of contradictory signs about femininity, as well as definitions about the 'value' of food to be consumed.

The bulimic may want to consume the meaning of food (the signified) but she literally expels the food (the sign) from her body. She does this so as to be able to cope, to live with the contradictory messages defined by patriarchal discourse, which demand that women should be slender, petite, small; the messages that tell her on the one hand to desire/consume everything in order to live the 'good life', but somehow, paradoxically, on the other, to remain thin. This is the logic of materialism in the West, which has given women contradictory messages culminating in the idea that 'you can never be too rich or too thin'.

Susie Orbach's writing, and the work of the Women's Therapy Centre, have contributed an astute understanding of the slender ideal, as we mentioned in chapter five. However, other writers we have examined supply some of the missing ingredients from their analysis. Crucially, in *Fat is a Feminist Issue*,[13] Orbach misses the point identified in Lacanian psychoanalysis, that there is no 'real self' that can be reclaimed when women become 'more realistic' about body shape. And what Baudrillard can tell us about eating disorder that Freud and psychiatry can't might be that it is *logical* to find women suffering from it in epidemic proportions. Unfortunately, fetishism is part of the logic of post-industrial capitalism, which may be seen as perverse in nature: and this perverse post-modern condition has always been women's condition.

We would argue, therefore, that post-modernism probably can tell us as much about fetishism and other forms of eating disorder as psychoanalysis. The complicated relationship of women to signs about their own identity, and the way material culture informs lived experience (including the experience of fantasy), is perhaps something that

Western medicine, as well as psychiatry, needs to conceptualise and take on board in more sophisticated terms. Excessive regulation of the body to conform to ideal stereotypes, and excessive consumption of food and objects, perhaps reflects a search for what has been lost in consumer culture − meaning and value.

The Post-Modern Predicament

Hilary Lawson has summarised that the post-modern 'predicament' lies in the fact that all the truths and beliefs we hold most dear, in philosophy, in sociology, literary criticism, physics, anthropology, history, and a host of other disciplines have no meaning outside the text;[14] that we are all locked into the self-referring play of signifiers. Such an extreme model of cultural life, when for most people real events continue to have real meanings, has angered many critics.[15] Clearly, post-modern theories of culture are open to challenge, as are its central concerns and obsessions, which are often imperialistically first-world in direction.

We would not want to discount the very real problems that have been raised about Baudrillard's work by many critics. Nevertheless the concepts of hyper-reality and simulation, as they have been elaborated within theories of post-modernism, have allowed us to connect epidemics of food and sexual fetishism in Europe and America with contemporary cultural structures of representation and experience. And like typical post-modernist critics, we have taken an eclectic approach to our analysis of femininity and its relationship to post-modern culture because there is not time or space to do otherwise. Like smash and grab artists we have taken the best, or just what we needed, and have left the rest behind.

When we started to research the subject of female fetishism for the book, and started to look for evidence of women as practitioners of it, we had no idea that we would end up linking individual 'psychosis' around food with cultural neurosis about 'meaning'. But when we started to question the epidemic proportions of women suffering from eating disorder it was impossible to stay within psychoanalytic arguments, and not to move out to look at 'cultural politics'.

However, we are painfully aware that our own argument, drawing as it does predominantly from first world discourses and phenomena, requires more substantiation than there is space for in this tentative conclusion. The implications of the theories of post-modernism we have outlined may only apply to specific media-saturated, late-capitalist sites in Europe and America, as well as to the experiences of specific women.

We have no desire to make the case for Baudrillard, or to make any claims for post-modernism as an appropriate world-view or meta-narrative. We offer our reading of fetishism in post-modern culture in the spirit of a case-study of the effects of the crisis of representations of femininity in the West.

Post-modernism has been open to a charge of ultimate conservatism, constantly playing with the crisis of values, unable to move forward. We would argue that a similar charge could be levelled against fetishism. Being locked into the continuous oscillation of 'I know ... but all the same ...' is a structure of immobility that most fetishists will recognise only too well. We have argued that it is a healthier compromise than whatever threatens the individual psyche (since it still allows pleasure) but it is, nevertheless, still a compromise.

A more positive assessment of the experience of fetishism might suggest that the spirit of fetishistic compromise contains the germ of what Gramsci meant when he argued for 'pessimism of the intellect, optimism of the will' in regard to engaging with national, or perhaps even sexual, politics. Clearly, fetishism assumes there is a 'whole' (woman or nation) that can be substituted for a 'part', whereas most contemporary thinkers appear to be telling us the opposite, that communities are imaginary, and that there is no 'whole' self that can ever be unified, because unity is an illusory experience, the subject of fiction. Indeed, in the face of such pessimistic accounts of subjectivity, it could be argued that the fetishist is always the optimist. He or she exhibits a faith in the whole that many individuals would be embarrassed to admit because of the fear of sounding politically naive.

But fetishism is often a private and secret activity, rather than a public and political one. It is difficult to remain optimistic about the significance of food fetishism for very long in light of the damaging effects associated with eating disorder; or in the context of the damaging effects associated with legal regulations that posit individual fetishists as deviants and 'perverts'. We have tried to argue against the current conservative legal crackdowns on sexual subcultures, but that does not mean that we think that sexual fetishism itself (as distinct from sado-masochism), is simply a 'progressive' phenomenon. The practitioner, in demanding that society tolerantly takes account of his or her preferences, may be an agent of progress. But the structure of fetishism itself, oscillating continually between knowing and un-knowing, doesn't exactly create a positive or stable space that can easily accommodate creative advancement. Fetishism as personal practice does not bring with it change or revolution. Instead, it offers oscillation and compromise, and perhaps at best what has been described by Jonathan Dollimore as a sort of 'dissidence' about sexual matters.[16]

We would, nevertheless, try to maintain a positive approach to the meaning of fetishism. The analysis of *the discourses* surrounding fetishism can, we believe, prove radical. Through questioning the usefulness of existing theoretical concepts as tools to chart female experience, we have been led to recognise that, to develop an adequate model of female sexuality a whole range of disciplines must re-examine the phallocentrism inherent in them; and through our analysis of these discourses, we have gestured towards a strong vision for cultural change.

Notes

1 Suzanne Moore, 'Getting a Bit of the Other — the Pimps of Post-modernism', in *Male Order: Unwrapping Masculinity*, Rowena Chapman and Johnathan Rutherford (eds), Lawrence and Wishart, London 1988, p182.

2 Freudian, object relations and Lacanian.

3 Mark Poster defines hyper-reality, in Baudrillard's usage, as the new linguistic condition of society, rendering impotent theories that still rely on materialist reductionalism or rationalist referentiality ... the strange mixture of desire and fantasy that is unique to late twentieth century culture. *Jean Baudrillard: Selected Writings*, Mark Poster (ed), Stanford University Press, Stanford California,1988, p2.

4 *Ibid*, chapter 5.

5 *Ibid*, chapter 7.

6 *Ibid*, chapter 3.

7 Moore, *op cit*, p177.

8 Fredric Jameson *Postmodernism — or the Cultural Logic of Late Capitalism*, Verso, London 1991, pp26–7.

8 Poster, (ed), *op cit*, p166.

10 Moore is extremely critical of what she calls the 'pimps of postmodernism' and suggests that critics like Baudrillard can afford to celebrate the feminine because they have power in the first place. She suggests that such discourse 'becomes a way of men exploring, rejecting and reconstructing their masculinity, "or getting a bit of the other" at the expense of women'. Moore, *op cit*.

11 Christine Di Stefano, 'Dilemmas of Difference: Feminism, Modernity & Postmodernism', Linda J. Nicholson (ed), *Feminism / Postmodernism*, Routledge, London 1990, pp63–82.

12 Michèle Barrett, 'Feminism and the Definition of Cultural Politics', in Rosalind Brunt and Caroline Rowans (eds), *Feminism, Culture and Politics*, Lawrence & Wishart, London 1982.

13 Kim Chernin, *Womansize: The Tyranny of Slenderness*, Women's Press, London 1983, and *The Hungry Self*, Virago, London 1986.

13 Susie Orbach, *Fat Is A Feminist Issue,* Hamlyn, London1979; see full discussion in our chapter five.

14 Hilary Lawson, *Reflexivity: The Postmodern Predicament,* Hutchinson, London 1985.

15 Mark Poster identifies that the main criticism against Baudrillard's writings is that 'he fails to define his major terms, such as the code; his writing style is hyperbolic and declarative, often lacking sustained, systematic analysis when it is appropriate; he totalizes his insights, refusing to qualify or delimit his claims. He writes about particular experiences, television images, as if nothing else in society mattered, extrapolating a bleak view of the world from that limited base. He ignores contradictory evidence such as the many benefits afforded by the new media ... ' *Jean Baudrillard: Selected Writings,* pp7–8.

16 Jonathan Dollimore, *Sexual Dissidence: Augustine to Wilde, Freud to Foucault,* Clarendon Press, Oxford 1991.

Bibliography

Abraham, S. and Llewellyn-Jones, D., *Eating Disorders: The Facts,* Oxford University Press, Oxford 1987.

Ackroyd, Peter, *Dressing Up: Transvestism and Drag; The History of an Obsession,* Thames & Hudson, London 1979.

Adams, Parveen, 'The art of Analysis: Mary Kelly's *Interim* and the Discourse of the Analyst', *October,* 58, 1991.

Adams, Parveen, 'On Female Bondage', in *Between Feminism and Psychoanalysis,* Teresa Brennan (ed), Routledge, London 1989, Chapter 14.

Agras, W. Stewart, *Eating Disorders: Management of Obesity, Bulimia and Anorexia Nervosa,* Pergamon, Oxford 1987.

Alibhai-Brown, Yasmin, 'Having it and Flaunting It', *Guardian,* 27.8.92.

Althusser, Louis, *Lenin, Philosophy and Other Essays,* New Left Books, London 1970.

Amos, Valerie, and Parmar, Pratibha, 'Challenging Imperial Feminism', *Feminist Review* 17, Autumn 1984.

Apter, Emily, *Feminising the Fetish: Psychoanalysis and Narrative Obsession in Turn of the Century France,* Cornell, New York 1991.

Apter, Emily, 'Splitting Hairs: Female Fetishism and Post Partum Sentimentality in the Fin de Siècle' in *Eroticism and the Body Politic,* Lynne Hunt (ed), 1990.

Ash J. and Wilson, E., *Chic Thrills: A Fashion Reader,* Pandora, London 1992.

Bak, R., 'Fetishism', *Journal of American Psychoanalytic Association,* 1, (1953).

Bartky, Sandra Lee, 'Foucault, Femininity and the Modernization of Patriarchal Power', *Feminism and Foucault: Reflections on Resistance,* I. Diamond and L. Quinby (eds), Northeastern University Press, Boston 1989.

Barrett, Michèle, 'Feminism and the Definition of Cultural Politics', R. Brunt and C Rowan (eds), *Feminism, Culture & Politics,* Lawrence & Wishart, London 1982.

Baudrillard, Jean, *Selected Writings,* Mark Poster (ed), Polity, Cambridge 1988.

Becquer, M. and Gatti J., 'Elements of Vogue', *Third Text,* 16/17, Autumn/Winter, 1991.

Belsey, Catherine, *Critical Practice* New Accents Series, Methuen, London 1980.

Berger, John, *Ways of Seeing,* BBC/Penguin, Harmondsworth 1972.

Bersani, L. and Dutoit, U., *The Forms of Violence* Schocken, New York 1985.

Bilich, Marion A., 'Demographic Factors Associated with Bulimia in College Students: Clinical and Research Implications', *Bulimic College Student,* L. Whitaker and W. Davies.

Binet, Alfred, 'Le fetichisme dans l'amour', in *Etudes de Psychologie Experimentale,* Octave Doin, Paris 1888.

Boffin, T. and Fraser, J. (eds), *Stolen Glances: Lesbians Take Photographs*, Pandora, London 1991.

Bonnet, G., 'Fetichisme et exhibitionnisme chez un sujet feminin', *Psychoanalyse a l'Universite*, 2, (1977). Reprinted in *Voir, etre vu: Etudes cliniques sur l'exhibionnisme*, Presses Universitaires de France, Paris 1981, Vol 1.

Bonnet, W. and Gurin, J., *The Dieter's Dilemma*, Harper Row, New York 1982.

Bordo, Susan, 'Material Girl: The Effacements of Post-modern Culture', in *The Madonna Connection: Representational Politics, Subcultural Identities, and Cultural Theory*, C.Schichtenberg (ed).

Boskind-Lodahl, M., 'Cinderella's Stepsisters: A Feminist Perspective on Anorexia Nervosa and Bulimia', *Signs*, 2, Winter 1976.

Boskind-Lodahl, M. and White, W., *Bulimarexia: The Binge/Purge Cycle*, Norton, New York 1983.

Bovey, Shelley, *Being Fat is not a Sin*, Pandora, London 1989.

Brande, Ilse, 'Perette et son gai (d'un cas de phobie d'impulsion et de comportment fetichiste chez une femme)', Memoir de candidature au titre de Membre adherent a la Societe Psychoanalytic de Paris, 1962.

Brierley, H., *Transvestism: A Handbook with Case Studies for Psychologists, Psychiatrists and Counsellors*, Pergamon, Oxford 1979.

Bronski, M., *Culture Clash: the Making of a Gay Sensibility*, South End Press, Boston Mass. 1984.

Brosses, Charles de, *Due culte des dieux fetiches, ou Parallele degre l'ancienne Religio de L'Egypete avec la Religion actuelle Nigritie*, Geneva 1769.

Browne, R.B., *Objects of Special Devotion: Fetishes and Fetishism in Popular Culture*, Bowling Green University Popular Press, 1989.

Bruch, Hilde, *Eating Disorders: Obesity, Anorexia Nervosa, and the Person Within*, Routledge, London 1974.

Brunt, Ros and Rowan, Caroline (eds), *Feminism, Politics and Culture*, Lawrence & Wishart, London 1982.

Butler, Judith, *Gender Trouble: Feminism and the Subversion of Identity*, Routledge, London 1990.

Califia, Pat, 'Love and the Pefect Sadist', *Skin Two*, 12, 1992.

Califia, Pat, *Macho Sluts*, Allyson Press, Boston, Mass.1988.

Califia, Pat, 'The Power Exchange', *Skin Two Retro*, Tim Woodward Publishing, London 1991.

Carter, Angela, 'Lorenzo as Closet Queen', *Nothing Sacred*, Virago, London 1982.

Cataldo, Janine, 'Obesity: A New Perspetive on An Old Problem', *Health Education Journal*, Vol 44, 1985.

Champ Freudien a Paris, *Traits de Perversion dans Les Structures Cliniques*, Rapports de La Recontre Internationale 1990 du Champ Freudien a Paris, Navarin, Paris 1990.

Chernin, Kim, *The Hungry Self: Women, Eating and Identity*, Virago, London 1986.

Chernin, Kim, *Womansize: The Tyranny of Slenderness*, Women's Press, London 1981.

Chodorow, Nancy, *The Reproduction of Mothering: Psychoanalysis and the Sociology of Gender*, University of California, London 1979.

Cixous, Hélène, 'Castration or Decapitation?', transl. Annette Kuhn, *Signs* 7 (1), Autumn 1981, pp41–55.

Cixous, Hélène, 'The Laugh of the Medusa', in *New French Feminisms:An Anthology*, Elaine Marks and Isabelle de Courtivron (eds), Harvester, London 1981.

Cixous, Hélène, and Clement, Catherine, *The Newly Born Woman*, transl. Betsy Wing, Manchester University Press, Manchester 1986.

Chorlton, Penny, 'Where Do the Pounds Go', *Sunday Observer*, 20.1.91.

Cline, Cheryl, 'Essays from Bitch: The Woman's Rock Newsletter with Bite', in Lewis, L., *The Adoring Audience*, Routledge, London 1992.

Clover, Carol, *Men, Women and Chainsaws: Gender in the Modern Horror Film*, BFI, London 1992.

Cooper, Troy, 'Anorexia and Bulimia: The Political and the Personal', in *Fed Up and Hungry*.

Copjec, Joan, 'The Sartorial Superego', *October*, Fall 1989.

Cosgrove, Stuart, 'Erotomania', *New Statesman*, 27.7.90.

Coward, Ros, *Female Desire*, Paladin, London 1984.

Crowley, H. and Himmelweit, S., *Knowing Women: Feminism and Knowledge*, Polity/Open University, Cambridge 1992.

Daly, Mary, and Caputo, Jane, *Websters' First New Intergalactic Wickedary of the English Language*, Beacon Press, Boston, Mass. 1987.

Dana, M. and Lawrence, M., *Women's Secret Disorder: A New Understanding of Bulimia*, Grafton, London 1988.

Debord, Guy, *Comments on Society of the Spectacle*, Transl. Malcolm Imrie, Verso, London 1988.

Dekker, R. and van de Pol, L., *The Tradition of Female Transvestism in Early Modern Europe*, Macmillan, London 1989.

Delacoste, F. and Alexandra, P. (eds), *Sex Work: Writings by Women in the Sex Industry*, Cleis Press, New York 1987.

Deleuze, G.and Guattari, F., *Anti-Oedipus: Capitalism and Schizophrenia*, trans. Hurley, R., Seem, M. and Lane, H., Viking, New York 1977.

Diamond, Nicki, 'Thin is a Feminist Issue', *Feminist Review*, 19, Spring, 1985.

Di Stefano, Christine, 'Dilemmas of Difference: Feminism, Modernity and Postmodernism', Linda J. Nicholson (ed), *Feminism/Postmodernism*, Routledge, London 1990.

Doane, Mary Anne, 'Masquerade Reconsidered: Further Thoughts on the Female Spectator', *Discourse* 11, Fall/Winter 1988–89.

Dollimore, Jonathan, *Sexual Dissidence*, Clarendon Press, Oxford 1991.

Dudley, G. A., 'A Rare Case of Female Fetishism', *International Journal of Sexology*, 8 (1954).

Durkheim, E., *Les Forms Elementaires de la via Religieuse: Le systeme totemique en Australie*, Paris 1912.

Dworkin, Andrea, *Intercourse*, Martin & Secker, London 1987.

Dyer, Geoff, *Ways of Telling: The Work of John Berger*, Pluto, London 1986.

Ehrenreich, B. *et al*, 'Beatlemania: Girls Just Want to Have Fun', in Lewis, L. (ed), *The Adoring Audience: Fan Culture and Popular Media*, Routledge, London 1992.

Ellis, Havelock, *Studies in the Psychology of Sex*, Random House, New York 1910.

Ellman, Lucy, 'Love and the Coffee Mates', *New Statesman and Society*, 14.2.92.

Evans, Caroline, 'Femininity as Perversion', Paper at '*Preaching to the Perverted*', ICA, July 1992.

Evans, C. and Thornton, M., *Women and Fashion: A New Look*, Quartet, London 1989.

Faderman, Lillian, *Odd Girls and Twilight Lovers: A History of Lesbian Life in 20th Century America*, Penguin, Harmondsworth 1992.

Fallon, R., and Rogin, P., 'Sex Differences in Perception of Desirable Body Shape', *Journal of Abnormal Psychology*, 94, 1985.

Fanon, Frantz, *Black Skin, White Masks*, trans. C Markmann, Pluto, London 1986.

Fiske, John, 'The Cultural Economy of Fandom' in Lewis, L. (ed), *The Adoring Audience*, Routledge, London 1992.

Fiske, John, *Understanding Popular Culture*, Unwin Hyman, London 1989.

Flugel, J., *The Psychology of Clothes*, Institute of Psychoanalysis, London 1930.

Foucault, Michel, *The History of Sexuality*, Vol 1, Penguin, Harmondsworth 1979.

Foucault, Michel, *Power/Knowledge: Selected Interviews and Other Writing 1972–1977*, Colin Gordon (ed), Harvester, Brighton 1980.

Frazer, J.G., *Totemism and Exogamy*, 4 Vols, Macmillan & Co, London 1910.

French, Barbara, *Coping with Bulimia: The binge/purge syndrome*, Thorsons, Wellingborough 1984.

Freud, Sigmund, '"Civilised" Sexual Morality and Modern Nervous Illness', *Standard Edition of The Complete Works*, trans. James Strachey, Hogarth, London 1953–64, Vol 9.

Freud, Sigmund, 'The Dissolution of the Oedipus Complex', *Standard Edition*, Vol 19, pp173–82.

Freud, Sigmund, 'Fetishism', *Standard Edition*, Vol 7.

Freud, Sigmund, 'Outline of Psycho-Analysis', *Standard Edition*, Vol 23.

Freud, Sigmund, 'Screen Memories,' *Standard Edition*, Vol 3.

Freud, Sigmund, 'Three Essays on Sexuality', *Standard Edition*, Vol 7.

Freud, Sigmund, *Totem and Taboo*, Routledge, London 1950.

Friday, Nancy, *My Secret Garden: Women's Sexual Fantasies*, Virago/Quartet, London 1975.

Friedan, Betty, *The Feminine Mystique*, Gollancz, London 1963.

Fuller, Peter, *Seeing Through Berger*, Claridge Press, London 1988.

Galford, Ellen, *Moll Cutpurse*, Virago, London 1992.

Gamman, L. and Marshment, M., *The Female Gaze: Women as Viewers of Popular Culture*, Women's Press, London 1988.

Gamman, Lorraine, 'Watching the Detectives', *The Female Gaze*, L. Gamman and M. Marshment (eds).

Garber, J. and McRobbie, A., 'Girls and Subculture', in S. Hall (ed), *Resistance Through Ritual*, Hutchinson, London 1978.

Garber, Marjorie, 'Fetish Envy', *October* 54, Fall 1990.

Garber, Marjorie, *Vested Interests: Cross-Dressing and Cultural Anxiety*, Routledge, London 1991.

Garner, David, *et al*, 'Cultural Expectations of Thinness in Women', *Psychological Reports*, 47 (1980).

Gebhard, P., 'Fetishism and Sado-Masochism', *Science & Psychoanalysis*, Vol 25, 1969.

Gerahty, C., *Women and Soap Opera: A Study of Prime Time Soaps*, Polity, Cambridge 1991.

Gilbert, Sara, *Pathology of Eating: Psychology and Treatment*, Routledge, London 1986.

Gillespie, W.H., 'A Contribution to the Study of Fetishism', *International Journal of Psycho-Analysis*, 21 (1940).

Gilligan, Carol, *In a Different Voice: Psychological Theory and Women's Development*, Harvard, Cambridge, Mass. 1982.

Gleick, Elizabeth, 'Food on the Brain', in *Cosmopolitan*, Aug 1990.

Glucksman, M.L.,'Psychiatric Observations of Obesity', *Advances in Psychosomatic Medicine*, 7 (1972).

Goodsitt, Alan, 'Self-Regulatory Disturbances in Eating Disorders', *International Journal of Eating Disorders* 2, Spring 1983.

Gordon, L. and Dubois, E., 'Seeking Ecstasy on the Battlefield: Danger & Pleasure in 19th Century Feminist Sexual Thought', *Feminist Review* 13, Spring 1983.

Gordon, R.A., *Anorexia and Bulimia: Anatomy of a Social Epidemic*, Blackwells, London 1990.

Gordon, R.A., 'Bulimia: A Sociocultural Interpretation', *The Bulimic College Student*.

Gosselin, C. and Wilson, G., *Sexual Variations: Fetishism, Sado-Masochism and Trans- vestism*, Faber, London 1980.

Grace, Della, *Love Bites*, Editions Aubrey Walters, London 1991.

Gramsci, Antonio, *Selections from the Prison Notebooks*, edited and translated by Hoare, Q. and Nowell Smith, G., Lawrence and Wishart, London 1971.

Greenacre, Phyllis, 'Perversions: General Considerations regarding their Genetic and Dynamic Background', *Psychoanalytic Study of the Child*, 23, (1968).

Grosz, Elizabeth, 'Fetishization', *Feminism and Psychoanalysis*, E. Wright (ed), Blackwell, Oxford 1992.

Grosz, Elizabeth, 'Lesbian fetishism', *differences*,3/2 (1991).

Hamilton, C., *Marriage as Trade*, Women's Press, London l981.

Hamilton, Gilbert, *A Research into Marriage*, Boni, New York 1929.

Heidensohn, Frances, *Women and Crime*, Macmillan, London l985.

Henderson, Lisa, 'Justify Our Love: Madonna and the Politics of Queer Sex', Cathy Schwichtenberg (ed), *The Madonna Connection*.

Hite, Shere, *Women and Love – A Cultural Revolution in Progress*, Penguin, London 1988.

Hunt, Lynn (ed), *Eroticism and the Body Politic*, Johns Hopkins, Baltimore 1990.

Irigaray, Luce, 'And one does not stir without the other', transl. Helene Wenzel, *Signs* 7 (1), Autumn 1981.

Irigaray, Luce, *Speculum of the Other Woman*, transl. Gillian Gill, Cornell, New York 1985.

Irigaray, Luce, 'When our lips speak together', transl C. Burke, *Signs* 6 (1), Autumn 1980.

Isaak, Jo-Ann, 'Our Mother Tongue: Post-Partum Document', *Vanguard*, April 1982, reprinted in the Appendix to *Post-Partum Document*, Kelly.

Iversen, Margaret, 'The Bride Stripped Bare by Her Desire: Reading Mary Kelly's Post-Partum Document', *Discourse* 4, (1981); reprinted in the Appendix to *Post Partum Document*, Kelly.

Jackson, Cath, 'Fast Food Feminism', *Trouble and Strife* 7, Winter 1985.

Jakobson, Roman, *On Language*, Linda R. Waugh and Monique Monville-Burston (eds), Harvard University Press, Cambridge, Mass. 1990.

Jameson, Fredric, *Postmodernism – or the Cultural Logic of Late Capitalism*, Verso, London 1991.

Jhalley, S., Kline, S. and Leiss, W., 'Magic in the Marketplace: an empirical test for commodity fetishism', *Canadian Journal of Political and Social Theory*, 9, Fall 1985.

Jouve, Nicole Ward, *The Street Cleaner: The Yorkshire Ripper Case on Trial*, Marion Boyars, London 1986.

Kaplan, Ann E., 'Madonna Politics: Perversion, Repression or Subversion? Or Masks, and/as Master–y', in *The Madonna Connection*, Cathy Schwichtenberg.

Kaplan, Louise, *Female Perversions*, Pandora, London 1991.

Katzman, Melanie, 'Is it true eating makes you feel better?': A Naturalistic Assessment of Food Consumption and its Effect on Stress', *Bulimic College Student*, pp75–87.

Kelly, Mary, *Interim*, Fruitmarket Gallery, Kettle's Yard and Riverside Studios, 1986.

Kelly, Mary, *Post-Partum Document*, Routledge, London 1984.

Kerridge, Roy, 'Sex Rampages of the Feminist Porn Queens', *New Statesman and Society*, 23.2.92.

Kershaw, Alex, 'The Limits of Liberty', *Weekend Guardian*, 28.11.92.

Kinsey Institute for Sex Research, *Sexual Behaviour in the Human Female*, Indiana University Press, Bloomington 1953.

Klein, Melanie, *The Selected Melanie Klein*, Juliet Mitchell (ed), Penguin, Harmondsworth 1986.

Kofman, Sara, 'Ca Cloche', in *Les fins de l'homme: A partir du travail de Jacques Derrida*, Galilee, Paris 1981.

Kofman, Sara, *The Enigma of Woman: Woman in Freud's Writings*, transl. Catherine Porter, Cornell Ithaca 1985.

Krafft Ebing, R. von, *Psychopathesis Sexualis*, 10th Ed., trans F.J. Rebman, Rebman, London 1899.

Kristeva, Julia, 'About Chinese Women', *The Kristeva Reader*, Toril Moi (ed).

Kristeva, Julia, *Desire in Language*, trans. Leon Roudiez, Blackwell, Oxford 1980.

Kristeva, Julia, *The Kristeva Reader*, Toril Moi (ed), Blackwell, Oxford 1987.

Kunzle, D., *Fashion and Fetishism: A Social History of the Corset, Tightlacing and Other Forms of Body Sculpture in the West*, Ravan & Littlefield, New York 1982.

Lacan, Jacques, 'The Agency of the Letter', *Ecrits*, A. Shelston (ed), Routledge, London 1977.

Lacan, Jacques, *Feminine Sexuality: Jacques Lacan and the Ecole Freudienne*, Juliet Mitchell and Jacqueline Rose (eds), Macmillan, London 1982.

Lacan, Jacques, and Granoff, V., 'Fetishism:the symbolic, the imaginary and the real', in *Perversions: psychodynamics and therapy*, Sandor Lorand (ed), Ortolan, London 1965.

Lang, A., *The Secret of the Totem*, Longman & Co., London 1905.

Lau, Grace, 'The Voyeuristic Camera', *Skin Two*, Issue 2, 1984.

Lawrence, Marilyn (ed), *Fed Up and Hungry*, Women's Press, London 1987.

Lawson, Hilary, *Reflexivity: The Postmodern Predicament*, Hutchinson, London 1985.

Lewis, Lisa (ed), *The Adoring Audience: Fan Culture and Popular Media*, Routledge, London 1992.

Lidz, T. and Lidz, R., 'Masculinization in Papua New Guinea', *Psychoanalytic Review* 73, Winter 1986.

Lippard, Lucy, 'Issue and Tabu', introduction to *Issue: Social Strategies by Women Artists*, ICA, London 1980.

Lukàcs, Georg, *History and Class Consciousness*, MIT Press, Cambridge, Mass. 1971.

Masters, W.H., Johnson, V.E. and Kolodny, R.C., *On Sex and Human Loving*, Macmillan, London 1982.

Marx, Karl, *Capital* Vol 1, Pelican, London 1986.

Masud Khan, M., *Alienation in Perversion*, Hogarth Press, London 1979.

Mayne, Judith, 'Feminist Film Theory and Criticism', *Signs*, l, Autumn 1985.

MacClancy, Jeremy, *Consuming Culture*, Chapman, London 1992.

Mellencamp, Patricia, *High Anxiety: Catastrophe, Scandal, Age and Comedy*, Indiana University Press, Bloomington 1992.

Mercer, Kobena, 'Bad Object Choices', *How Do I Look: Queer Film and Video*, K. Mercer (ed), Bay Press, Seattle 1991.

Merck, Mandy, 'Transforming the Suit: A Century of Lesbian Self Portraits', in Boffin & Fraser, *Stolen Glances*, Pandora, London 1991.

Metz, C., *The Imaginary Signifier: Psychoanalysis and the Cinema*, Indiana University Press, Bloomington 1975.

Mintz, Ira, 'Psychoanalytic Description: The Clinical Picture of Anorexia Nervosa and Bulimia', *Fear of Being Fat: The Treatment of Anorexia Nervosa and Bulimia*, C. P. Wilson, C. Hogan and I. Mintz (eds), Aronson, New York 1985–88.

Mitchell, Juliet, 'Feminist Theory and Feminist Movements: The Past Before us', in *What is Feminism?*, Juliet Mitchell and Ann Oakley (eds), Blackwell, Oxford 1986.

Mitchell, Juliet, *Psychoanalysis and Feminism*, Allen Lane, London 1974.

Moi, Toril, *Sexual / Textual Politics*, Methuen, London 1985.

Moore, Suzanne, 'Deviant Laws', in *Looking For Trouble*.

Moore, Suzanne, 'Getting a Bit of the Other – the Pimps of Postmodernism', in *Looking For Trouble*.

Moore, Suzanne, 'Here's Looking at You Kid!' *The Female Gaze*, L. Gamman and M. Marchment (eds), Women's Press.

Moore, Suzanne, *Looking For Trouble: On Shopping, Gender and the Cinema*, Serpent's Tail, London 1991.

Moore, Suzanne, 'Reach for the Stars', *Women's Review*, 21, 1986.

Morgan, Robyn, *Sisterhood is Global: The Women's Movement Anthology*, Penguin, Harmondsworth 1985.

Mort, Frank, 'Men and shopping', *New Socialist*, Nov 1986.

Mulvey, Laura, 'Impending Time', *Interim*, M. Kelly.

Mulvey, Laura, 'Post-Partum Review', *Spare Rib*, 40 (1976); reprinted in the Appendix to *Post-Partum Document*, Kelly.

Mulvey, Laura, *Visual and Other Pleasures*, Macmillan, London 1989.

Mulvey, Laura, 'Visual Pleasure and Narrative Cinema', *Screen*, 16 (3), Autumn 1975.

Nedell, G., 'Still Cleaning After All These Years', *Guardian*, 16.8.92.

Norbeck, Edward, 'Psychiatric Fetishism', *Encyclopedia Americana*, Vol 11.

Norris, Christopher, *Uncritical ·Theory: Postmodernism, Intellectuals and the Gulf War*, Lawrence & Wishart, London 1992.

Ohmann, R., 'History and Literary History: The Case of Mass Culture', *Poetics Today*, Vol 9, 1988.

Oliveira Marques, H. de, *Daily Life in Portugal in the Late Middle Ages*, University of Wisconsin Press, London 1971.

Orbach, Susie, *Hunger Strike: The Anorectic Struggle as a Metaphor of our Age*, Faber, London 1986.

Orbach, S. and Eichenbaum, L., *Outside In ... Inside Out: Women's Psychology, a Feminist Psychoanalytic Approach*, Penguin, Harmondsworth 1982.

Parker, Rozika, and Pollock, Griselda, *Old Mistresses: Women, Art and Ideology*, Routledge, London 1981.

Payne, S.M., 'Some Observations on the Ego Development of the Fetishist', *International Journal of Psychoanalysis*, 20, (1939).

Person, Ethel Spector, 'Sexuality as the Mainstay of Identity: Psychoanalytic Perspectives', *Signs* 5 (1980).

'Perverse Politics: Lesbian Issues', *Feminist Review*, Vol 34, Spring 1990.

Pettinger, Alasdair, 'Why Fetish?', *New Formations*, Perversity Issue, Autumn 1993.

Pietz, W. 'The Problem of the Fetish, I', *Res*, 9, 1985.

Pietz,W. 'The Problem of the Fetish, II, The origins of the fetish', *Res* 13, Spring 1987.

Pietz, W. 'The Problem of the Fetish, IIIa, Bosman's Guinea and the Enlightenment Theory', *Res*, 16, 1988.

Pollock, Griselda, 'Anonymous Notes Towards a Show on Self Image', *Framing Feminism: Art and the Women's Movement 1970–1985*, R. Parker and G. Pollock (eds), Pandora, London 1987.

'Preaching to the Perverted' Conference, ICA, 12 July 1992.

Pribham, E.D.(ed), *Female Spectators*, Verso, London 1988.

Rayland-Sullivan, Ellie, 'Masochism', in *Feminism and Psychoanalysis*, E. Wright (ed).

Reynolds, Margaret (ed), *Erotica: An Anthology of Women's Writing*, Pandora, London 1990.

Riviere, Joan, 'Womanliness as Masquerade', *International Journal of Psychoanalysis*, 10.

Rose, Jacqueline, 'Introduction II', *Feminine Sexuality: Jacques Lacan and the Ecole Freudienne*, Juliet Mitchell and Jacqueline Rose (eds), Macmillan, London 1982.

Rose, Louis, 'Freud and Fetishism: Previously Unpublished Minutes of the Vienna Psychoanalytic Society', *Psychoanalytic Quarterly* 57 (1988).

Ross, W.A., *The Sex Life of the Foot and Shoe*, Routledge, London 1977.

Roth, G., *Feeding the Hungry Heart*, Grafton Books, London 1986.

Scott, Rosemary, *The Female Consumer*, Associated Business, London 1976.

Skin Two, Tim Woodward Publishing Ltd., London, Vol 10, 1991.

Schlesinger, Philip, *et al* (eds), *Women Viewing Violence*, BFI Publishing, London 1992.

Schor, Naomi, 'Female Fetishism: The Case of George Sand', in *The Female Body in Western Culture: Contemporary Perspectives*, Suleiman and Rubin (eds).

Schor, Naomi, 'Fetishism', *Feminism and Psychoanalysis*, E Wright.

Schor, Naomi, 'Fetishism and its ironies', *Nineteenth Century French Studies*, 17 (1), Fall 1988.

Schor, Naomi, *Reading in Detail: Aesthetics and the Feminine*, Methuen, London 1987.

Schwichtenberg, Cathy (ed), *The Madonna Connection: Representational Politics, Subcultural Identities, and Cultural Theory*, Westview Press, Oxford 1992.

Segal, Lynne, 'Lessons from the Past', in Carter, E. and Watney, S., *Taking Liberties: Aids and Cultural Politics*, Serpent's Tail/ICA, London 1989.

Showalter, Elaine, *The Female Malady*, Virago, London 1987.

Sights, J. and Richards, H., 'Parents of Bulimic Women', *International Journal of Eating Disorders*, 3 (4) Summer 1984.

Silverman, L., *et al*, 'Effect of Subliminal Stimulation of Symbiotic Fantasies on Behaviour Modification Treatment of Obesity', *Journal of Consulting and Clinical Psychology*, 46, (1978).

Simpson, David, *Fetishism and the Imagination*, Johns Hopkins, Baltimore 1982.

Sinclair, Y., *Transvestism Within A Partnership of Marriage and Families*, The TV/TS Group, London 1984.

Slochower, Joyce, *Excessive Eating: the role of emotions and the environment*, Human Sciences Press, New York 1983.

Smyth, Cherry, *Lesbians Talk: Queer Notions*, Scarlet Press, London 1992.

Sperling, Merlitta, 'Fetishism in Children', *International Journal of Psychoanalysis* 32, (1963).

Sperling, Melitta, 'Transference Neurosis in patients with psychosomatic disorders', *Psychoanalytic Quarterly* 36, (1967).

Sperling, Melitta, 'Trichotillomania, Trichopagy and Cyclic Vomiting', *International Journal of Psycho-Analysis* 49, (1968).

Spiegel, Nancy Tow, 'An Infantile Fetish and its Persistence into Young Womanhood', *Psychoanalytic Study of the Child*, 22 (1967).

Srikameswaran, S., *et al*, 'Sex Role Ideology among Women with Anorexia Nervosa and Bulimia', *International Journal of Eating Disorders* 3 (3) Spring 1984.

Steele, V., *Fashion and Eroticism: Ideals of Feminine Beauty From the Victorian Era to the Jazz Age*, Oxford University Press, Oxford l985.

Steiner, Wendy, 'Politically Correct Kinks', *The Independent on Sunday*, 13.10.91.

Stekel, Wilhelm, *Sexual Aberrations*, John Lane, London 1934.

Stoller, R.J., *Observing the Erotic Imagination*, Yale University Press, New Haven 1985.

Strauss, Claude Levi, *The Raw and the Cooked*, Trans J, and D. Weightman, Cape, London 1970.

Strober, M. and Yager, J., 'Some Perspectives on the Diagnosis of Bulimia Nervosa', in *The Bulimic College Student*.

Suleiman, S. and Rubin, R.S. (eds), *The Female Body in Western Culture: Contemporary Perspectives*, Harvard University Press, Cambridge, Mass. l986.

Taussig, Michael, *The Devil and Commodity Fetishism in South America*, University of North Carolina Press, 1983.

Thomas, David, *Not Guilty: Men, the Case for the Defence*, Weidenfeld, London 1993.

Tickner, Lisa, 'The Body Politic: Female Sexuality and Women Artists Since 1970', *Old Mistresses*, R. Parker and G. Pollock (eds), Routledge, London 1981.

Tylor, E.B., *Primitive Culture*, Vol 2, Murray, Albermarle 1891.

Vale, V. and Juno, A. (eds), *Modern Primitives: An Investigation of Contemporary Adornment & Ritual*, Re/Search Publications, New York 1989.

Veblen, Thorstein, *The Theory of the Leisure Class*, Macmillan, New York 1899.

Vermorel, Fred and Judy, *Starlust: The Secret Fantasies of Fans*, W H Allen, London 1985.

Villault, Nicholas, *Relatins de Costes d'Afrique, appelees Guinee*, Thiery, Paris 1669.

Weeks, Jeffrey, *Sexuality and its Discontents: Meaning, Myth and Modern Sexualities* Routledge, London 1985.

Welldon, Estella V., *Mother, Madonna, Whore*, Free Association Books, London 1988.

Wheelwright, J., *Amazons and Military Maids: Women who dressed as men in the pursuit of life, liberty and happiness*, Pandora, London l989.

Westwood, Vivienne, 'Sex is Fashion, Fashion is Sex' (interview), *Z/G*, l980.

Whitaker, L. and Davis, W., *The Bulimic College Student: Evaluation, Treatment and Prevention*, Haworth, New York 1989.

Williams, Linda, 'Pornographies on/scene', *Sex Exposed: Sexuality and the Pornography Debate*, L. Segal and M. McIntosh (eds), Virago, London 1992.

Williams, Raymond, 'Advertising: the Magic System', *Problems in Materialism and Culture*, Verso, London 1980.

Williamson, Judith, *Decoding Advertisements: Ideology and Meaning in Advertising*, Marion Boyars, London 1978.

Williamson, Judith, 'Lost in the Hypermarket', *City Limits*, December 1988.

Willis, P., 'Shop Floor Culture: Masculinity and the Wage Form', in C. Critcher *et al*, *Working Class Culture*, Hutchinson, London 1977.

Willis, Susan, *A Primer For Daily Life*, Routledge, London 1991.

Wilson, C., Hogan, C. and Mintz, I., *Fear of Being, Fat: The Treatment of Anorexia Nervosa and Bulimia*, Aronson, New York 1985–88.

Wilson, Elizabeth, *Adorned in Dreams*, Virago, London 1985.

Winnicott, D.W., *Through Paediatrics to Psycho-Analysis*, Hogarth Press, London 1975.

Winters, Shelley, Interviewed by Christina Appleyard, *Daily Mirror*, 2.10.89.

Wolf, Naomi, *The Beauty Myth*, Chatto & Windus, London 1990.

Woodhouse, Annie, *Fantastic Women: Sex, Gender and Transvestism*, Macmillan, London 1989.

Wright, Elizabeth (ed), *Feminism and Psychoanalysis: A Critical Dictionary*, Blackwell, Oxford 1992.

Zavitzianos, G., 'Fetishism and Exhibitionism in the Female and their Relationship to Psychopathology and Kleptomania', *International Journal of Psychoanalysis*, 52 (1971).

Index